Good Housekeeping

Complete Book of

CAKE BAKING
&
DECORATING

Good Housekeeping

Complete Book of
CAKE BAKING
—— & ——
DECORATING

A step-by-step guide to the essential techniques
with over 50 cake designs and recipes

JANICE MURFITT

NOVELTY CAKES: POLLY TYRER

LIMITED EDITIONS

This edition published by Limited Editions

First published 1994

1 3 5 7 9 10 8 6 4 2

ISBN 0 09 178885 4

**Janice Murfitt and Ebury Press would like to thank Squires Kitchen, Squire
House, 3 Waverley Lane, Farnham, Surrey GU9 8BB, for their help in
providing materials for photography.**

Editor: Barbara Croxford
Designer: Sara Kidd
Photography: Graham Tann
Food stylists: Janice Murfitt and Polly Tyrer
Photographic stylist: Antonia Gaunt

Typeset by SX Composing Ltd, Rayleigh, Essex
Printed and bound in Singapore by Tien Wah Press

CONTENTS

Introduction 6

Equipment for cake making 7

How to make cakes successfully 12

SIMPLE CAKES AND GÂTEAUX 18-41

Basic cake recipes 20

Basic icings and frostings 23

Simple cakes and gâteaux 28-41

CHOCOLATE 42-61

Chocolate cakes 48-61

CELEBRATION CAKES 62-181

Celebration cake recipes 64

Marzipan or almond paste 71-77

Marzipan cakes 74-77

Food colourings 78-79

Sugar paste 80-104

Sugar paste cakes 90-104

Royal icing 105-125

Royal iced cakes 112-125

Piping 126-151

Piped cakes 136-151

Flower paste 152-169

Flower paste cakes 160-169

Flowers 170-175

Flower cakes 172-175

Ribbons 176-179

Ribbon cake 178

NOVELTY CAKES 180-205

Novelty cakes 186-205

Templates 206

Index 212

Suppliers and useful addresses 216

INTRODUCTION

Cakes can give so much pleasure to so many people, either as a gift or as a centrepiece for a special occasion or celebration, and decorative cakes have been made throughout the centuries by many well-known chefs or cooks for the rich and famous. These classic cake designs and finishes were named after their creators or recipients and many are still used today.

Cake decorating is now an increasingly popular activity which attracts many people worldwide as a creative hobby or successful business. This has been made possible by the updated methods now used, the vast selection of equipment available, and, more importantly, the visual step-by-step guides which have been published to explain all the techniques.

There are no secrets to making a cake worthy of being iced or decorated – just following a few simple guidelines will ensure successful results. Once made, these un-assuming cakes may be turned into decorative cakes and gâteaux by the use of simple coatings, fillings and decorations. Others may be transformed into wonderful creations, real works of art, with the clever use of marzipan, royal icing and sugar paste.

This book has been carefully devised to give the less experienced cake decorator the opportunity to master the basic techniques and methods of cake making and icing, then progress to the more advanced and intricate skills. More experienced cake decorators can turn straight to these more advanced sections, where they will find plenty to test and expand their skills. Each chapter deals with a specific technique from beginning to end and is full of hints and tips, making the book a complete step-by-step guide to producing cakes, icings and decorations of the very highest standard.

Janice Murfitt

EQUIPMENT FOR CAKE MAKING

A selection of basic equipment is most important to have when making cakes to obtain the best results. All equipment is expensive so choose carefully and buy the best. It is false economy to buy inferior equipment which will not last and may produce bad results.

The equipment listed below includes a cross-section of items needed to produce consistently good cakes, so start with a few basic items and add to your collection as your skills increase. With care and careful storage, the equipment may never need replacing. Care of basic equipment is simple when it comes to bowls, jugs, spoons and knives, so long as they are kept spotlessly clean and dry.

● Ensure all tins, moulds, baking sheets, wire racks, sieves and cutters are clean and completely dry before storing; this will ensure the metal does not tarnish or rust, and the equipment will retain its new look.

● Weighing scales should be serviced or checked regularly to ensure accurate weighing of ingredients. Always keep metric and imperial weights separately to prevent any mistakes when weighing ingredients.

● Electric mixers and food processors must be cleaned and dried thoroughly after each use. Always ensure the area around the beaters or blades is kept clean as stale food particles may fall into mixtures such as royal icing.

● Glazing brushes should be thoroughly washed and dried to prevent the bristles from going hard or sticking together. Shake the brush well to separate the bristles and dry in a warm place. Care must be taken not to dip brushes into hot fat or glazes as the bristles will fuse together.

● Keep all papers rolled up and neatly secured with a rubber band. This ensures the paper is smooth and flat and does not have creases which could impair cake designs or cause a weakness in a fine cake mixture or meringue.

GENERAL EQUIPMENT

Weighing scales – this is the most essential piece of equipment for weighing all cake ingredients in metric and imperial measures. Without accurate scales, good cakes and consistent results cannot be achieved. Choose weighing scales with separate metric or imperial weights for the most accurate weighing. Spring balance scales may be used but ensure they are set accurately before using them. Always use either metric or imperial measurements; do not mix them.

Measuring jug – with metric and imperial measurements for accurate measuring of liquids in millilitres, fluid ounces or pints. This ensures consistent fluid measurements for all cake mixtures.

Standard measuring spoons – for spoon measurements which are constantly accurate use a standard set of measuring spoons for dry and liquid ingredients. General spoons used in the kitchen may vary in size, causing inaccurate measurement and in turn upset the balance of the cake mixture.

Bowls – a selection of small, medium and large heatproof bowls are essential for good cake making. Choose bowls in glass or china, with smooth rounded insides for thorough and even mixing when using a wooden spoon or an electric mixer.

Wooden spoons – choose a selection of different-sized wooden spoons with handles of varying lengths, suitable for beating all types of mixture in large or small quantities.

Whisks – a flexible wire whisk, balloon whisk or small hand rotary whisk is necessary for whisking all types of mixture to obtain the volume and give smooth consistencies to sponge mixtures, meringues or icings.

Hand mixers – this type of whisk or mixer is invaluable for all types of cake making – for quick cake mixtures, whisked sponges, meringues and icings. They ensure a good volume and quick results.

Electric mixer – these larger mixers are often necessary when making large quantities of cake mixtures or icings for wedding cakes or special occasion cakes. Care must be taken not to over-mix so do always follow the manufacturer's instructions.

Food processors – ideal for chopping ingredients quickly, beating butter cream or for some types of cake mixtures. Care must be taken not to over-process mixtures; always follow the manufacturer's instructions.

Spatulas – made in a variety of shapes and sizes, and have a very flexible plastic blade. Essential for folding in ingredients thoroughly to lightly whisked mixtures, cake batters and icings, and for removing all the mixture from the bowl.

Tins and moulds – whenever possible always choose the best quality tins for baking cakes. The thickness of the metal ensures the tins retain their shape without bending or warping during baking or storage. Cake mixtures bake evenly without over-cooking on the outside when the quality of the metal is good.

Baking sheets – choose heavy-duty baking sheets with flat edges which will not warp in the oven during cooking. These are necessary for meringues, pastry or sponge layers and are ideal for standing cakes on.

Papers – there are a variety of papers, such as greaseproof, non-stick baking parchment, waxed paper, rice paper and brown paper, which all have their own uses. Greaseproof paper, being all-purpose, is suitable for lining all cake tins. Non-stick baking parchment, which has a non-stick coating, is ideal for meringues, spreading melted chocolate, drying moulded or cut-out sugar decorations, ensuring they do not stick. Waxed paper, being fine and flexible, is ideal for icing run-outs and to trace over designs for piped decorations. Rice paper is used for biscuits, macaroons and meringue mixtures which stays intact with the mixture and is edible. Brown paper is used to fit around the outside of cake tins to protect the cake during long periods of baking.

Glazing brushes – available round or flat; choose a small or medium brush for simply brushing all tins and moulds with melted fat or oil, and larger sized flat brushes for coating cakes with apricot glaze. Always choose the best quality to give even brushing and no loss of bristles.

Ruler, pencil and scissors – always needed when making cakes, for measuring tin sizes accurately, drawing around the tin shapes for lining papers, designing and cutting out templates.

Palette knives – small, medium and large straight palette knives with flexible blades are necessary for loosening cakes from tins, spreading and smoothing icing. The small cranked-handle palette knives are ideal for lifting and transferring small and fragile icing decorations, spreading royal icing on to cakes and smoothing edges without touching the surface with your fingers.

Knives – a selection of small, medium and large knives with straight blades are useful for preparing ingredients or for cutting cakes into layers.

Wire racks – obtainable in different sizes, round or oblong, with wide or narrow mesh; each type has its own use so it is advisable to have a selection.

Cutters – a set of plain round and fluted metal cutters give a good clean cut and are useful for cutting out shapes for novelty cakes, gâteaux and small cakes. Fancy biscuit cutters are available in many sizes and you will find endless uses for them.

Sieves – a variety of fine wire mesh or nylon sieves are always needed especially for icing sugar and flour, removing any lumps or particles. Always keep icing sugar sieves separately.

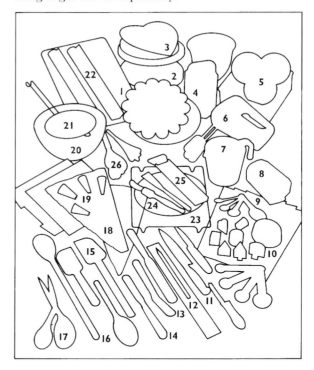

1. Tins and moulds   2. Turntable   3. Cake boards   4. Grater   5. Shaped tins   6. Hand mixer   7. Measuring jug   8. Brown paper   9. Standard measuring spoons   10. Cutters   11. Knives   12. Ruler and pencil   13. Cranked handle palette knife   14. Palette knives   15. Spatulas   16. Wooden spoons   17. Scissors   18. Nylon piping bags   19. Metal piping nozzles   20. Bowls   21. Sieve   22. Papers   23. Wire racks   24. Glazing brushes   25. Thermometer   26. Whisks

Turntable – there are many qualities to choose from, but it is essential for revolving the cake while icing and decorating to obtain good results.

Nylon piping bags – always have a selection of these ready-made washable bags which are ideal for piping dairy cream, butter cream and meringue.

Metal piping nozzles – choose the large variety of nozzles for piping creams and icings. Choose straight-sided metal nozzles which come in a variety of sizes and patterns.

Thermometer – an accurate sugar thermometer is needed for testing the temperature of sugar syrup when making some varieties of icing.

Cake boards – now available in many different shapes, sizes and colours, the most popular being round and square. Use the thick substantial cake boards for large iced cakes and wedding cakes which will keep them rigid and will support the weight of the cake. Thin cake boards are used for light sponge cakes with butter cream or cream and come in a variety of patterns and fluted edges.

Boxes – cardboard cake boxes are essential when making any cakes but especially celebration cakes. Once the cakes have been made and placed on a cake board, they can be stored in boxes during marzipanning, icing and decorating to keep them clean, dry and free from damage.

CAKE TINS

Cake tins are so important when it comes to baking all types of cakes. They vary tremendously in the quality and thickness of the metal, the finish, the sizing and the depth, so care must be taken when choosing them.

CHOOSING AND PREPARING CAKE TINS

• Always buy a fixed base cake tin unless the recipe states otherwise. This will ensure the tin will retain its shape during cooking and will not warp causing mixtures to bake unevenly.

• Good quality metal tins which feel rigid are preferable to the flimsy metal variety. These tins will last for ever and keep their shape with care and careful storage.

• Tin sizes vary according to the make and whether they are sold by metric or imperial measurement. Always measure the tin with a ruler across the base for an accurate measurement. Sometimes the sides of the tin may slope giving a wider measurement on the top but mixtures rarely come to the top of tins.

• Never be tempted to use a different shape or size

of tin than the recipe states, otherwise the baking time, texture, depth and appearance of the cake will be affected.

• Remember equivalent sizes in round and square tins take different quantities of mixture. A 20.5 cm (8 inch) round tin will take the same quantity as an 18 cm (7 inch) square tin, not a 20.5 cm (8 inch) square tin.

• Always prepare your cake tin according to the recipe you are making. Rich cake mixtures need double lining for protection during the long slow baking. Whisked sponge and quick mix cake mixtures need only the base of the tin lined so the sides of the cake adhere to the tin for even rising and a good shape.

• Light mixtures baked in Swiss roll tins need lining with one continuous sheet of greaseproof paper or non-stick baking parchment. This ensures a good shaped cake which may be turned out of the tin easily and the lining paper removed quickly and cleanly.

• All cake tins should be base lined so the base of the cake does not stick and the cake comes out of the tin in a good shape.

• Lined cake tins keep the tins clean and in good condition, often then will only need a wipe clean. Ensure all tins are washed and cleaned well, then dried thoroughly to prevent tarnishing or rusting. When the tins are completely dry, store them carefully in a dry cupboard.

SHAPED TINS

Although traditional round and square cake tins are used, the trend today is towards different shaped cakes. This has been made possible by the use of sugar paste which may be used to cover any shape imaginable whereas before with the use of royal icing this was not possible. Tins come in many shapes which may be purchased at cake icing and decorating suppliers or for a small fee tins may be borrowed. Lists are available of the various shapes. The most popular shapes are hexagonal, octagonal, petal, trefoil, oval, heart, horseshoe, diamond and triangle. The advantage of these tin shapes is that it gives more scope for unusual designs and fitting for certain occasions. Once covered with sugar paste, the soft lines of a petal, trefoil or heart shape cake need the minimum of decoration so as not to detract from these pretty shapes.

For a trefoil-shaped cake, see Chocolate Celebration Cake on page 58. For a heart-shaped cake, see Basket Weave Heart on page 28. For a triangular cake, see 18th Birthday Cake on page 116.

TO LINE A DEEP CAKE TIN OF ANY SHAPE

For rich or light fruit cakes, use good quality fixed base deep cake tins. Ensure you have the right sized tin for the quantity of cake mixture as this will affect the depth and baking time of the cake. Always measure the tin across the base, not the top.

Double line the inside of the tin with greaseproof paper or non-stick baking parchment, and the outside with double thickness brown paper. This protects the outside of the cake during the long baking time and prevents the cake from being overcooked. Always stand the tin on a baking sheet lined with three or four thicknesses of brown paper. This protects the cake and prevents overbaking.

1 Place the tin on a piece of double thickness greaseproof paper or non-stick baking parchment and draw around the base following the tin shape. Cut out the marked shape with a pair of scissors.

2 Measure and cut a strip of double thickness greaseproof paper or non-stick baking parchment long enough to wrap around the outside of the tin with a small overlap and to stand 2.5 cm (1 inch) above the top of the tin.

3 Brush the base and sides of the tin with melted white fat or oil. Place the cut out paper shapes in the base of the tin and press flat. Fit the double strip of greaseproof paper inside the tin, pressing well against the sides and making sharp creases where the paper fits into the corners of the tin shape being lined. Ensure the paper strip is level and fits neatly without any creases. Brush the base and side paper well with melted white fat or oil.

4 Line a baking sheet with three or four layers of brown paper and stand the tin on the centre of the lined baking sheet. Measure and fit a double thickness strip of brown paper around the outside of the tin. Tie with string.

TO LINE A SANDWICH TIN

1 Place the tin over a piece of greaseproof paper. Using a pencil, draw around the outside of the tin. Cut out the marked shape.

2 Brush the tin lightly with melted white fat or oil and fit the greaseproof paper disc over the base of the tin. Grease the paper.

3 For a whisked sponge or Genoese, lightly dust the sides of the tin with flour. This ensures the cake rises evenly and adheres to the side of the tin, keeping a good baked cake edge.

TO LINE A SWISS ROLL TIN

1 Place the tin in the centre of a piece of greaseproof paper, 2.5 cm (1 inch) larger all round than the tin. Cut from the corner of the paper to the corner of the tin using a pair of sharp scissors.

2 Lightly brush the tin with melted white fat or oil and fit the paper into the tin, neatly pressing into the corners. Brush the paper lightly with melted white fat or oil.

TO LINE A SHAPED TIN

1 Place the tin over a piece of greaseproof paper. Draw around the base following the tin shape and cut out.

2 Measure and cut a strip of greaseproof paper to fit around the side as before. Grease the tin, line with the base and side papers, then grease again.

HOW TO MAKE CAKES
SUCCESSFULLY

T here are a few simple guidelines which must be followed to achieve the very best results when making all types of cake. Unlike many recipes, the ingredients and measurement of quantities must be followed accurately as there is a very fine balance between all the ingredients.

Always make sure you have the correct tin shape and size according to the recipe you are making, otherwise this will affect the end result of the cake. A round tin instead of a square tin a centimetre or an inch larger or smaller will not only affect the baking time of the cake but also the volume, texture and appearance.

• Ensure the tin is properly prepared and lined for baking the recipe you have chosen to make. Different cake mixtures require different tin linings to ensure even cooking and a good shape.

• Check that you have all the necessary ingredients that are stated in the recipe, and that they are at the right temperature.

• Measure all the ingredients accurately using scales, measuring spoons and a measuring jug.

• Check that the eggs are the size stated in the recipe, do not use other sized eggs as this will upset the balance of the mixture.

• Ensure soft margarine is kept chilled in the refrigerator for the right consistency; if it is too soft it will cause the mixture to sink in the centre. Use unsalted butter for the best results when making cakes; always leave the butter out of the refrigerator to become room temperature and soft for creaming.

• Sift all dry ingredients to help aerate the mixture and to disperse lumps. Store flours and raising agents in well sealed packets or airtight containers in a dry place.

• When making cakes by hand, beat well with a wooden spoon until the mixture is light and glossy; scrape down the mixture during beating with a spatula to ensure even mixing.

• If the cakes are being made in a food processor or an electric mixer, be very careful not to over-process or over-beat the mixture. This will cause the structure of mixture to over-rise and then collapse and dip in the centre during baking. Remember to scrape down the mixture with a spatula during mixing. Follow the manufacturer's instructions accurately for the best results.

• If ingredients have to be folded into a cake mixture, use a spatula with a flexible blade which will cut cleanly through the mixture; keep turning it over and at the same time moving the bowl until all the ingredients have been incorporated and the mixture is light and smooth. Do not be tempted to stir or over-handle the cake mixture in any way or it will lose the air, causing the mixture to become heavy.

• Spoon or pour the cake mixture into the centre of the prepared tin. Use a small palette knife to spread the mixture evenly from the centre to the edge. Level the mixture in the tin before baking.

• Always set a timer 5 or 10 minutes before the end of the baking time as ovens do vary and the times stated in the recipe are only a guide. Test the cake always before removing it from the oven.

HOW TO BAKE
THE PERFECT CAKE

Many problems do arise when baking cakes, mainly because all ovens do vary, depending on the fuel you use; some are hot, others are slow, others are circotherm or fan assisted. Recipes always give cooking times, but you must remember the times are simply a guide. Check the instruction book with your oven.

• Do check that your oven is preheated to the temperature stated in the recipe.

• If the cake appears to be cooked before the given time, it may indicate that the oven is rather hot, or if it takes longer it means the oven is slow.

• The temperature of the cake mixture can also cause the baking time to vary. If conditions are very cold, the mixture will be cold and take longer to cook; in the same way, if it is a very hot day, ingredients may be warmer and the baking time will be slightly quicker.

● For sponge, Madeira and light fruit cake mixtures, the surface of the cake should be evenly browned and level. If the cake is overcooked on one side, the heating of the oven is uneven due to overheating on one side of the cooker. If the mixture has risen unevenly, the cooker or oven shelf is not level, or the cake tin may be warped.

These guidelines are assuming tin sizes are correct and recipes have been followed correctly.

TO TEST COOKED CAKES

● Always check the cake five or ten minutes before the given baking time just in case the oven is a little fast. It is always better to slightly undercook a cake as the mixture continues to cook in the tin after removing it from the oven.

● Always test the cake before removing it from the oven, just in case it is not cooked.

● For all cakes, other than fruit cakes, test the cake by pressing very lightly on the centre of the cake with the fingers; if it springs back, the cake is cooked. Otherwise it will leave a slight depression or fingerprint in the centre of the cake, and will need to be returned to the oven. Re-test at five-minute intervals.

● Fruit cakes are best tested as above and with a warm skewer inserted into the centre of the cake. If the skewer comes out clean, the cake is ready. Otherwise return the cake to the oven and re-test at ten-minute intervals.

● Once the cake is baked, if it is a sponge mixture loosen the edge of the cake using a small palette knife and leave the cake to rest for 5 minutes in the tin. Turn out on to a wire rack, remove the lining

paper, invert the cake and leave until really cold.

● Fruit cakes or cakes cooked in fully lined tins are best left to cool in the tins. When removed, some cakes are better stored with their lining paper intact. Otherwise, peel off the paper carefully.

TO STORE CAKES

● Everyday cakes such as sponge mixtures may be kept in an airtight container or simply wrapped in greaseproof paper or foil. This will ensure they keep moist and fresh with the exclusion of the air. Store the cakes in a cool, dry place for up to a week.

● To store fruit cakes, leave the lining paper on the cakes as this is sealed on to the surface during cooking and keeps the cakes moist and fresh. Wrap the cakes in a double layer of greaseproof or waxed paper with a final layer of foil. Place the cake on a cake board, base side uppermost, to keep the top flat, in a cardboard cake box. Store in a cool, dry place. Never seal a fruit cake in an airtight plastic container for long periods of time as this may encourage mould growth.

● Rich fruit cakes keep well because of their high fruit content; although they are moist and full of flavour, they taste their best when they are first made. Fruit cakes do mature with keeping, but all fruit cakes are best eaten within three months. If you are going to keep a fruit cake for several months before marzipanning or icing it, add the alcohol a little at a time at monthly intervals.

● Light fruit cakes and Madeira cakes may be stored in the same way as rich fruit cakes, but their keeping qualities are not as good.

● For long-term storage, all cakes are better kept in the freezer in their double wrapping and foil, keeping their flavour in peak condition until they are required. For a decorated celebration cake, freeze the cake in the cake box, ensuring the lid is sealed with tape. Thaw the cake slowly out of its box in a cool, dry place. When the cake has thawed, keep it in a warm, dry place to ensure the icing dries completely. Wedding cakes which have been kept for a long time may need re-icing and decorating.

● When the cake has been marzipanned and iced, the cake must remain in a covered cardboard cake box in a warm, dry place. This ensures the icing is kept dry and at peak condition without discolouring or becoming damaged. Damp and cold are the worst conditions for decorated cakes as the icing absorbs the moisture from the air causing condensation on the surface of the cake. This in turn will cause the colours to run and the design to be spoilt.

● If a cake covered with sugar paste is being kept for a later date and has acrylic skewers inserted into the surface, it is advisable to remove the skewers and to fill these holes with a little alcohol. Plug the holes with a small piece of sugar paste to seal.

TO CALCULATE CAKE SERVINGS

A problem which we are often faced with when making a celebration cake is what size to make the cake or cakes, and how many portions it will yield.

To calculate the number of servings from a cake is extremely simple. It depends if you require just a small finger of cake – this is quite usual for a rich fruit cake at a reception – or a more substantial slice. Whether the cake is round, square, heart-shaped or hexagonal, it is always cut into slices. Cut across the cake from edge to edge into about 2.5 cm (1 inch) slices (not wedges), or thinner if desired. Then cut each slice into 4 cm (1½ inch) pieces, or to the size you require. It is then easy to calculate the number of cake slices you can cut from a given size cake. A square cake is larger than a round cake of the same size, and will yield more slices. As you cut across a round cake, the slices become smaller

at either side as the edges curve. Unusual shaped cakes may vary in the quantities they yield so simply work out the slices in the same way.

Sometimes if time is short or the cake has to be produced on a small budget, it is quite acceptable to have just one beautifully iced and decorated cake for the centrepiece. The remaining cake required

may be made as one large slab cake with just the top marzipanned and iced. This will not be seen by guests but may be cut into fingers for the occasion.

CAKE PORTION CHART

Cake Sizes	Round Cake Portions	Square Cake Portions
12.5 cm (5 inch)	16	20
15 cm (6 inch)	25	30
18 cm (7 inch)	36	42
20.5 cm (8 inch)	45	56
23 cm (9 inch)	64	72
25.5 cm (10 inch)	81	90
28 cm (11 inch)	100	120
30.5 cm (12 inch)	120	140

PLANNING THE CAKE FOR THE OCCASION

When you are making any type of celebration cake, it is really important to think through and plan every single detail of the cake carefully. So often it is easy to rush into making the cake with little thought of who the cake is for, the type of cake mixture used, the shape, size or even the finish.

There are so many factors which relate to the finished cake so it is wise to take these points into consideration at the beginning before you even buy the ingredients.

- For whom the cake is being made, the type of person he or she is and their age.
- The cake mixture required for the cake, if it needs to be kept or if it will be eaten immediately.
- The shape and size of the cake, taking into consideration how many guests there will be.
- The type of occasion for which the cake is being made, whether it is formal or informal.
- The colour scheme and type of icing required.
- The design and the time available to complete the cake.
- Transportation of the cake and the distance of its destination.

The type of person for whom you are making the cake always has a strong influence and quite often determines many factors. The most obvious is the age of the recipient, whether it is a young girl or boy, or an adult woman or man. The person may have a particular interest, skill or hobby which may relate to the finished cake; also people's tastes vary.

Many a cake needs to be made in advance so choose a fruit cake which will keep for months, or an instant birthday cake would suit a quick mix.

The shape of the cake is very important. Now there are so many different shaped tins to choose from : hexagonal, round, square, horseshoe, heart-shaped, petal, oval, to name just a few. These shaped tins may be hired from kitchen shops or cake specialists for a small charge or hire fee. Make sure the corresponding shaped cake boards are obtainable, or can be ordered.

The occasion for which the cake is being made often dictates the type of cake you are making, whether it is a wedding cake, christening, anniversary, novelty or birthday cake. For formal occasions, especially for weddings, the colour schemes are most important. Discuss the base colour of the cake and the colours or shades of the decorations. If it is possible, acquire fabric samples or swatches, thread, flowers or ribbons, so that you have a guide to the colour scheme.

The design is always a personal aspect of cake decorating, and everyone knows their strong points and which skills they are happiest working with. This should influence the design as the cake must be beautifully finished; it is always the centrepiece and is viewed from every angle.

The time factor can also affect the design – if time is short, obviously a simple cake well finished is better than an intricate cake which is rushed.

It is also necessary to know the destination of the finished cake as this can relate to the decorations. A cake which has to travel miles for the occasion would be better with a substantial decoration rather than a delicate and fragile piping design which may get damaged in transit. Repair work may always be carried out but sometimes the person making the cake does not accompany it.

When all these factors have been considered, you will be able to make the cake with confidence.

CAKE SIZES AND CAKE BOARDS

The balance of a tiered cake is most important, and aesthetically it should look pleasing to the eye. All the cakes must be of the same depth so to ensure this measure the depth of the uncooked mixture in the first cake tin. Take a note of this and ensure each subsequent cake mixture measures the same.

The following cake sizes give a balanced appearance for a three-tiered cake:

12.5 cm,	18 cm,	23 cm,	(5 inch,	7 inch,	9 inch)
15 cm,	20.5 cm,	25.5 cm,	(6 inch,	8 inch,	10 inch)
15 cm,	23 cm,	30.5 cm,	(6 inch,	9 inch,	12 inch)

Although cake charts are given to ensure that all the cakes are the same depth, problems may arise when unusual shaped tins are used.

The graduation of the cake tiers must be considered carefully; cakes may look heavy and solid if the graduation is too steep. Likewise an unbalanced effect will occur if the gaps between vary or are too great.

The number of tiers used to make the cake must be considered and if they are to be supported by pillars or stacked immediately on top of each other similar to an American style cake. A good tip is to stack the cake tin sizes, base side uppermost, on top of each other to give yourself a helpful visual to work from.

Allow between 5-7.5 cm (2-3 inches) between each cake tier for cakes which will be supported by pillars and 7.5-10 cm (3-4 inches) for cakes which will be stacked one upon another.

Cake boards also play an important part in the cake design and overall appearance. The cake boards need to be 5-7.5 cm (2-3 inches) larger than the cake to allow for the addition of the marzipan, icing and decoration. Sometimes the cake boards are graduated to give a better balance – 5 cm (2 inches) larger on the top tier, 7.5 cm (3 inch) on the second tier, and 10 cm (4 inches) on the base tier. The design of the cake must be considered when selecting cake boards, the colour of the cake boards, the shape and the size. If the design includes run-out collars, extension work or sugar pieces, allow extra width on the cake board to prevent any damage to the decoration. If in any doubt about the size, allow more rather than less.

TIME PLAN FOR CAKE MAKING

When you are committed to making a celebration cake, this can often be quite a worry, wondering how much time to allow for making, icing and decorating the cake. I find the best way is to work backwards from the date the cake is required.

● Firstly I always finish a cake a week before it is required, just in case the person needs the cake earlier, or the collection or delivery cannot be made on the day. Then you can relax in knowing that the cake is at its destination.

● Calculate how long it will take you to decorate one or more cakes; this very much depends on the design you have chosen. Take into consideration how long the decoration will take you, for example. Allow an extra week or two for intricate run-out collars which must include the drying time, remembering that if there is a lot of moisture in the air or if it is winter, they will take much longer to dry out. The cake design may include making hundreds of sugar flowers or sprays. These may always be made months in advance if colours have been decided. Stored carefully in tissue-lined boxes, they will come to no harm.

● Working with sugar paste is much quicker than covering a cake with royal icing, so work out the time it will take to complete either of these icing finishes. Then allow one or two days for marzipanning plus drying time which will take two to three days in a warm dry place, and two days for making the cakes plus extra time if you need to make them in advance.

● To give a rough estimate of time, allow yourself one week to make one simple cake covered with marzipan and sugar paste, or two weeks to complete a cake covered with marzipan and three thin coats of royal icing, both with simple designs.

● To lighten the load and the worry, if you are a beginner to this craft, plan everything well in advance to save any last-minute panic. Make the cakes and store them (see page 13) so that they are ready to marzipan. Each day make a few sugar decorations such as simple sugar flowers, sprays and cut-out sugar pieces or piped flowers.

● Run-out collars or pieces being fitted to a cake cannot be completed until the cake has been smoothly iced with royal icing to obtain accurate measurements, so ice the cake well ahead of time to allow for these decorations to dry out and be fitted to the cake in plenty of time.

● Once the time plan has been worked out, you may work on the cake in a calm relaxed manner which produces good results.

TO ASSEMBLE
TIERED CAKES ON PILLARS

Royal-iced cakes – these are really quite easy to assemble as the cake pillars are placed directly on to the surface of the base cake, and positioned accordingly before placing the next cake on top. The position of the cakes often can relate to the design. Sometimes the pillars support the extreme corners of the cake and cake board above. If the position looks wrong, the cake may be lifted up and the pillars moved in towards the centre of the cake.

Aesthetically a cake looks better if the pillars are just underneath the corners of the cake with the cake board proud of the pillars. If they are positioned too close to the centre, the cake looks unbalanced. Choose pillars made of plaster to match the whiteness and finish of a royal iced cake. They are made round or square to suit the cake shape. Four pillars are used for a square cake and three to support a round cake.

To be more accurate when assembling a square cake, cut out a paper template to the same size as the cake being supported above. Fold the template into four and place one pillar on to the open corner of the template. Draw around the shape of the pillar and cut out neatly. Open the template and place it on the centre of the cake, position the four pillars on the cut spaces of the template. Remove the template and carefully position the cake.

On a round cake, it looks more balanced to have only three pillars in the centre which look like columns. Use the same procedure with the template, but fold the circular template into three, making a cone shape. Place one pillar in the centre edge of the broad end of the cone and cut out the shape. Open the template and position the pillars.

Sugar-pasted cakes – cakes covered with sugar paste may be placed directly on top of each other, producing a soft rounded effect, and are simply supported by their own cake boards. If a sugar paste cake is to be supported by pillars, acrylic skewers must be inserted into the cake as the icing will not support the weight of the subsequent tiers. Preformed hollow cake pillars are then slipped over the skewers to conceal them and to support the cakes.

Arrange the hollow cake pillars on the top of the cake until the position is right. Use a paper template if required, as described before.

Insert one skewer into the centre of the pillars and press right through the icing into the cake until it is resting on the cake board. Repeat inserting the skewers into the remaining pillars. Mark the skewers level with the top of each pillar. Carefully re-

move each pillar and skewer, and cut the skewers to the correct height following the marked lines. Replace the skewers and the pillars and position the cake. Repeat for the other tiers.

Always assemble the cakes before they have to be delivered so you are happy with the appearance. Dismantle the cakes leaving the skewers in position, and pack them into their boxes; pack the pillars separately.

TO DESIGN A CAKE

Cake designing is the most important aspect of cake decorating. The overall design of the cake is seen and admired by everyone. As a centrepiece, the craft is observed at all angles so no part of the cake must be overlooked. Always display the cake in a prominent position as the centrepiece on a table with a matching fabric, beautiful flowers and a silver cake knife.

Once the shape and size of the cake has been decided, this gives you a base on which to plan your design. It is often easier if the design is left to you.

The base colour of the cake has a strong impact on the finished design. White or champagne base colours are the safest choice.

When it comes to choosing the icing for the cake, there are two main choices for formal cakes – the clean, sharp, classical lines of royal icing, or the rounded, smooth finish of sugar paste. These two very different mediums dramatically change the overall appearance of the cakes and also the choices of the decoration.

The actual design of the cake can be chosen at this stage, so it may be a good idea to look at fabric and wallpaper books for unusual designs, china or ceramic patterns, embroidery patterns – all these designs may be interpreted in icing. Reference books will show finished cakes to provide ideas.

SIMPLE CAKES AND GÂTEAUX

BASIC CAKE RECIPES

C ake recipes vary greatly not only by the methods used to make the cakes but also the balance of the various ingredients. The basic aim of all cake making is to incorporate air into the ingredients so that during baking the mixture rises and a light aerated texture is formed.

C akes may be made by whisking together eggs and sugar creating a very light sponge but structurally not very strong. Other cake mixtures are created by creaming together sugar and butter to make a light creamy batter, resulting in a light sponge cake with a firm texture.

Always select the correct recipe for the finished cake you require. Victoria sandwich and quick mix cakes are ideal for decorated sponges, birthday and novelty cakes. They are ideal for cutting, layering and shaping.

Whisked sponges are light as a feather and wonderful for Swiss rolls or flavoured roulades, whereas the Genoese mixture is more suitable for layered gâteaux or dainty iced cakes as the texture is slightly firmer and more moist.

The basic recipes which follow are suitable for all types of cakes.

VICTORIA SANDWICH CAKE

A traditional English cake which may be made in different shapes and flavours to suit plain, fancy or novelty cakes.

175 g (6 oz) butter or block
 margarine, softened
175 g (6 oz) caster sugar
3 eggs, size 3, beaten
175 g (6 oz) self-raising flour,
 sifted
45-60 ml (3-4 tbsp) jam
caster sugar, to dredge (optional)

....

1 Grease and base line two 18 cm (7 inch) sandwich tins. (see page 11).

2 Beat the butter and sugar together until pale and fluffy. Add the eggs, a little at a time, beating well after each addition, scraping down the mixture from time to time. Fold in half the flour, using a spatula, then fold in the remainder until all the flour has been incorporated.

3 Divide the mixture evenly between the tins and level with a palette knife. Bake in the centre of the oven at 180°C (350°F) mark 4 for about 25-30 minutes until they are well risen and the cakes spring back when lightly pressed in the centre. Loosen the edges of the cakes with a palette knife and leave in the tins for 5 minutes. Turn out, remove the lining paper, invert and cool on a wire rack.

4 When the cakes are cool, sandwich them together with the jam and sprinkle the top with caster sugar, if using. Or use as required.

VARIATIONS

Chocolate – Replace 45 ml (3 tbsp) flour with cocoa powder. Sandwich the cakes with vanilla or chocolate butter cream (see page 25).

Coffee – Blend together 10 ml (2 tsp) instant coffee granules with 15 ml (1 tbsp) boiling water. Cool and add to the creamed mixture with the eggs. Sandwich the cakes with vanilla or coffee butter cream (see page 25).

Citrus – Add the finely grated rind of an orange, lime or lemon to the mixture. Sandwich the cakes together with orange, lime or lemon butter cream (see page 25).

ONE STAGE QUICK MIX CAKE

A quick method to produce a light traditional sponge cake which may be flavoured as a Victoria sandwich cake and cooked in many different sized tins. For chocolate, coffee or citrus flavour, see Victoria sandwich cake variations opposite.

175 g (6 oz) self-raising flour
5 ml (1 tsp) baking powder
175 g (6 oz) caster sugar
175 g (6 oz) soft margarine
3 eggs, size 3, beaten
45-60 ml (3-4 tbsp) jam
caster sugar, to dredge (optional)

....

1 Grease and base line two 18 cm (7 inch) sandwich tins (see page 11).

2 Sift the flour and baking powder into a bowl. Add the sugar, margarine and eggs. Mix together with a wooden spoon, then beat for 1-2 minutes until smooth and glossy, or use an electric mixer or food processor until smooth.

3 Divide the mixture evenly between the tins and level with a palette knife. Bake in the centre of the oven at 180°C (350°F) mark 4 for about 25-30 minutes until they are well risen and the cakes spring back when lightly pressed in the centre. Loosen the edges of the cakes with a palette knife, leave to cool in the tins for 5 minutes. Turn out, remove the lining paper, invert and cool on a wire rack.

4 When the cakes are cool, sandwich them together with the jam and sprinkle the top with caster sugar, if using. Or use as required.

GENOESE SPONGE

A whisked sponge mixture with the addition of melted butter to give the cake a moist firm texture. It is ideal for making into small fancy cakes or layering for gâteaux.

40 g (1½ oz) unsalted butter
3 eggs, size 2
75 g (3 oz) caster sugar
65 g (2½ oz) plain flour
15 ml (1 tbsp) cornflour

....

1 Grease and base line two 18 cm (7 inch) sandwich tins or one 18 cm (7 inch) deep round cake tin and dust with a little flour or with a mixture of flour and caster sugar (see page 11).

2 Put the butter into a saucepan and heat gently until melted, then remove from the heat and leave to stand for a few minutes to cool slightly.

3 Put the eggs and sugar in a bowl, whisk until well blended using an electric whisk. Place the bowl over a pan of hot water and whisk until pale and creamy and thick enough to leave a trail on the surface when the whisk is lifted. Remove the bowl from the saucepan and whisk until cool and thick.

4 Sift the flours together into a bowl. Sift, then fold the flour into the egg mixture using a plastic bladed spatula until all the flour has been incorporated.

5 Pour the cooled butter around the edge of the mixture leaving the sediment behind. Gradually fold in the butter very lightly, cutting through the mixture until all the butter has been incorporated. Pour into tins.

6 Bake in the oven at 180°C (350°F) mark 4 for 25-30 minutes, or the deep cake for 35-40 minutes, until well risen and the cakes spring back when lightly pressed. Loosen the cake edge and leave for 5 minutes. Turn out, remove paper and cool on a rack.

WHISKED SPONGE CAKE

A quick and easy light sponge mixture suitable for gâteaux, Swiss rolls or novelty cakes.

3 eggs, size 2
125 g (4 oz) caster sugar
75 g (3 oz) plain flour
45-60 ml (3-4 tbsp) strawberry or
   apricot jam, to fill
caster sugar, to dredge (optional)
....

1 Grease and base line two 18 cm (7 inch) sandwich tins and dust with a little flour or with a mixture of flour and caster sugar (see page 11).

2 Put the eggs and sugar in a bowl, whisk until well blended using an electric whisk. Place the bowl over a pan of hot water and whisk until pale and creamy, and thick enough to leave a trail on the surface when the whisk is lifted. Remove the bowl from the saucepan and whisk until cool and thick.

3 Sift half the flour over the mixture and fold it in very lightly, using a plastic spatula. Sift in the remaining flour and fold in until all the flour has been incorporated.

4 Pour the mixture into the tins, tilting the tins to spread the mixture evenly. Do not use a palette knife or spatula to smooth the mixture as this will crush out the air bubbles.

5 Bake in oven at 190°C (375°F) mark 5 for 20-25 minutes until well risen and the cakes spring back when lightly pressed in the centre. Turn out and cool on a wire rack.

SWISS ROLL

3 eggs, size 2
125 g (4 oz) caster sugar
125 g (4 oz) plain flour
caster sugar, to dredge (optional)
125 g (4 oz) jam, warmed
....

1 Grease and line a 33 × 23 cm (13 × 9 inch) Swiss roll tin (see page 11); grease the paper. Dust with caster sugar and flour.

2 Put the eggs and sugar in a bowl, whisk until well blended using an electric hand whisk. Place the bowl over a pan of hot water and whisk until pale and creamy, and thick enough to leave a trail on the surface when the whisk is lifted. Remove the bowl from the saucepan and whisk until cool and thick.

3 Sift half the flour over the mixture and fold it in very lightly using a plastic bladed spatula. Sift in the remaining flour and fold in until all the flour has been completely incorporated. Lightly and carefully fold 15 ml (1 tbsp) hot water into the Swiss roll mixture.

4 Pour the mixture into the tin and tilt the tin backwards and forwards to spread evenly.

Bake in the oven at 200°C (400°C) mark 6 for 10-12 minutes until pale golden, well risen and the cake springs back when pressed.

5 Meanwhile, place a sheet of greaseproof paper on a work surface. Dredge the paper thickly with caster sugar.

6 Quickly turn out the cake on to the paper and remove the lining paper. Trim off the edges and spread the cake with jam.

7 Roll up the cake with the aid of the paper. Make the first turn firmly so that the whole cake will roll evenly and have a good shape when finished, but roll more lightly after this turn.

8 Place seam-side down on a wire rack and dredge with sugar, if using.

BASIC ICINGS AND FROSTINGS

*E*ach icing or frosting has its own characteristics in texture, flavour, colour and consistency, and may be used to fill, cover and decorate cakes. Some icings are satin smooth and may be poured over the cake to give a smooth glossy finish, whereas other varieties may need spreading or swirling to give a textured appearance.

*B*utter cream or dairy cream may be smoothed flat, textured with a palette knife or piped to give a professional finish. Whichever choice is made to fill, cover or decorate the cake, have the base well prepared so that the cake keeps a good shape throughout.

CUTTING CAKES INTO LAYERS

A well prepared cake must consist of evenly baked cake layers, or one deep cake cut into several thin even layers.

Once the cakes are baked satisfactorily and cooled, cut them into layers. Place the cake on a thin cake board on a turntable at eye level. Using a long sharp knife, mark the number of layers required on the side of the cake. Cut into the side of the cake in a sawing movement cutting backwards and forwards and slowly revolve the cake as you are cutting, keeping the cut even. Once you have cut through all the side of the cake, continue the sawing movement to separate the layers. Repeat to cut into more layers if necessary.

If the layers have to be cut across an oblong cake, measure accurately before cutting; a good guide is to measure twice, cut once.

It is necessary to coat the cake with an icing which will complement the texture, flavour and filling of the cake. The same mixture used to fill the cake can often be used as the covering. It may be necessary to dilute, thicken or warm the filling to obtain the desired finish to the cake.

FILLING CAKES WITH ICING AND FROSTINGS

Fillings come in different textures, consistencies, flavours and colours. It is the essential part of assembling a layered cake or gâteau as it offers moisture, flavour and a way of sandwiching the layers back together to give the cake a good shape.

Some fillings team better with some cakes than others; if a cake is light and delicate in texture, it needs to be filled with a light cream filling or frosting. A more substantial cake will tolerate a richer type of filling; this factor is quite important when cutting a cake as often a heavy filling can cause a cake to fall apart once cut as it cannot support the filling.

There are many types of filling which may be used to fill cakes – whipped dairy cream with added coffee, chocolate or fruit zests; frosting flavoured with coffee, chocolate or citrus fruits; butter cream, which is the most popular, or crème au beurre and chocolate fudge icing, not forgetting a variety of jams which team well with all frostings and icings. *To fill a cake* – place the cake on a thin cake board, decide on the filling required and ensure the consistency is ideal for spreading on to a cut surface of a fresh cake. If the filling is too firm, it will pull the crumbs from the cake, making an untidy layer. On the other hand, fillings which are too soft will cause the cake layers to slip and move around, and ooze out of the side of the cake.

Use a palette knife dipped in hot water before spreading the filling evenly over the cake. This prevents the filling from sticking to the knife and pulling up the cake crumbs. Re-dip the knife to obtain a smooth, level finish. Place the next cake layer in position, making sure it is level, then repeat the procedure to fill the remaining cake. Always keep the cake on a thin cake board during filling to ensure the cake remains level and even at all times.

When dairy cream is being used to fill a cake or gâteau, the most even way to fill the layers is to pipe the whipped cream through a 5 mm (¼ inch) plain piping nozzle evenly over the surface. Place the next cake layer evenly in position and gently press to level. Repeat the procedure and add the remaining layers of cake.

Jam should be heated gently to warm it and to make the consistency softer for spreading over the cake layers. If it is spread from the jar, it will pull up the cake crumbs and cause holes in the cake.

The most important point to remember when layering and filling cakes is to work at eye level to ensure the cake is level. If the layers are even and the filling spread evenly throughout the layers, and when the cake is re-assembled ensure all the layers are accurately put together, the end result should then be a good shaped cake ready for frosting or coating. Place the cake in a cool place to set before frosting or icing to ensure the cake is firm and retains a good shape.

COVERING A CAKE USING BASIC ICINGS AND FROSTINGS

To cover a cake with butter cream or crème au beurre icing – this is a different process to filling as the icing will need to be spread evenly over the surface of the cake. Make sure the icing is well beaten, smooth and soft in texture so that it does not pull up the surface crumbs of the cake. Keep the cake on the thin cake board and place it on the turntable. Place a spoonful of icing on top of the cake and use a small cranked palette knife to spread the icing smoothly. Have a jug of hot water to dip the knife into as the icing is spread so that the icing does not stick to the palette knife and pull up the crumb surface. Simply coat the cake as evenly as possible with the icing to obtain a smooth coating. Then, using the palette knife dipped into hot water, add some more icing and spread smoothly to obtain a good, even surface. It looks most attractive to paddle the palette knife backwards and forwards to give a lined effect instead of a perfectly smooth coat.

Another way of producing a pattern is to swirl the palette knife on the surface of the icing to produce a textured finish. Alternatively, pipe a design directly on to the surface of the cake; the most obvious choice is a basket weave design (see page 28), or a piped scroll, shell or swirl edging.

To cover a cake with frosting – this gives you a choice of a smooth surface or a textured finish. If the cake is to be smooth, keep it on a thin cake board the same size, or slightly smaller, than the cake and place it on a wire rack over a plate or a turntable.

Make the frosting and ensure it is of the right consistency, thick enough to evenly coat the back of a spoon. Frostings are often warm at this stage; if it is too thick, the bowl will need to be placed over hot water to melt the frosting, or have a little water added to dilute the consistency. On the other hand, if the frosting is too slack, allow it to cool and as it does so the frosting will thicken.

Before frosting the cake, make sure everything is ready and there is a palette knife to hand. Pour the frosting all at once over the top of the cake and allow the frosting to fall over the sides. Do not be tempted to spread the frosting or it will mark, but gently tap or shake the cake to encourage the frosting to fall evenly from the top.

Once the frosting has stopped falling, run a palette knife around the base of the cake board to neaten the edge and allow the covering to dry. Carefully lift the cake on to a cake plate and add the finishing touches.

To finish – once any cake has been covered with icing or frosting, it adds flavour and texture to coat the sides with toasted nuts, crushed ratafias or meringues; pistachio nuts particularly add colour, or crushed praline or grated chocolate.

The cake is now ready for the finishing touches, so use any simple decorations such as flowers, fruit, chocolate leaves or cut-out shapes.

BUTTER CREAM

75 g (3 oz) unsalted butter,
softened
175 g (6 oz) icing sugar, sieved
few drops of vanilla flavouring
15-30 ml (1-2 tbsp) milk or water

....

> ### HINT
> It can be used as a filling or
> icing. Spread it over the top of
> the cake only, or over the top
> and sides. Decorate by making
> swirls with a palette knife and
> mark with the prongs of a fork.
> For more elaborate decoration,
> butter cream can be piped on
> top of the cake as well.

1 Put the butter in a bowl and
beat with a wooden spoon
until it is light and fluffy.

2 Gradually stir in the icing
sugar, vanilla and milk or
water. Beat well until light and
smooth.
Makes 250 g (9 oz)

VARIATIONS
Orange, lime or lemon – Replace
the vanilla flavouring with a little
finely grated orange, lime or lemon
rind. Add a little juice from the fruit
instead of the milk, beating well to
avoid curdling the mixture. If the
mixture is to be piped, omit the fruit
rinds.
Coffee – Replace the vanilla flavouring with 10 ml (2 tsp) instant coffee
granules dissolved in 15 ml (1 tbsp)
boiling water; cool before adding to
the mixture.
Chocolate – Blend 15 ml (1 tbsp)
cocoa powder with 30 ml (2 tbsp)
boiling water and cool before adding
to the mixture.

CRÈME AU BEURRE

75 g (3 oz) caster sugar
60 ml (4 tbsp) water
2 egg yolks, beaten
175 g (6 oz) unsalted butter,
softened

....

1 Place the sugar and water in a
heavy pan and heat gently to
dissolve sugar, without boiling.

2 When the sugar has
dissolved, boil steadily for 2-3
minutes to reach thread stage, a
temperature of 107°C (225°F) as
registered on a sugar thermometer.
To test, remove the pan from the
heat and place a little syrup on the
back of a dry teaspoon. Press the
back of a second teaspoon on to
the syrup and pull them apart. The
syrup should form a fine thread.

3 Pour the syrup in a thin
stream on to the yolks in a
bowl, whisking with an electric
hand whisk until thick and cold.

4 In another bowl, whisk the
butter until light and fluffy.

Gradually add the egg yolk
mixture, whisking well after each
addition.
Makes about 275 g (10 oz)

VARIATIONS
Chocolate – Melt 50 g (2 oz) plain
chocolate. Cool slightly and beat
into the crème au beurre mixture.
Fruit – Crush 225 g (8 oz) fresh
strawberries, raspberries, etc., or
thaw, drain and crush frozen fruit.
Beat into the crème au beurre mixture.
Orange or lemon – Add freshly
grated rind and juice to taste to the
crème au beurre mixture.
Coffee – Dissolve 15-30 ml (1-2 tbsp)
coffee granules in 15 ml (1 tbsp)
boiling water. Cool, then beat into
the crème au beurre mixture.

GLACÉ ICING

225 g (8 oz) icing sugar
few drops of vanilla or almond
    flavouring (optional)
30-45 ml (2-3 tbsp) boiling water
food colouring (optional)

....

1 Sift the icing sugar into a bowl. Add a few drops of flavouring if wished.

2 Using a wooden spoon, gradually stir in enough water until the mixture is the consistency of thick cream. Beat until white and smooth and the icing is thick enough to coat the back of the spoon. Add colouring, if liked, and use at once.
Makes about 225 g (8 oz)

VARIATIONS

Orange or lemon – Replace the water with strained orange or lemon juice.

Mocha – Dissolve 5 ml (1 tsp) cocoa powder and 10 ml (2 tsp) instant coffee granules in 15 ml (1 tbsp) of the boiling water.

Liqueur – Replace 10-15 ml (2-3 tsp) of the water with the same amount of any liqueur.

Chocolate – Sift 10 ml (2 tsp) cocoa powder with the icing sugar.

Coffee – Flavour with 5 ml (1 tsp) coffee essence or dissolve 10 ml (2 tsp) instant coffee granules in 15 ml (1 tbsp) of the hot water.

Rosewater – Use 10 ml (2 tsp) rose-water instead of water.

COFFEE FUDGE FROSTING

50 g (2 oz) butter or margarine
125 g (4 oz) light soft brown sugar
30 ml (2 tbsp) single cream or
    milk
15 ml (1 tbsp) coffee granules
30 ml (2 tbsp) boiling water
200 g (7 oz) icing sugar, sifted

....

1 Put the butter, sugar and cream in a saucepan. Blend together the coffee and boiling water and add to the saucepan. Heat gently until the sugar dissolves. Boil briskly for 3 minutes.

2 Remove the saucepan from the heat and gradually stir in the icing sugar. Beat with a wooden spoon for 1 minute until

smooth. Use immediately, spreading with a wet palette knife, or dilute with a little water and use as a smooth coating frosting.
Makes about 400 g (14 oz)

VARIATION

Chocolate fudge frosting – Omit the coffee and add 75 g (3 oz) plain chocolate or plain chocolate flavoured cake covering with the butter in the pan.

SEVEN-MINUTE FROSTING

1 egg white
175 g (6 oz) caster sugar
30 ml (2 tbsp) water
pinch of salt
pinch of cream of tartar

....

1 Put all the ingredients into a bowl and whisk lightly using an electric hand whisk.

2 Place the bowl over a pan of hot water and heat, whisking continuously, until the mixture thickens sufficiently to stand in peaks. This will take about 7 minutes.

3 Pour the frosting over the top of the cake and spread with a palette knife.
Makes about 175 g (6 oz)

VANILLA FROSTING

150 g (5 oz) icing sugar, sifted
25 ml (5 tsp) vegetable oil
15 ml (1 tbsp) milk
few drops of vanilla flavouring

....

1 Put the icing sugar in a bowl and, using a wooden spoon, beat in the oil, milk and vanilla flavouring until smooth.
Makes about 175 g (6 oz)

CHOCOLATE FROSTING

25 g (1 oz) plain chocolate or
plain chocolate flavoured cake
covering
25 g (1 oz) butter or margarine
1 egg, beaten
150 g (5 oz) icing sugar, sifted
2.5 ml (½ tsp) vanilla flavouring

....

1 Break the chocolate into pieces and place in a bowl with the butter over a saucepan of hot water. Stir occasionally until the chocolate has melted, then remove the bowl from the pan.

2 Stir in the egg, icing sugar, and vanilla flavouring. Beat until the frosting is smooth.
Makes about 200 g (7 oz)

AMERICAN FROSTING

1 egg white
225 g (8 oz) caster or granulated
sugar
60 ml (4 tbsp) water
pinch of cream of tartar

....

1 Whisk the egg white until stiff. Place the sugar, water and cream of tartar in a saucepan. Heat gently, stirring until the sugar has dissolved. Bring to the boil, without stirring, and boil until it reaches a temperature of 115°C (240°F).

2 Remove the syrup from the heat and immediately, when the bubbles subside, pour the syrup on to the egg white in a thin stream, whisking the mixture using an electric hand whisk until thick and white. Leave to cool slightly.

3 When the mixture starts to go dull around the edges and is almost cold, pour quickly over the cake and spread evenly with a palette knife.
Makes about 225 g (8 oz)

BASKET WEAVE HEART

*J*ust a basic orange-flavoured quick mix cake simply transformed by the use of two nozzles to create this basket weave of butter cream. Tint the butter cream to match the flowers available for the cake.

4-egg quantity orange-flavoured quick mix cake mixture (see page 21)
2½ quantities butter cream, using orange juice (see page 25)
gooseberry green food colouring
fresh flowers, to decorate

....

1 Grease and line the base and side of a 20.5 cm (8 inch) heart-shaped cake tin. Make the orange-flavoured quick cake mixture, omitting the baking powder. Turn the mixture into the prepared tin. Bake in the oven at 180°C (350°F) mark 4 for 1½ hours until well risen and the cake springs back when lightly pressed in the centre. Leave the cake to cool in the tin, then turn out, remove the paper and place in the centre of the cake board.

2 Cut the cake horizontally into three layers. Spread each with a layer of butter cream and re-assemble the layers. Spread the top and sides smoothly with a thin layer of butter cream. Place in the refrigerator for 15 minutes to set the butter cream.

3 Tint a quarter of the butter cream green with a few drops of gooseberry green food colouring. Fit one large greaseproof paper piping bag (see page 129) with a basket weave nozzle, half-fill with plain butter cream and fold down the top. Fit a medium-sized greaseproof paper piping bag with a No. 43 rope nozzle and half-fill with green butter cream.

4 Pipe the side of the cake first, starting at the back of the heart with a vertical green line from top to bottom. Then pipe four horizontal lines each spaced apart with the basket weave nozzle, starting at the top edge and working towards the base of the cake.

5 Repeat this pattern to cover the side of the cake, piping vertical green lines and horizontal basket weave lines (see page 129).

6 Pipe the top in just the same way, starting at the point of the heart and working across the top of the cake from side to side. Just before serving, decorate with fresh flowers.

HINT
Use any flavour cake mixture of your choice to make the heart shaped cake.

COFFEE COCONUT BOMBE

This rather spectacular-looking cake is made in an ice cream bombe mould and is full of surprises. Inside the smooth coffee frosting is a moist coffee cake with a white coconut filling.

1 egg white
50 g (2 oz) caster sugar
75 g (3 oz) fresh coconut, grated
15 ml (1 tbsp) cornflour
3-egg quantity coffee-flavoured
  quick mix cake mixture (see
  page 21)
DECORATION
1 quantity coffee fudge frosting
  (see page 26)
ribbons of fresh coconut
10 chocolate coffee beans
cocoa powder and icing sugar, to
  dust

....

> ### HINT
> Omit the baking powder when
> using a deep mould to keep the
> mixture more stable. Use a
> pudding basin if you do not
> have a mould. Desiccated
> coconut may be used instead of
> fresh if preferred.

1 Grease and base line an 18
   cm (7 inch), 1.7 litre (3 pint)
bell or ice cream bombe mould.
Whisk the egg white in a bowl until
stiff. Gradually add the sugar,
whisking well after each addition
until the meringue is thick. Mix
together the coconut and cornflour
and add to the meringue. Using a
plastic-bladed spatula, gently fold
in until all the coconut has been
incorporated.

2 Make the coffee-flavoured
   quick cake mixture, omitting
the baking powder. Turn half the
mixture into the prepared mould.
Drop spoonfuls of coconut mixture
on to the coffee cake mixture and
place the remaining cake mixture
on top. Smooth with a palette
knife.

3 Bake in the oven at 180°C
   (350°F) mark 4 for 1½ hours
until well risen and the cake
springs back when lightly pressed
in the centre. Loosen the edge of
the cake with a palette knife and
leave the cake to cool in the tin.
Turn out on to a wire rack and
remove the lining paper.

4 Make the coffee frosting and
   ensure the consistency will
easily coat the back of a wooden
spoon. If it is too thick, add
enough cold water to dilute it, or if
it is too slack allow the frosting to
cool.

5 Place a tray underneath the
   cake and pour the frosting
over the cake all at once to coat
evenly. Tap the rack to allow the
frosting to fall evenly. Run a palette
knife around the base of the cake
and place it on a serving plate.

6 Using a potato peeler, peel
   off thin ribbons of coconut
and arrange around the base of the
cake in loops. Decorate with the
coffee beans and dust with sifted
cocoa powder and icing sugar.

FROSTED FRUIT RING

A chocolate maraschino ring cake covered with
American frosting and filled with a selection of
sugar frosted fruits and flowers.

3-egg quantity chocolate-flavoured
  quick mix cake mixture (see
  page 21)
125 g (4 oz) maraschino flavoured
  cherries, drained and sliced
1 quantity American frosting (see
  page 27)
450 g (1 lb) assorted sugar-frosted
  fruits – physalis, cherries, white
  grapes, strawberries (see page
  170)
fresh flowers and leaves

```
HINT
Drain the maraschino cherries
well and dry on absorbent
kitchen paper before slicing.
```

1 Grease and base line a 23 cm
(9 inch) ring mould. Dust the
sides with flour. Make the
chocolate flavoured quick cake
mixture and fold in the maraschino
cherries. Turn the mixture into the
prepared mould.

2 Bake in the oven at 180°C
(350°F) mark 4 for 50-55
minutes until well risen and the
cake springs back when lightly
pressed in the centre. Loosen the
edge of the cake with a palette
knife and cool in the tin for 5
minutes. Invert on to a wire rack,
remove the lining paper and leave
until cold.

3 Make the American frosting
and spread evenly over the
ring cake to cover completely.
Swirl with a palette knife and leave
to set.

4 Leave the stems on the
fruits, twist back the physalis
leaves and sugar frost the fruit (see
page 170). Leave until dry.

5 Place the cake on a serving
plate, arrange the fruit in the
centre of the cake and pile high
into an attractive arrangement,
using fresh or sugar frosted flowers
and leaves of your choice if
desired.

KIWI AND BLUEBERRY GÂTEAU

*T*he fresh flavour and colours of kiwi fruit and
blueberries make this gâteau irresistible. Try a
different combination of fruits to suit the season.

1 quantity of Genoese sponge
  mixture (see page 21)
finely grated rind of 1 lime
300 ml (½ pint) whipping cream
60 ml (4 tbsp) apricot fruit spread
4 kiwi fruit, skinned and sliced
175 g (6 oz) blueberries
75 g (3 oz) pistachio nuts,
  skinned and finely chopped

· ·

HINT
If the pistachio nuts are not a
good colour, add a drop of green
food colouring to the chopped
nuts and mix until evenly
coloured.

1   Grease and base line a 23 cm
(9 inch) sandwich tin. Dust
the sides with flour. Make the
Genoese sponge mixture, folding in
the grated lime rind with the
butter. Turn the mixture into the
prepared tin.

2   Bake in the oven at 180°C
(350°F) mark 4 for 30
minutes until well risen and the
cake springs back when lightly
pressed in the centre. Loosen the
edge of the cake with a palette
knife and cool in the tin for 10
minutes. Turn out, remove the
lining paper and cool on a wire
rack.

3   Whip the cream until it softly
peaks, place one-third of the
cream into a nylon piping bag
fitted with a star nozzle. Cut the
cake into two layers horizontally.
Spread the base layer with apricot
fruit spread and cover with one-
third of kiwi fruit slices, one-third
blueberries and one-third of the
cream.

4   Place the top layer of cake in
position and spread the sides
of the cake evenly with the
remaining cream. Cover the side
with pistachio nuts and place the
cake on a serving plate.

5   Cover the top of the cake
with the remaining fruit
spread. Cut the kiwi slices from
the centre to the edge and twist.
Arrange twists of kiwi fruit all
around the edge of the gâteau and
fill the centre with a pile of
blueberries.

6   Pipe a reverse scroll edging
of cream around the top edge
to decorate (see page 128). Chill
until required.

RITZY MOCHA GÂTEAU

*A*n eye-catching gâteau with a wonderful mixture of flavours. Decorate with three-flavoured crème au beurre and top with chocolate cut-out pieces.

15 ml (1 tbsp) coffee granules
30 ml (2 tbsp) boiling water
3-egg quantity whisked sponge
  mixture (see page 22)
15 g (½ oz) cocoa powder
125 g (4 oz) plain chocolate,
  melted
2 quantities crème au beurre (see
  page 25)

....

1 Grease and line a 33 × 23 cm
(13 × 9 inch) Swiss roll tin.
Blend together the coffee granules
and boiling water and leave until
cool. Make the sponge mixture,
replacing 15 g (½ oz) of the flour
with the cocoa powder, and fold in
half the coffee liquid until evenly
blended. Pour the mixture into the
prepared tin, tilt to level the
mixture.

2 Bake in the oven at 190°C
(375°F) mark 5 for 20-25
minutes until well risen and the
cake springs back when lightly
pressed in the centre. Cool the
cake in the tin, then invert on to a
wire rack and remove the lining
paper. Cut the cake into three
short strips.

3 Melt the chocolate while
making the crème au beurre.
Divide the crème au beurre in
three equal portions. Add half of
the melted chocolate to one
portion and beat until smooth.
Beat the remaining coffee into
another portion of crème au
beurre. Spread the base layer of
sponge with chocolate, the second
layer with coffee and the top layer
with plain crème au beurre.
Sandwich the three layers together.

4 Fit a nylon piping bag with a
small star nozzle and fill with
plain crème au beurre. Pipe a line
across the top edge of the cake and
leave a gap for the coffee and

chocolate lines to follow. Repeat to
pipe more lines at intervals across
the top of the cake. Match up the
top lines with vertical side and end
lines of plain crème au beurre.

5 Repeat with the same size
nozzle to pipe chocolate lines
and coffee lines across the top and
down the sides and ends of the
gâteau.

6 Spread the remaining melted
chocolate over a piece of
non-stick baking parchment until
smooth. When the chocolate has
only just set, cut out eight petal
shaped pieces of chocolate using a
small cutter (see chocolate cut-
outs on page 47). Arrange the
chocolate cut-outs down the length
of the cake. Leave to set.

LEMON GERANIUM CELEBRATION CAKE

T he subtle lemon flavour of this cake is imparted from fresh lemon geranium leaves lining the base of the cake tin. The decoration is simply smooth butter cream and the leaf border which is piped from a greaseproof paper piping bag.

4-egg quantity quick mix cake
  mixture (see page 21)
6 fresh lemon geranium leaves
  or the grated zest of 1 lemon
2½ quantities butter cream, using
  lemon (see page 25)
gooseberry green and claret red
  food colourings
1 metre (1 yard), 4 cm (1½ inch)
  wide fancy claret ribbon
fresh dark pink or red flowers

....

1 Grease and line the base and side of a 20.5 cm (8 inch) round cake tin. Arrange the geranium leaves over the base. Make the quick cake mixture and add the lemon zest if the leaves are not available. Turn into the tin.

2 Bake in the oven at 180°C (350°F) mark 4 for 1 hour 20 minutes until well risen and the cake springs back when lightly pressed. Leave to cool in the tin, then turn out and remove paper.

3 Cut the cake horizontally into three layers. Sandwich the layers together using one-third of the butter cream. Spread the sides and the top evenly with a thin layer of butter cream. Place the cake in the refrigerator for 15 minutes to set the butter cream.

4 Spread a second layer of butter cream over the cake to cover evenly and smooth the surface with a side scraper and a palette knife. Dip the side scraper and palette knife into hot water to help smooth the surface. Leave to set.

5 Divide the remaining butter cream in half and colour rich green and claret colours, using the two food colourings. Using two medium-sized greaseproof paper piping bags, half-fill each with green and claret butter cream. Fold down the tops. Press the butter cream to the end of each piping

bag and press flat. Using a pair of sharp scissors, cut each side of the point to shape an inverted 'V'.

6 Pipe alternate green and claret butter icing leaves around the top and base of the cake. Pipe one colour at a time, leaving a space in between for the remaining colour. Fit the ribbon around the side of the cake and secure into folds with a stainless steel pin. Decorate with fresh flowers and a lemon geranium leaf.

PRALINE PYRAMID

A sensational centrepiece for a special celebration.
Melt-in-the-mouth japonnaise layers with orange
praline flavoured crème au beurre, glistening with
caramel threads.

JAPONNAISE
175 g (6 oz) toasted hazelnuts,
* finely ground*
15 ml (1 tbsp) cornflour
4 egg whites
250 g (9 oz) caster sugar
PRALINE
50 g (2 oz) caster sugar
50 g (2 oz) skinned hazelnuts
CARAMEL
125 g (4 oz) granulated sugar
60 ml (4 tbsp) water

2 quantities crème au beurre (see
* page 25)*
finely grated zest of 1 orange

....

1   Line two baking sheets with
    non-stick baking parchment
and draw five decreasing circles –
20.5 cm (8 inches), 16 cm (6½
inches), 12.5 cm (5 inches), 9 cm
(3½ inches), 5 cm (2 inches).
Invert the paper.

2   To make the japonnaise, mix
    together the hazelnuts and
cornflour. Whisk the egg whites
until stiff. Gradually add the sugar
and continue whisking well after
each addition until all the sugar is

incorporated. Add the hazelnut
mixture and fold in carefully using
a plastic-bladed spatula until all
the hazelnuts are incorporated.

3   Fit a large nylon piping bag
    with 1.5 cm (⅝ inch) plain
piping nozzle and fill with
japonnaise mixture. Pipe a
continuous ring of mixture just
inside the marked line of each
circle. Fill in the circles with a coil
of mixture, piping from the outside
ring into the centre of each. Pipe
any leftover mixture into small
rounds in between the circles on
the paper.

4   Bake the japonnaise layers in
    the oven at 170°C (325°F)
mark 3 for 1¼ hours or until the
smaller rounds lift easily off the
paper. Cool the japonnaise layers
on the paper on wire racks.

5   To make the praline, place
    the sugar and hazelnuts in a
non-stick frying pan and heat
gently until the sugar melts and
turns a rich golden brown. Pour

the mixture on to a well buttered
baking sheet and leave until cold.
Crush finely in a food processor or
between two sheets of greaseproof
paper with a rolling pin.

6   Make the crème au beurre
    and place one-third into a
nylon piping bag fitted with a small
star nozzle. Stir the praline and
orange zest into the remaining
crème au beurre.

7   Place the base japonnaise
    layer in the centre of a cake
board or serving plate and spread
generously with praline and orange
crème au beurre. Cover with the
next layer and repeat until all the
layers are in position. Pipe coils of
crème au beurre around the edge
of each layer with a swirl on the
top. Position four tiny rounds of
japonnaise on top of the pyramid.
Leave in a cool place until 1 hour
before serving.

8 Place the sugar and water into a saucepan and heat gently, stirring occasionally until the sugar has dissolved. Cover a baking sheet with foil and butter generously. Boil rapidly until the syrup turns a rich golden brown. Remove the saucepan from the heat and allow the bubbles to subside. Using a spoon, drizzle 20 abstract pieces of caramel on to the foil, allowing the thread to fall then move the spoon back and forth producing neat shapes. Arrange these pieces on to the pyramid.

9 Warm the remaining caramel so it is just liquid. Add a little water if necessary to melt the caramel. Using a fork, dip into the caramel and touch on to one of the caramel pieces. Pull to form a thread and wind around the gâteau. Repeat until the gâteau is covered in fine caramel threads.

10 Place in the refrigerator until required. Decorate with fresh flowers if desired.   To serve the praline pyramid, start at the top and lift off one or two layers at a time. Cut into wedges.

HINT
Assemble the gâteau, cover with cling film and keep refrigerated overnight. Pipe and decorate with caramel the next day.
   When making the meringue circles use egg whites which are at least one week old. This produces a meringue which will keep for several weeks.

CHOCOLATE

CHOCOLATE

*R*ich, dark, exotic, a sheer luxury, almost addictive
qualities are all summed up in the one word
'Chocolate'. Being an expensive and highly processed
ingredient, it needs care when being used for cooking.

*C*hocolate varies greatly in quality, flavour and texture depending on the type of chocolate chosen. Sometimes it is quite daunting to know which type to use for certain recipes, but this becomes much clearer once you have an idea how chocolate is made and formed into bars of white, plain and milk chocolate.

When the cocoa beans have been roasted, the skin is removed together with the gum leaving what are known as 'cocoa nibs'. These are ground into a thick paste and processed into about half cocoa butter and half chocolate liquor.

SELECTING CHOCOLATE

White chocolate – made only from the cocoa butter and sugar with no addition of the chocolate liquor, hence the colour.

Couverture chocolate – made from cocoa butter and chocolate liquor with no added sugar, producing a very dark, brittle chocolate suitable only for chocolate work and cooking. This chocolate is ideal for hand-made chocolates, gâteaux, desserts and decorations. It must be tempered before use.

Plain and semi-sweet chocolate – also made from cocoa butter, chocolate liquor and sweetened with some sugar.

Milk chocolate – made the same way as plain chocolate but has the addition of dried milk powder which gives the chocolate a lighter colour and texture and a sweeter flavour.

Cocoa – made from the chocolate liquor which has been pressed and dried to form an unsweetened chocolate powder.

Other less expensive forms of chocolate are made with some of the cocoa butter being replaced with vegetable fat. This makes the chocolate softer in texture and not such a good flavour. If more than 50 per cent of the cocoa butter has been replaced, it may no longer be called chocolate.

All these qualities of chocolate are suitable for cooking and may be purchased as plain, milk or white chocolate; the plainer the chocolate, the harder the texture and stronger the flavour will be.

MELTING CHOCOLATE

Care must be taken when melting chocolate as it is an exacting process and determines the set appearance of the chocolate, giving it either a smooth glossy finish or a dull streaked appearance. Once melted, the chocolate may be used for dipping, coating, spreading or for cut-out chocolate pieces and piped decorations. Always choose a good quality chocolate if melted chocolate is being used and set, as the flavour and texture are important.

TO MELT CHOCOLATE

1 Break fresh chocolate into small pieces and place in a large, dry, clean bowl over a saucepan of *hand-hot* water.

2 Ensure the base of the bowl does not touch the water and there are no spaces between the bowl and the saucepan rim which may cause steam and condensation to get into the chocolate which will render it thick and unusable.

3 Do not beat, but stir occasionally while the chocolate is melting. This you cannot hurry and the chocolate temperature should not exceed 38-43°C (100-110°F), otherwise when it eventually sets, the surface will be dull and covered in streaks.

4 Leave the bowl over hand-hot water during use, unless you require the chocolate thicker.

5 For speed use a microwave to melt the chocolate. Place the chocolate, broken into small pieces, into a bowl and place in the microwave on the lowest setting. Heat for 3-4 minutes until the chocolate has almost melted, then stir until smooth. If the temperature of the chocolate becomes too warm it will result in a streaked surface. This method is ideal for cakes which need melted chocolate added to them.

CHOCOLATE FOR COATING

1 Stand cakes or biscuits on a wire rack, spaced a little apart, making sure all the items to be coated are at room temperature for smooth even coating.

2 Place a large piece of non-stick baking parchment underneath the wire rack to catch the excess chocolate.

CHOCOLATE FOR DIPPING

This is ideal for small sweets, fruit and nuts.

1 Have everything ready before starting and ensure all the items to be dipped are at room temperature, otherwise the chocolate will set before smoothly coating.

2 Use two confectioners' dipping forks or two dinner forks with fine prongs and have several sheets of non-stick baking

3 Depending on the size of the items being coated, use a ladle full of chocolate that will coat the whole area at one coating for small cakes and biscuits, or pour the chocolate directly from the bowl, ensuring the base is completely dry.

parchment ready to take the dipped items.

3 Take one piece at a time and immerse in the melted chocolate, turn once with the dipping fork to coat evenly.

4 Lift out of the chocolate with the fork and tap gently on the side of the bowl to allow the excess chocolate to fall.

4 Quickly pour the chocolate over all at once, allowing the excess to fall on to the paper. Tap or gently shake the wire rack to level the chocolate. Repeat with another layer of chocolate after the first one has set, if desired, returning the fallen chocolate from the baking parchment back into the bowl.

5 Place the coated item on to the paper, push off carefully using a small palette knife and leave to set. Trim off the bases to neaten if necessary.

6 To half coat fruit, nuts or sweets, simply immerse half the item being dipped, lift out and allow the excess chocolate to fall (see page 52). Leave to set on the paper.

TO MAKE CHOCOLATE LEAVES

Choose real fresh leaves which are small, firm and have well-defined veins, from flowers, herbs and plants. (See also page 56.)

1 Pick the leaves as freshly as possible and dry them thoroughly on absorbent kitchen paper. Line a tray with non-stick baking parchment and melt the chocolate.

HINT

Any leftover melted chocolate may always be re-used so there is no waste. Set leftover chocolate on a piece of foil, exclude all the air and wrap tightly. Store for up to 1 month in a cool dry place.

2 Using a medium-sized paint brush, dip into the melted chocolate and brush the underside of each leaf with melted chocolate, taking care not to paint the chocolate over the edges of each leaf or the fresh leaf will not peel away from the chocolate.

3 Place the leaves to set on the baking parchment with the chocolate side uppermost in a cool place. If the chocolate coating needs to be thicker, brush a second layer of chocolate over the first layer. Just before using, peel the leaves away from the chocolate.

PIPING CHOCOLATE

There are easy ways of piping chocolate; one is by using chocolate and hazelnut spread which is the ideal consistency. When placed in a greaseproof paper piping bag fitted with a small star nozzle, borders or shells, stars or whirls may be piped.

Melted chocolate is much more difficult to pipe through a metal piping nozzle as the coldness of the metal begins to set the chocolate almost before you start piping. Allow the chocolate to cool and thicken slightly, quickly fill a greaseproof paper piping bag fitted with a warm piping nozzle, then pipe as quickly as possible. If the chocolate does start to set, warm the piping nozzle in your hands.

For piping threads or lines of chocolate, use only a greaseproof paper piping bag half filled with chocolate, snip off the point to the size of the hole required. Pipe fine threads of chocolate in straight or zig-zag lines directly on to the surface being decorated or leave the patterns to set on non-stick baking parchment. Carefully remove the piped chocolate pieces with a palette knife and use for all kinds of decorating.

TO MAKE PIPED CHOCOLATE DECORATIONS

1 Draw the chosen designs on to a piece of plain paper. Place a piece of waxed paper over the top and secure the corners with tape.

2 Half-fill a greaseproof paper piping bag with cooled melted chocolate and fold down the top. Snip off the end with a pair of sharp scissors to the size of hole required.

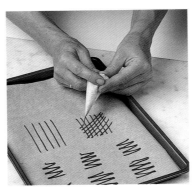

3 Pipe fine threads of chocolate following the designs, or pipe free-hand designs. Leave to set in a cool place, then carefully slide a thin palette knife under each chocolate piece to release them from the paper, and use for decorating.

4 To produce curved or waved pattern pieces, pipe the desired shape or design on to a piece of non-stick baking parchment. Place the paper over a curved shape, such as a rolling pin, wooden spoon handle, bun tins or small moulds, while the chocolate is setting.

CHOCOLATE CURLS AND FRILLS

When making any form of chocolate curls, frills, flakes or caraque, the temperature of the set chocolate is most important. Always allow the melted chocolate to set at room temperature and keep testing the edge to see if the chocolate has set enough and is ready to curl. Chocolate which is too soft will not curl but just wrinkle, and hard set chocolate is too brittle and will break. The chocolate is at the right temperature when the edge of the chocolate will begin to curl when a knife is drawn across the surface from the edge. At this stage be positive and work quickly and precisely to form the chocolate into large or small curls. Chocolate curls make simple yet effective decorations.

TO MAKE CHOCOLATE FRILLS

1 Using a side scraper or knife, press the end of the scraper or point of the blade slightly more into the chocolate at the top edge.

2 Pull the blade at this tilted angle down the edge of the chocolate just under the surface to form narrow frilled lengths. Lift off and set before using.

To make chocolate shavings – prepare in the same way but let the chocolate set a little harder, then draw the knife only half way across the surface to shave off fine flakes.

To make tiny chocolate curls – use a potato peeler to shave the curls off the side of a block of chocolate, which must be at room temperature; chocolate flavoured cake covering is just the right texture for curling directly from the bar.

TO MAKE CHOCOLATE CURLS

1 Pour the melted chocolate on to a rigid surface such as marble, wood or plastic laminate. Spread the chocolate evenly backwards and forwards with a palette knife until thinly spread and even.

2 When the chocolate has set but is not too hard, test the edge with a knife to see if the chocolate will curl.

3 Using a sharp knife held at a 45° angle to the chocolate, draw the knife towards you across the surface to shave off a thin layer of chocolate which forms into a curl.

4 If the chocolate is too soft, it will not curl; if it is too hard, it will be brittle and will break.

5 To make long chocolate curls or caraque, draw a long-bladed knife down the whole length and width of the set chocolate to form long thin curls.

6 To make large loose curls of chocolate, use a metal side scraper with a flexible blade instead of a knife and push it against the chocolate to form loose wide curls.

TO MAKE DECORATIVE CHOCOLATE CUT-OUT PIECES

1 Melt the chocolate (see page 44) and pour on to a piece of non-stick baking parchment. Spread as evenly as possible with a palette knife.

2 Pick up the corners of the paper and shake a few times to level the chocolate and remove air bubbles from the surface. Leave the chocolate at room temperature.

3 When the chocolate is almost set and can be touched with the fingers without sticking to the surface, turn the whole sheet of chocolate over on to another piece of paper and peel off the backing paper.

4 Cut out the shapes using any shaped cocktail or biscuit cutters. Press the cutter on to the surface of the chocolate; remove the shape by using a soft paint brush to push the chocolate shape out of the cutter. Work quickly while the chocolate is still pliable. Cut out as many shapes as you require. Once the chocolate has set too hard, it will become brittle and the shapes may break, so work in a warm place rather than somewhere which is too cold for the chocolate.

5 To cut out squares or triangles, carefully measure and mark the size of the squares required. Using a fine sharp knife or scalpel and a ruler, cut along the marked lines and remove the shapes. Cut diagonally in half for triangular shapes.

6 Leave the chocolate cut-out pieces in a cool place to set hard before using.

HINT

White chocolate is very versatile and may be used for all chocolate work. Being white, it lends itself to being coloured, especially for decorating or making assorted chocolates. Use only powdered food colourings as any liquids added to chocolate will cause it to thicken and become unusable.

BLACK AND WHITE GÂTEAU

T he blend of dark and white chocolate makes an impressive presentation, swirled softly to give a feathered effect. The dark chocolate cake with equal contrast is marbled with sweetened white soft cheese.

200 g (7oz) light soft cheese
50 g (2 oz) caster sugar
275 g (10 oz) self-raising flour
2.5 ml (½ tsp) baking powder
25 g (1 oz) cocoa powder
225 g (8 oz) light soft brown sugar
100 ml (4 fl oz) vegetable oil
300 ml (½ pint) water
7.5 ml (1½ tsp) lemon juice
DECORATION
30 ml (2 tbsp) apricot glaze (see page 70)
350 g (12 oz) white marzipan
125 g (4 oz) white chocolate
125 g (4 oz) plain chocolate
150 ml (¼ pint) whipping cream

....

1 Grease and base line a 23 cm (9 inch) spring form tin. Dust the sides with flour. Put the soft cheese and sugar into a bowl and beat with a wooden spoon until smooth. Sift the flour, baking powder and cocoa into a mixing bowl. Stir in the sugar to blend the ingredients evenly. Blend together the oil, water and lemon juice in a measuring jug. Pour into the mixing bowl and mix together with a wooden spoon. Beat for 1 minute until smooth.

2 Place the cake mixture into the prepared tin. Drop spoonfuls of cheese mixture evenly over the surface. Draw a knife through the mixture to give the mixture a marbled effect. Bake in the oven at 180°C (350°F) mark 4 for about 1-1¼ hours until well risen and the cake springs back when lightly pressed in the centre. Loosen the edges with a palette knife and leave to cool in the tin.

3 Invert the cake on to a thin cake board and remove the paper. (Decorate the cake inverted as the top may have slight depressions due to the soft cheese mixture.) Brush evenly with glaze. Cover with marzipan.

4 Place each chocolate into a bowl over a saucepan of hot water. Add half the cream to each and leave until melted. Stir to blend. Place the cake on a wire rack over a plate or baking sheet. Pour the white chocolate over to cover half of the cake in a crescent shape, coating the top and the sides evenly.

5 Pour the plain chocolate over the remaining cake surface to evenly cover, allowing the excess chocolate to fall on to the plate.

6 Working quickly, draw a cocktail stick through the dark chocolate into the white chocolate to give a feathered effect. Then come back in the opposite direction from the white to the dark chocolate to form the design. When the chocolate has set, place the cake on to a serving plate.

CHOCOLATE BOX GÂTEAU

A rich moist cake topped with assorted truffles and contained in a milk chocolate box. Choose a dainty ribbon as a finishing touch to this decadent gâteau.

90 ml (6 tbsp) golden syrup
30 ml (2 tbsp) black treacle
105 ml (7 tbsp) vegetable oil
125 g (4 oz) caster sugar
150 ml (¼ pint) milk
200 g (7 oz) plain flour
25 g (1 oz) cocoa powder
2.5 ml (½ tsp) bicarbonate of soda
1 egg

CHOCOLATE TRUFFLE MIXTURE
275 g (10 oz) plain chocolate, melted
300 ml (½ pint) whipping cream

DECORATION
45 ml (3 tbsp) each of milk, plain and white grated chocolate
75 g (3 oz) milk chocolate, melted
1 metre (1 yard), 3 cm (1¼ inch) wide fancy brown ribbon

1 Grease and line the base and sides of an 18 cm (7 inch) square cake tin. Put the golden syrup, treacle, vegetable oil, sugar and milk into a saucepan. Heat very gently, stirring occasionally, until the sugar has dissolved. Remove from the heat.

2 Sift the flour, cocoa and bicarbonate of soda into a mixing bowl. Make a well in the centre, add the egg and melted mixture. Mix together with a wooden spoon and beat until smooth. Pour the mixture into the prepared tin.

3 Bake in the oven at 170°C (325°F) mark 3 for 1¼ hours until well risen and the cake springs back when lightly pressed in the centre. Leave the cake to cool in the tin. Turn out of the tin, remove the paper and cool on a wire rack.

4 To make the chocolate truffle mixture, cool the melted chocolate. Whip the cream until it peaks softly. Add the chocolate quickly all at once and whip until the cream is thick and evenly blended. Place 25 separate teaspoonfuls of truffle mixture on to a greaseproof paper-lined baking sheet in a cool place.

5 Cut the cake horizontally into two layers. Using two-thirds of the remaining truffle mixture, sandwich the layers together and spread over the top and sides evenly. Place the cake on a 20.5 cm (8 inch) cake board, if liked.

6 Shape the spoonfuls of truffle mixture into neat balls and coat seven with grated milk chocolate, eight with grated plain, and ten with grated white.

7 Spread the melted milk chocolate over a piece of non-stick baking parchment measuring 23 × 20.5 cm (9 × 8 inches). Make the surface even by lifting the corners of the paper. When the chocolate has just set, invert the chocolate on to another piece of paper and peel away the paper. Use a knife and a ruler to cut the chocolate into four strips and trim to fit the cake side. Place the strips in position.

truffle mixture into a nylon piping bag fitted with a medium star nozzle and pipe a rope of chocolate cream between the chocolate edge and the truffles. Fit the ribbon around the edge of the gâteau and tie a pretty bow.

HINT
If the truffles stick when rolling into balls, use wetted hands to shape them.

8 Arrange the chocolate truffles in the centre of the gâteau. Place the remaining chocolate

CHOCOLATE FRUIT RING

Colourful chocolate-dipped fruits make a spectacular decoration for the centre of this moist almond chocolate sponge ring cake, covered with a glossy chocolate icing. Select your favourite fruits for dipping, using milk or plain and white chocolate.

150 g (5 oz) self-raising flour

7.5 ml (1½ tsp) baking powder

75 g (3 oz) ground almonds

175 g (6 oz) caster sugar

175 g (6 oz) butter, softened

3 eggs

125 g (4 oz) plain chocolate, melted

CHOCOLATE ICING

50 g (2 oz) unsalted butter

75 ml (5 tbsp) whipping cream

175 g (6 oz) plain chocolate, melted

DECORATION

275 g (10 oz) assorted chocolate dipped fruits – physalis, strawberries, cherries, grapes (see page 45)

....

1 Grease and base line a 19 cm (7½ inch), 1.4 litre (2½ pint) ring mould. Dust the sides with flour. Using the ingredients above, follow the recipe for making a quick mix cake mixture (see page 21), adding the ground almonds with the flour and the melted chocolate at the end. Turn the mixture into the prepared ring mould.

2 Bake in the oven at 180°C (350°F) mark 4 for 1¼ hours until well risen and the cake springs back when lightly pressed in the centre. Loosen the edge of the cake with a palette knife, cool in the tin for 10 minutes, then invert on to a wire rack and remove the lining paper.

3 To make the chocolate icing, add the butter and cream to the chocolate and leave until melted. Stir to blend.

4 Place a tray under the wire rack and pour the chocolate all at once over the top and outside of the cake to coat evenly. Spread the inside of the ring cake using the icing which has fallen on to the plate. Leave to set.

5 Dip the fruits in chocolate, following the instructions on page 45, using 25 g (1 oz) each of white, plain and milk chocolate.

6 Place the ring cake on a serving plate and fill the centre with chocolate-dipped fruits. Leaves and flowers may also be added to the fruits.

CHOCOLATE RIBBON CAKE

A softly marbled sponge flavoured with chocolate and orange, smoothly coated with orange butter cream and covered with smooth white chocolate. Ribbons of chocolate adorn the top, drizzled with find threads of white chocolate.

15 ml (1 tbsp) cocoa powder
25 ml (1½ tbsp) boiling water
3-egg quantity quick mix cake mixture (see page 21)
10 ml (2 tsp) finely grated orange rind
1 quantity orange butter cream (see page 25)

DECORATION
225 g (8 oz) white chocolate, melted
125 g (4 oz) milk chocolate, melted

....

1 Grease and base line two 20.5 cm (8 inch) sandwich tins. Blend together the cocoa powder and boiling water until smooth and leave to cool. Make the quick mix cake mixture and divide evenly in half. Fold the cocoa mixture evenly into one half and the orange rind into the remaining mixture.

2 Place alternate spoonfuls of mixture into each tin so the mixtures are evenly divided. Smooth the top and draw a knife through each of the mixtures to marble. Bake in the oven at 180°C (350°F) mark 4 for 35-40 minutes until well risen and the cakes spring back when lightly pressed in the centre. Loosen the edges of the cakes with a palette knife, turn out of the tins, remove the paper and cool on a wire rack.

3 Use the orange butter cream to sandwich the cakes together and evenly cover the outside of the cake. Leave to set. Place the cake on a wire rack over a plate. Pour the white chocolate all at once over the cake to coat evenly. Using a palette knife, spread the chocolate evenly, allowing the excess chocolate to fall on to the plate. Pattern the surface with a palette knife.

4 Using a greaseproof paper piping bag, half-fill with white chocolate from the plate and fold down the top. Cut out strips of non-stick baking parchment 10 × 4 cm (4 × 1½ inches). Cut the ends into 'V' shapes. Set three cardboard tubes or similar shapes on the board evenly spaced apart.

5 Spread each strip of paper thinly with milk chocolate. Snip the point off the end of the piping bag and pipe threads of white chocolate in a zig-zag design.

6 Drape the chocolate ribbons over the cardboard tubes so they bend as the chocolate dries.

7 Carefully peel the paper away from the chocolate ribbons and arrange attractively on top of the cake.

HINT
To obtain a good cake shape, dip the palette knife in hot water to smooth the butter cream.

ROSE LEAF GÂTEAU

*S*oft layers of chocolate sponge assembled with fruit, jam and cream, encased in chocolate cream and rich glossy icing. The decoration is a design of different coloured chocolate leaves.

---

125 g (4 oz) self-raising flour
25 g (1 oz) cocoa powder
125 g (4 oz) caster sugar
4 eggs, separated
30 ml (2 tbsp) vegetable oil
45 ml (3 tbsp) boiling water
CHOCOLATE CREAM ICING
300 ml (½ pint) whipping cream
125 g (4 oz) plain chocolate,
   melted
90 ml (6 tbsp) peach and apricot
   fruit spread
DECORATION
28 assorted chocolate rose leaves
   (see page 45)

····································

1 Grease and base line a 20.5 cm (8 inch) moule à manque mould. Dust the side with flour. Sift the flour and cocoa powder into a bowl, stir in the sugar until the ingredients are well mixed. Put the egg yolks, oil and boiling water into another bowl and whisk until well blended. Pour on to the dry ingredients, mix together with a wooden spoon and beat for 1 minute until smooth and glossy.

2 Whisk the egg whites in a bowl until stiff, give the cake mixture another stir and add half the egg whites to the cake mixture. Fold in gently using a plastic bladed spatula. Fold the remaining egg whites into the mixture until all the egg whites have been incorporated. Pour the mixture into the prepared tin.

3 Bake in the oven at 180°C (350°F) mark 4 for 35-40 minutes until well risen and the cake springs back when lightly pressed in the centre. Loosen the edge of the cake with a palette knife and leave to cool in the tin. Invert on to a wire rack and remove the lining paper.

4 To make the chocolate cream icing, add 90 ml (6 tbsp) of the measured cream to the melted chocolate. Leave over the heat to warm the cream before mixing together to form a smooth glossy icing. Whip the remaining cream until it peaks softly.

5 Cut the cake horizontally into three thin layers. Re-assemble the cake layers together using peach and apricot fruit spread and half of the cream. Spread the remaining cream over the top and side of the cake and place it on a wire rack. Set the cream for 5 minutes in the refrigerator.

6 Put the wire rack over a tray and pour the chocolate icing all at once over the cake to cover evenly. Tap the wire rack gently to level the icing. Leave in a cool place to set.

7 Using 25 g (1 oz) each of white, plain and milk chocolate, make the chocolate leaves (see page 45).

8 Using a cranked palette knife, arrange the chocolate leaves over the top of the gâteau.

CHOCOLATE CELEBRATION CAKE

T his cake is fitting for almost any celebration for someone who loves chocolate. A light chocolate sponge covered with chocolate icing and decorated with hand-made roses.

5-egg quantity quick mix cake
  mixture (see page 21)
50 g (2 oz) cocoa powder
25.5 cm (10 inch) trefoil shaped
  cake board
60 ml (4 tbsp) apricot glaze (see
  page 70)
700 g (1½ lb) chocolate flavoured
  sugar paste
50 g (2 oz) white sugar paste
4 chocolate sugar paste roses (see
  page 89)
10 chocolate sugar paste leaves
  (see page 89)
sifted cocoa powder, to dust
1 metre (1 yard), 5 mm (¼ inch)
  wide brown ribbon

....

1 Grease and line the base and
   sides of a 20.5 cm (8 inch)
trefoil shaped tin. Make the quick
mix cake mixture but only use
10 ml (2 tsp baking powder and
add the cocoa powder. Turn the
mixture into the prepared tin.

2 Bake in the oven at 180°C
   (350°F) mark 4 for 1½ hours
until well risen and the cake
springs back when lightly pressed
in the centre. Leave to cool in the
tin, then turn out and remove the
lining paper. Place the cake in the
centre of the cake board and brush
evenly with apricot glaze.

3 Using an acrylic board and
   rolling pin, roll out the
chocolate sugar paste to 5 mm

(¼ inch) thickness and trim to a
round 7.5 cm (3 inches) larger
than the top of the cake. Support
the sugar paste over the rolling pin
and place centrally over the cake.
Gently smooth over the top and
down the sides of the cake, so the
excess sugar paste is at the base of
the cake on the board. Trim away
the excess sugar paste at the base.
Knead the trimmings together.
Knead a walnut sized piece of
chocolate sugar paste into the
white sugar paste to tint it a
creamy colour. Roll out this sugar
paste thinly and trim to an oblong
25.5 × 5 cm (10 × 2 inches). Roll
out a matching oblong in chocolate
sugar paste.

5 Brush the indentation on the
   top of the cake with a little
water. Drape the twisted strips
around the outside and press. Roll
out and cut three chocolate strips
of sugar paste.

4 Place the chocolate oblong
   on top of the other. Trim to
shape. Cut the oblong into three
strips 25.5 cm (10 inches) long by
1 cm (½ inch) wide. Twist the
strips evenly.

6 Loop the strips into three
   bows. Secure to the cake
with a little water. Twist the tails.
Mould the roses using trimmings.
Make the rose leaves by kneading
the cream and dark chocolate
sugar paste together. Arrange roses
and leaves on cake and dust board
with cocoa. Trim with ribbon.

FILIGREE GÂTEAU

A chocolate Genoese soaked in a liqueur syrup and frosted with a chocolate icing. Fine threads of chocolate are piped to make these filigree pieces which finish the gâteau.

50 g (2 oz) unsalted butter
90 g (3½ oz) plain flour
15 g (½ oz) cornflour
4 eggs
125 g (4 oz) caster sugar
75 g (3 oz) plain chocolate
LIQUEUR SYRUP
125 g (4 oz) caster sugar
150 ml (¼ pint) water
45 ml (3 tbsp) apricot brandy
CHOCOLATE FROSTING
25 g (1 oz) unsalted butter
125 g (4 oz) plain chocolate,
 melted
1 egg, beaten
125 g (4 oz) icing sugar, sifted
DECORATION
25 g (1 oz) plain chocolate, melted
25 g (1 oz) white chocolate, melted
sifted icing sugar and cocoa
 powder, to dust
....

HINT
These chocolate pieces are very fragile. Use the broken ones to trim the base of the cake.

1 Grease and base line an 18 cm (7 inch), 1.7 litre (3 pint) mould. Using the ingredients above, make a Genoese sponge (see page 21), adding the chocolate to the butter to melt. Turn the mixture into the mould. Bake in the oven at 180°C (350°F) mark 4 for 40-45 minutes until well risen and the cake springs back when pressed. Loosen the edge and cool in the tin.

2 To make the syrup, put the sugar and water into a saucepan and heat gently, stirring occasionally, until the sugar has dissolved. Boil rapidly for 2-3 minutes, cool slightly. Add the apricot brandy to the syrup and pour over the cake in the mould.

3 To make the chocolate frosting, add the butter to the chocolate and leave until melted. Add the egg and stir the mixture together with a wooden spoon until evenly blended. Gradually stir in the icing sugar and beat until smooth and glossy.

4 Invert the cake on to a wire rack over a plate and remove the lining paper. Pour the frosting over the cake and spread evenly with a palette knife. Place the cake on a serving plate.

5 Cover a rolling pin with baking parchment. Using two piping bags, half-fill one with plain and the other with white chocolate. Fold down the top and snip off the point of the plain chocolate one. Pipe zig-zag lines of chocolate across the rolling pin. Make 12 shapes and leave to set; repeat with white chocolate.

6 Carefully peel the paper away from the chocolate shapes and arrange them alternately on the top of the cake. Use half pieces of filigree chocolate to decorate around the base. Dust with a little sifted icing sugar and cocoa.

CELEBRATION CAKES

CELEBRATION CAKE RECIPES

These cake mixtures are generally used for special occasion cakes. This often demands a much richer and substantial type of cake as they are usually covered with marzipan and sugar paste or royal icing. The advantage of a rich fruit cake is its keeping qualities. Light fruit or Madeira cake may be used instead.

RICH FRUIT CAKE

This recipe makes a very moist rich cake suitable for any celebration cake. It allows the cake to be made in stages, especially if time is short or if you are making more than one cake. All the dried fruit these days has been pre-cleaned and dried so it is only necessary to look over the fruit before using it. The fruit may be prepared and mixed together and left to soak overnight in brandy and the cake made the following day. Once the mixture is in the tin, the surface may be covered with greaseproof paper and the cake stored in a cool place overnight if baking is not possible on the same day. The quantities have been carefully worked out so that the depth of each cake is the same. This is so important when making several tiers for a wedding cake as they must all be the same depth to look aesthetically correct. For sizes and quantities, see the Rich Fruit Cake Chart on page 66.

Note: All cakes must always be made in a spotlessly clean environment. All utensils must be clean and well cared for; ingredients must be freshly purchased; tins carefully lined and prepared.

RICH FRUIT CAKE (QUICK MIX METHOD)

1 Grease and line the cake tin for the size of cake you wish to make, using a double thickness of greaseproof paper. Tie a double band of brown paper round the outside. Stand the tin on a baking sheet, double lined with brown paper (see page 11).

2 Prepare the ingredients for the appropriate size of cake according to the chart on page 66. Into a large mixing bowl, place the currants, sultanas, raisins, glacé cherries, mixed peel, flaked almonds, lemon rind and brandy. Mix all the ingredients together until well blended, then cover the bowl with cling film. Leave for several hours or overnight in a cool place if desired.

3 Sift the flour, mixed spice and cinnamon together into another mixing bowl. Add the sugar, butter and eggs. Mix together with a wooden spoon, then beat for about 2-3 minutes until smooth and glossy. Alternatively, beat for about 1 minute using an electric mixer, especially if large quantities are being made.

4 Gradually add the mixed fruit and fold into the cake mixture using a spatula until all the fruit has been evenly distributed throughout the mixture.

5 Spoon the mixture into the prepared tin and spread evenly. Give the tin a few sharp bangs to level the mixture and to remove any air pockets. Smooth the surface with the back of a metal spoon, making a slight depression in the centre. The cake surface may be covered with greaseproof paper and left overnight in a cool place if required.

6 Bake in the centre of the oven at 150°C (300°F) mark 2, following the chart baking time as a guide. If the cake has been made and left overnight in a cool place, this will make the baking time slightly longer. Test the cake to see if it is cooked 15 minutes before the end of the baking time. If cooked, the cake should feel firm and when a fine skewer is inserted into the centre, it should come out quite clean. If the cake is not cooked, re-test it at 15-minute intervals. Remove the cake from the oven and allow it to cool in the tin.

7 Turn the cake out of the tin but do not remove the lining paper as it helps to keep the cake moist. Spoon half the quantity of brandy, according to the recipe size, over the top of the cooked cake and wrap in double thickness foil.

8 Store the cake on its base with the top uppermost in a cool dry place for a week. Unwrap the cake and spoon over the remaining brandy. Re-wrap well and invert the cake and store it upside down, so the brandy moistens the top of the cake and helps to keep it flat.

9 The cake will store well for up to 2-3 months; if it is going to be kept for a longer time, it will be better to freeze it to ensure the cake has a good flavour. Make sure it is completely thawed before applying the marzipan and icing.

> **HINT**
> Rich fruit cakes are so easy to make especially if they are made in stages. It makes the task much quicker if the fruit is weighed and mixed a day ahead, the tins prepared and lined in advance and the remaining ingredients weighed ready to mix. On the day of baking simply make the cake and bake.
>
> Use the same amount of brandy used in the cake to spoon over the cake when baked. Add half the amount after baking and the remainder about a week later.

RICH FRUIT CAKE (TRADITIONAL METHOD)

1 Grease and line the cake tin for the size of cake you wish to make, using a double thickness of greaseproof paper. Tie a double band of brown paper round the outside. Stand the tin on a baking sheet, double lined with brown paper (see page 11).

2 Prepare the ingredients for the appropriate size of cake according to the chart on page 66. Look over all the fruit if necessary, chopping any over-large pieces, and mix well together in a large bowl. Add the flaked almonds. Sift flour and spices into another bowl with a pinch of salt.

3 Put the butter, sugar and lemon rind into a bowl and cream together until pale and fluffy. Add the beaten eggs gradually, beating well after each addition.

4 Gradually fold the flour lightly into the mixture with a plastic-bladed spatula, then fold in the brandy. Finally fold in the fruit and nuts.

5 Turn the mixture into the prepared tin, spreading it evenly and making sure there are no air pockets. Make a depression in the centre to ensure an even surface when cooked.

6 Bake in the centre of the oven at 150°C (300°F) mark 2 for the time given in the chart until a fine warmed skewer inserted in the centre comes out clean.

7 When cooked, leave the cake to cool in the tin before turning out on to a wire rack. Prick the top all over with a fine skewer and slowly pour over the brandy (see above).

8 Wrap the cake in a double thickness of greaseproof paper and overwrap with foil. Store in a cool dry place to prevent mould growth.

RICH FRUIT CAKE CHART

When baking large cakes, 25.5 cm (10 inch) and upwards, it is advisable to reduce the oven heat to 130°C (250°F) mark 1 after two-thirds of the baking time.

CAKE TIN SIZE	12.5 cm (5 in) square 15 cm (6 in) round	15 cm (6 in) square 18 cm (7 in) round	18 cm (7 in) square 20.5 cm (8 in) round	20.5 cm (8 in) square 23 cm (9 in) round
Currants	225 g (8 oz)	350 g (12 oz)	450 g (1 lb)	625 g (1 lb 6 oz)
Sultanas	100 g (4 oz)	125 g (4½ oz)	200 g (7 oz)	225 g (8 oz)
Raisins	100 g (4 oz)	125 g (4½ oz)	200 g (7 oz)	225 g (8 oz)
Glacé cherries	50 g (2 oz)	75 g (3 oz)	150 g (5 oz)	175 g (6 oz)
Mixed peel	25 g (1 oz)	50 g (2 oz)	75 g (3 oz)	100 g (4 oz)
Flaked almonds	25 g (1 oz)	50 g (2 oz)	75 g (3 oz)	100 g (4 oz)
Lemon rind, grated	a little	a little	a little	¼ lemon
Plain flour	175 g (6 oz)	215 g (7½ oz)	350 g (12 oz)	400 g (14 oz)
Mixed spice	1.25 ml (¼ tsp)	2.5 ml (½ tsp)	2.5 ml (½ tsp)	5 ml (1 tsp)
Cinnamon	1.25 ml (¼ tsp)	2.5 ml (½ tsp)	2.5 ml (½ tsp)	5 ml (1 tsp)
Butter	150 g (5 oz)	175 g (6 oz)	275 g (10 oz)	350 g (12 oz)
Brown soft sugar	150 g (5 oz)	175 g (6 oz)	275 g (10 oz)	350 g (12 oz)
Eggs, beaten	2½	3	5	6
Brandy	15 ml (1 tbsp)	15 ml (1 tbsp)	15-30 ml (1-2 tbsp)	30 ml (2 tbsp)
Baking time (approx.)	2½-3 hours	3½ hours	3½ hours	4 hours
Weight when cooked	1.1 kg (2½ lb)	1.5 kg (3¼ lb)	2.1 kg (4¾ lb)	2.7 kg (6 lb)

CAKE TIN SIZE	23 cm (9 in) square 25.5 cm (10 in) round	25.5 cm (10 in) square 28 cm (11 in) round	28 cm (11 in) square 30.5 cm (12 in) round	30.5 cm (12 in) square 33 cm (13 in) round
Currants	775 g (1 lb 12 oz)	1.1 kg (2 lb 8 oz)	1.5 kg (3 lb 2 oz)	1.7 kg (3 lb 12 oz)
Sultanas	375 g (13 oz)	400 g (14 oz)	525 g (1 lb 3 oz)	625 g (1 lb 6 oz)
Raisins	375 g (13 oz)	400 g (14 oz)	525 g (1 lb 3 oz)	625 g (1 lb 6 oz)
Glacé cherries	250 g (9 oz)	275 g (10 oz)	350 g (12 oz)	425 g (15 oz)
Mixed peel	150 g (5 oz)	200 g (7 oz)	250 g (9 oz)	275 g (10 oz)
Flaked almonds	150 g (5 oz)	200 g (7 oz)	250 g (9 oz)	275 g (10 oz)
Lemon rind, grated	¼ lemon	½ lemon	½ lemon	1 lemon
Plain flour	600 g (1 lb 5 oz)	700 g (1 lb 8 oz)	825 g (1 lb 13 oz)	1 kg (2 lb 6 oz)
Mixed spice	5 ml (1 tsp)	10 ml (2 tsp)	12.5 ml (2½ tsp)	12.5 ml (2½ tsp)
Cinnamon	5 ml (1 tsp)	10 ml (2 tsp)	12.5 ml (2½ tsp)	12.5 ml (2½ tsp)
Butter	500 g (1 lb 2 oz)	600 g (1 lb 5 oz)	800 g (1 lb 12 oz)	950 g (2 lb 2 oz)
Sugar	500 g (1 lb 2 oz)	600 g (1 lb 5 oz)	800 g (1 lb 12 oz)	950 g (2 lb 2 oz)
Eggs, beaten	9	11	14	17
Brandy	30-45 ml (2-3 tbsp)	45 ml (3 tbsp)	60 ml (4 tbsp)	90 ml (6 tbsp)
Baking time (approx.)	4½ hours	6 hours	6-6½ hours	6½ hours
Weight when cooked	3.8 kg (8½ lb)	4.8 kg (10¾ lb)	6.1 kg (13½ lb)	7.4 kg (16½ lb)

LIGHT FRUIT CAKE

This is a light moist fruit cake, which may be made to replace the rich fruit cake if a lighter cake is required. As there is less fruit in this cake, it has a tendency to dome slightly during the cooking time so ensure a deep depression is made in the centre of the uncooked mixture before baking. This cake will keep for up to one month once it has been marzipanned and iced.

For sizes and quantities, see the Light Fruit Cake Chart on page 68.

1 Place a deep cake tin on a piece of double thickness greaseproof paper or non-stick baking parchment and draw around the base following the tin shape. Cut out the marked shape with a pair of scissors.

2 Measure and cut a strip of double thickness greaseproof paper or non-stick baking parchment long enough to wrap around the outside of the tin with a small overlap and to stand 2.5 cm (1 inch) above the top of the tin.

3 Brush the base and sides of the tin with melted white fat or oil. Place the cut out paper shapes in the base of the tin and press flat. Fit the double strip of greaseproof paper inside the tin, pressing well against the sides and making sharp creases where the paper fits into the corners of the tin shape being lined. Ensure the paper strip is level and fits neatly without any creases. Brush the base and side paper well with melted white fat or oil.

4 Measure and fit a double thickness strip of brown paper around the outside of the tin. Tie securely with string.

5 Place the mixed dried fruit, glacé cherries, lemon rind and juice in a large mixing bowl. Mix all the ingredients together until well blended.

6 Sift the flour, baking powder, mixed spice and sugar into another mixing bowl, add the butter or margarine and eggs. Mix together with a wooden spoon, then beat for 2-3 minutes until smooth and glossy. Alternatively, beat for 1 minute with an electric mixer, especially for large quantities.

7 Gradually add the mixed fruit and fold into the cake mixture using a spatula until all the fruit is evenly mixed. Spoon the mixture into the prepared cake tin and spread evenly. Give the tin a few sharp bangs to level the mixture and remove any air pockets. Smooth the surface with the back of a metal spoon, making a fairly deep depression in the centre. Line a baking sheet with three or four layers of brown paper and stand the tin on the centre of the lined baking sheet.

8 Bake in the centre of the oven at 150°C (300°F) mark 2 according to the quantity you are making, following the chart baking time as a guide. Test the cake 15 minutes before the end of the given baking time. If cooked, the cake should feel firm and when a fine skewer is inserted into the centre of the cake, it should come out quite clean. If the cake is not cooked, re-test at 15-minute intervals.

9 Remove the cake from the oven and leave to cool in the tin. Wrap in foil and store in a cool place for up to 2 weeks.

HINT

Always a good alternative to a rich fruit cake. It has moisture and flavour but not the richness of a darker fruit cake. The cost of the cake is far cheaper to make as it has less fruit but the keeping time is shorter.

LIGHT FRUIT CAKE CHART

CAKE TIN SIZE	12.5 cm (5 in) square / 15 cm (6 in) round	15 cm (6 in) square / 18 cm (7 in) round	18 cm (7 in) square / 20.5 cm (8 in) round	20.5 cm (8 in) square / 23 cm (9 in) round
Mixed dried fruit	350 g (12 oz)	450 g (1 lb)	525 g (1 lb 3 oz)	775 g (1 lb 12 oz)
Glacé cherries, quartered	25 g (1 oz)	25 g (1 oz)	50 g (2 oz)	75 g (3 oz)
Lemon rind, coarsely grated	5 ml (1 tsp)	7.5 ml (1½ tsp)	10 ml (2 tsp)	15 ml (3 tsp)
Lemon juice	15 ml (1 tbsp)	22.5 ml (1½ tbsp)	30 ml (2 tbsp)	37.5 ml (2½ tbsp)
Plain flour	225 g (8 oz)	275 g (10 oz)	350 g (12 oz)	450 g (1 lb)
Baking powder	2.5 ml (½ tsp)	4 ml (¾ tsp)	5 ml (1 tsp)	6.5 ml (1¼ tsp)
Ground mixed spice	5 ml (1 tsp)	7.5 ml (1½ tsp)	10 ml (2 tsp)	12.5 ml (2½ tsp)
Light soft brown sugar	175 g (6 oz)	225 g (8 oz)	275 g (10 oz)	400 g (14 oz)
Butter	175 g (6 oz)	225 g (8 oz)	275 g (10 oz)	400 g (14 oz)
Eggs, size 3	3	4	4	5
Baking time	2-2¼ hours	2¼-2½ hours	2½-3 hours	3-3¼ hours

CAKE TIN SIZE	23 cm (9 in) square / 25.5 cm (10 in) round	25.5 cm (10 in) square / 28 cm (11 in) round	28 cm (11 in) square / 30.5 cm (12 in) round	30.5 cm (12 in) square / 33 cm (13 in) round
Mixed dried fruit	1.1 kg (2 lb 6 oz)	1.4 kg (3 lb)	1.8 kg (4 lb)	2.2 kg (4 lb 14 oz)
Glacé cherries, quartered	100 g (4 oz)	150 g (5 oz)	175 g (6 oz)	225 g (8 oz)
Lemon rind, coarsely grated	20 ml (4 tsp)	25 ml (5 tsp)	30 ml (6 tsp)	40 ml (8 tsp)
Lemon juice	45 ml (3 tbsp)	52.5 ml (3½ tbsp)	60 ml (4 tbsp)	75 ml (5 tbsp)
Plain flour	550 g (1 lb 4 oz)	700 g (1 lb 8 oz)	900 g (2 lb)	1.1 kg (2 lb 8 oz)
Baking powder	7.5 ml (1½ tsp)	9 ml (1¾ tsp)	10 ml (2 tsp)	12.5 ml (2½ tsp)
Ground mixed spice	15 ml (3 tsp)	17.5 ml (3½ tsp)	20 ml (4 tsp)	22.5 ml (4½ tsp)
Light soft brown sugar	475 g (1 lb 1 oz)	550 g (1 lb 4 oz)	750 g (1 lb 11 oz)	950 g (2 lb 2 oz)
Butter	475 g (1 lb 1 oz)	550 g (1 lb 4 oz)	750 g (1 lb 11 oz)	950 g (2 lb 2 oz)
Eggs, size 3	6	7	9	11
Baking time	3¼-3¾ hours	3¼-4 hours	4-4½ hours	4¾-5¼ hours

MADEIRA CAKE

This is a good moist plain cake which may be made as an alternative to a rich or light fruit cake. It has a firm texture, therefore making it a good base for a celebration cake. There are many variations for flavouring this cake and once covered with marzipan, royal icing or sugar paste, it may be decorated for any occasion.

For sizes and quantities, see Madeira Cake Chart.

MADEIRA CAKE (QUICK MIX METHOD)

1 Grease and line a deep cake tin following the instructions on page 67.

2 Sift the flours into a mixing bowl, add the butter or margarine, sugar, eggs and lemon juice or milk. Mix together with a wooden spoon, then beat for 1-2 minutes until smooth and glossy. Alternatively, use an electric mixer and beat for 1 minute only, depending on the quantity of the mixture.

3 Add any flavourings if required and mix until well blended.

4 Turn the mixture into the prepared tin, spread evenly. Give the tin a sharp tap to remove any air pockets. Make a depression in the centre of the mixture to ensure a level surface.

5 Bake in the centre of the oven at 170°C (325°F) mark 3 following the chart baking times as a guide, or until the cake springs back when lightly pressed in the centre.

6 Leave the cake to cool in the tin, then remove and cool completely on a wire rack. Wrap in cling film or foil and store in a cool place until required.

MADEIRA CAKE (TRADITIONAL METHOD)

1 Grease and line a deep cake tin following the instructions on page 67.

2 Sift the flours together. Cream the butter and sugar in a bowl until pale and fluffy. Add the eggs, a little at a time, beating well after each addition.

3 Fold in the flour with a plastic spatula, adding a little lemon juice or milk if necessary to give a dropping consistency.

4 Add any flavourings if required and mix until well blended.

5 Turn the mixture into the prepared tin, spread evenly. Give the tin a sharp tap to remove any air pockets. Make a depression in the centre of the mixture to ensure a level surface.

6 Bake in the centre of the oven at 170°C (325°F) mark 3 following the chart baking times as a guide, or until the cake springs back when lightly pressed in the centre.

7 Leave the cake to cool in the tin, then remove and cool completely on a wire rack. Wrap in cling film or foil and store in a cool place until required.

VARIATIONS

These flavourings are for a 3-egg quantity Madeira cake: increase the suggested flavourings to suit the quantities being made.

Cherry – add 175 g (6 oz) glacé cherries, halved.

Coconut – add 50 g (2 oz) desiccated coconut.

Nut – replace 125 g (4 oz) flour with ground almonds, hazelnuts, walnuts or pecan nuts.

Citrus – add the grated rind of 1 lemon, orange or lime with the freshly squeezed juice.

MADEIRA CAKE CHART

CAKE TIN SIZE	15 cm (6 in) square / 18 cm (7 in) round	18 cm (7 in) square / 20.5 cm (8 in) round	20.5 cm (8 in) square / 23 cm (9 in) round	23 cm (9 in) square / 25.5 cm (10 in) round
Plain flour	125 g (4 oz)	175 g (6 oz)	225 g (8 oz)	250 g (9 oz)
Self-raising flour	125 g (4 oz)	175 g (6 oz)	225 g (8 oz)	250 g (9 oz)
Unsalted butter, softened, or soft margarine	175 g (6 oz)	275 g (10 oz)	400 g (14 oz)	450 g (1 lb)
Caster sugar	175 g (6 oz)	275 g (10 oz)	400 g (14 oz)	450 g (1 lb)
Size 3 eggs	3	5	7	8
Lemon juice or milk	30 ml (2 tbsp)	45 ml (3 tbsp)	52.5 ml (3½ tbsp)	60 ml (4 tbsp)
Baking time (approx.)	1¼-1½ hours	1½-1¾ hours	1¾-2 hours	1¾-2 hours

CAKE TIN SIZE	25.5 cm (10 in) square / 28 cm (11 in) round	28 cm (11 in) square / 30.5 cm (12 in) round	30.5 cm (12 in) square / 33 cm (13 in) round
Plain flour	275 g (10 oz)	350 g (12 oz)	450 g (1 lb)
Self-raising flour	275 g (10 oz)	350 g (12 oz)	450 g (1 lb)
Unsalted butter, softened, or soft margarine	500 g (1 lb 2 oz)	625 g (1 lb 6 oz)	725 g (1 lb 10 oz)
Caster sugar	500 g (1 lb 2 oz)	625 g (1 lb 6 oz)	725 g (1 lb 10 oz)
Size 3 eggs	10	12	13
Lemon juice or milk	67.5 ml (4½ tbsp)	75 ml (5 tbsp)	82.5 ml (5½ tbsp)
Baking time (approx.)	2-2¼ hours	2¼-2½ hours	2½-2¾ hours

APRICOT GLAZE

It is always a good idea to make a large quantity of apricot glaze, especially when making a celebration cake.

450 g (1 lb) apricot jam
30 ml (2 tbsp) water

....

1 Place the jam and water into a saucepan, heat gently, stirring occasionally until melted.

2 Boil the jam rapidly for 1 minute, then strain through a sieve. Rub through as much fruit as possible, using a wooden spoon. Discard the skins left in the sieve.

3 Pour the glaze into a clean, hot jar, then seal with a clean lid and cool. Refrigerate for up to 2 months.

4 Use to brush the cakes with apricot glaze before applying the marzipan, and for glazing fruit finishes on gâteaux and cakes. **Makes 450 g (1 lb) apricot glaze**

MARZIPAN OR ALMOND PASTE

Marzipan or almond paste is a pliable paste made
from an amalgamation of ground almonds, caster
or icing sugar, eggs and flavouring. The consistency,
texture and colour varies to how the paste is made, but
the end result is used for covering cakes to preserve
them, to keep in the moisture and flavour, and to give a
smooth, flat surface for royal icing or sugar paste.

Used as a cake covering on its own, it offers colour, texture and flavour without the sweetness of icing sugar. Once the cake has been covered in marzipan or almond paste, it may be decorated very simply by crimping or embossing the edges, applying marzipan cut-outs, moulded leaves and flowers, animals or fruit.

Home-made marzipan – this has a wonderful taste and texture of its own, being made with equal quantities of ground almonds to sugar, and can be made in easily manageable quantities. Care must be taken when making marzipan not to over-knead or over-handle the mixture as this encourages the oils to flow from the ground almonds. This makes an oily covering to a celebration cake, and these oils will eventually seep through the iced surface of the cake, causing unsightly staining, which cannot be rectified.

Ready-made marzipan – always use the white marzipan for all cakes as it is the best and most reliable type to use. It looks like home-made but has a slightly firmer texture. Once the cake has been covered with this type of marzipan, sugar paste may

be applied immediately without allowing the surface to dry. The yellow marzipan has added yellow food colouring and may be used for covering rich fruit cakes, but the yellow colour may show through if the icing is thinly applied, or may cause yellow staining on the surface. This marzipan does not take food colourings so well as the white marzipan when used for modelling work and decorations.

Always use fresh, pliable marzipan to obtain the very best results, for modelling and especially for covering a cake. Once the marzipan has been used, knead the trimmings together and seal well in a polythene bag for further use, so there is no waste. Be sure to dry the marzipanned cake before applying the icing by storing the cake in a cardboard cake box in a warm, dry room. Set marzipan always ensures a good cake shape during icing and prevents any moisture from seeping through and staining the surface of the cake. Sugar paste may be applied immediately after the cake has been marzipanned but take care of the shape. Otherwise allow at least 24 hours for the marzipan to set before applying any form of icing, and 48 hours for smooth royal icing.

MARZIPANNING A CAKE FOR ROYAL ICING

To marzipan a cake ready for royal icing is a very exacting process as the finished shape of the cake determines the smooth flat finish of the royal icing. The shape of the cake when covered with marzipan should look clean, sharp and smooth; ensuring the royal icing will look the same.

To obtain this appearance the top of the cake is marzipanned first, then the cake is placed on a cake board before applying the marzipan to the sides. Round shaped cakes may be covered with one long strip of marzipan measured to the exact height and

length of the side of the cake. Square cakes need four single pieces, one applied to each side of the cake and cut accurately for shape to ensure good square corners. All the seams and joins at the corners and top edge should be smoothed together with a palette knife.

The cake is placed in a cardboard cake box and left in a warm, dry place to dry for at least 48 hours. Once the marzipan has become dry and set, this will ensure a good shape when applying the coats of royal icing.

MARZIPAN

Home-made marzipan has a wonderful flavour and texture. Alternatively use ready-made white marzipan which is quick and convenient.

---

225 g (8 oz) icing sugar
225 g (8 oz) caster sugar
450 g (1 lb) ground almonds
5 ml (1 tsp) vanilla flavouring
2 egg whites, lightly beaten
10 ml (2 tsp) lemon juice

....

1 Sift the icing sugar into a bowl and mix in the caster sugar and ground almonds.

2 Add the vanilla flavouring, egg whites and lemon juice, and mix to a stiff dough. Knead lightly, then shape into a ball. Cover until ready to use.
Makes 900 g-1 kg (2-2¼ lb)

HINT

As an alternative to raw egg whites, use water mixed with a little sherry or brandy and the lemon juice to bind the mixture.

TO MARZIPAN A CAKE FOR ROYAL ICING

1 Unwrap the cake and remove the lining paper. Roll the top with a rolling pin to give a flat surface.

2 Brush the top of the cake evenly with apricot glaze (see page 70). Lightly dust the surface with icing sugar.

3 Using two-thirds of the marzipan, knead it into a smooth ball. Roll out the marzipan to a thickness of 5 mm (¼ inch) to match the shape of the top of the cake. Make sure the marzipan moves freely before inverting the cake on to the centre of the marzipan.

4 Trim off the excess marzipan to within 1 cm (½ inch) of the cake, knead the trimmings and set aside. Using a small flexible palette knife, push the marzipan level to the side of the cake until all the marzipan is neat around the edge of the cake.

5 Invert the cake ensuring the surface is flat and place in the centre of a matching shaped cake board about 5 cm (2 inches) larger than the cake. Brush the sides with apricot glaze. Knead the trimmings and remaining one-third of marzipan together, taking care not to include any crumbs from the cake.

6 Measure and cut a piece of string the length of the side of the cake. Measure and cut another piece of string the depth of the side of the cake from the board to the top.

7 Roll out the marzipan to the thickness of 5 mm (¼ inch) and to the shape of the side of the cake. Cut out one side piece for a round cake, and four pieces for a square cake, to match the length and width of the pieces of string. Knead the marzipan trimmings together and re-roll them if necessary to cut out more side pieces.

8 Carefully fit the marzipan on to the side of the cake and smooth the joins and then the top and sides with a palette knife until smooth. Place the cake in a cardboard cake box and leave in a warm, dry place for at least 48 hours before icing.

MARZIPANNING A CAKE FOR SUGAR PASTE

When applying marzipan to a cake which is being covered with sugar paste, it is necessary to smooth the marzipan to the contours and shape of the cake being covered to give a rounded but smooth finish.

It is a very quick and easy method to do as long as the marzipan is fresh and pliable, and carefully fitted over the cake. Care must be taken not to stretch or tear the marzipan as it is eased into corners, over the sides and cake edges.

Round or oval shaped cakes are the most simple shapes to cover with sugar paste as they have the top and only one side to cover smoothly. Make sure there are no air bubbles trapped between the marzipan and the top of the cake before easing the marzipan over the sides and down to the base of the cake. Once the marzipan is eased in to fit the base, trim the excess with a knife.

Square, hexagonal or unusual shaped cakes are

slightly more difficult to cover with marzipan because of the shaped sides or corners. Care must be taken to cup your hands around the base of the corners, gently easing the marzipan up towards the top of the cake. This prevents the marzipan from stretching or tearing over the top edge.

TO MARZIPAN A CAKE FOR SUGAR PASTE

1 Unwrap the cake and remove the lining paper. Place the cake on a matching shaped cake board about 5 cm (2 inches) larger than the cake. Roll the top with a rolling pin to give a flat surface.

2 Brush the top and sides of the cake evenly with apricot glaze (see page 70), then dust the surface lightly with sifted icing sugar.

3 Knead the marzipan into a smooth ball. Roll out the marzipan to match the shape of the top of the cake, and large enough to cover the top and sides, allowing 5-7.5 cm (2-3 inches) larger and 5 mm (¼ inch) in thickness. Make sure the marzipan moves freely, then roll the marzipan loosely around the rolling pin.

4 Place the supported marzipan centrally over the top of the cake and carefully unroll so that the marzipan falls evenly over the cake. Working from the centre of the cake, carefully smooth the marzipan over the top of the cake, ensuring there are no air pockets trapped, and smoothing down the sides. Lift the edges slightly to allow the marzipan to be eased in to fit the base of the cake without stretching or tearing the top edge.

5 Using a sharp knife, trim the excess marzipan from the base of the cake, cutting down on to the board.

6 Using clean, dry hands, or a cake smoother, gently rub the top of the cake in circular movements to make a smooth glossy rounded finish to the marzipan.

7 Place the cake in a cardboard cake box in a warm, dry place for at least 2 hours, or preferably 24 hours, before covering with sugar paste.

MARZIPAN QUANTITY CHART

CAKE SIZES	12.5 cm (5 in) square 15 cm (6 in) round	15 cm (6 in) square 18 cm (7 in) round	18 cm (7 in) square 20.5 cm (8 in) round	20.5 cm (8 in) square 23 cm (9 in) round
Marzipan or almond paste	450 g (1 lb)	550 g (1¼ lb)	700 g (1½ lb)	800 g (1¾ lb)
CAKE SIZES	23 cm (9 in) square 25.5 cm (10 in) round	25.5 cm (10 in) square 28 cm (11 in) round	28 cm (11 in) square 30.5 cm (12 in) round	30.5 cm (12 in) square 33 cm (13 in) round
Marzipan or almond paste	1 kg (2¼ lb)	1.1 kg (2½ lb)	1.25 kg (2¾ lb)	1.6 kg (3½ lb)

HAPPY BIRTHDAY CAKE

Bright vibrant colours on this marzipanned cake make it suitable for different occasions and for all ages. Simply cut out the coloured strips and roll them together to create this amazing effect.

---

18 cm (7 inch) square light fruit cake mixture (see page 67)
20.5 cm (8 inch) square cake board
30 ml (2 tbsp) apricot glaze (see page 70)
1 kg (2 lb) white marzipan
bitter lemon, violet, red and ice blue food colourings

....

HINT
Cut the marzipan strips with a wet knife to obtain clean cut strips. Invert the cake before decorating if the top is not level.

1 Prepare an 18 cm (7 inch) square tin (see page 11). Make the light fruit cake mixture and place in the tin. Bake according to the cake chart on page 68. Place the cake in the centre of the cake board and brush the sides with apricot glaze.

2 Cut off one-third of the marzipan and colour yellow using the bitter lemon food colouring. Roll out two-thirds thinly to fit the top of the cake, cut to size and reserve. Knead the trimmings together with the remaining yellow marzipan.

3 Cut the remaining two-thirds marzipan into three pieces and colour each piece bright purple, red and turquoise blue using the food colourings. Roll out each coloured piece thinly and cut to an oblong 18 × 10 cm (7 × 4 inches). Knead the trimmings together, keeping the colours separate.

4 Cut each colour into 1 cm (½ inch) strips. Separate the strips and lay them on the work surface, alternating the colours to give enough strips to fit the depth and one side of the cake. Lightly roll the strips together to join them, keeping them straight. Run a palette knife underneath the strips to ensure they move freely.

5 Hold the top and base of the cake and place one side on to the marzipan strips. Trim the marzipan to size using a long-bladed knife. Invert the cake. Repeat to alternate the strips of marzipan to fit each side of the cake and trim to size. Place the yellow square of marzipan to cover the top of the cake and fit alternate coloured strips of marzipan around the top edge.

6 Place the leftover strips from the side pieces together and roll to join them. Using alphabet cutters, cut out the letters HAPPY BIRTHDAY and arrange in the centre of the cake. Mould the remaining marzipan into balloon shapes with strings and arrange them on top of the cake. Leave to dry in a warm place.

EASTER CAKE

This lattice marzipan is created by using a special pastry cutter; a similar effect may be created by cutting out strips of marzipan. Sugar eggs are well worth making but, if time is short, buy hand-blown eggs as an alternative decoration.

18 cm (7 inch) round light fruit
  cake mixture (see page 67)
20.5 cm (8 inch) round silver
  cake board (optional)
30 ml (2 tbsp) apricot glaze (see
  page 70)
550 g (1¼ lb) white marzipan
green and yellow food colourings
1 quantity flower paste (see page
  154)
icing sugar and cornflour to dust
½ quantity royal icing (see page
  108)
1 metre (1 yard), 2.5 cm (1 inch)
  wide Easter ribbon

....

1 Prepare an 18 cm (7 inch) round cake tin (see page 11). Make the light fruit cake mixture and place in the tin. Bake according to the cake chart on page 68. Place the cake in the centre of the cake board and brush with apricot glaze.

2 Colour two-thirds of the marzipan pale green and the remaining one-third yellow, using the green and yellow food colourings. Roll out the green marzipan thinly and smoothly cover the cake, trimming off the excess at the base of the cake.

3 Dust the surface with icing sugar and roll out the yellow marzipan to an oblong 25.5 cm (10 inches) by 18 cm (7 inches), ensuring it moves freely on the surface. Using the lattice pastry

cutter, well dusted with icing sugar, start at the base of the short edge in the centre, roll the cutter over the surface of the marzipan to cut. Repeat to lattice the rest.

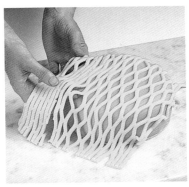

4 Carefully lift the latticed marzipan over the cake, opening the pattern in the centre, allowing the lattice to fit around the side of the cake. Press gently to secure the lattice and trim off the excess at the base. Leave to set.

5 Make the flower paste, reserve a tiny piece and cut the remainder in half. Tint one half

pale green and the other half pale yellow. Using a set of six plastic egg mould tray, dust well with cornflour. Roll out the green paste very thinly and use to line two of the half egg moulds. Trim the paste level with the edge of the mould and ensure the paste moves freely. Knead the trimmings together and return to a polythene bag. Repeat with the yellow paste to line another two half egg moulds and leave in a warm dry place until completely dry.

6 Roll out a small piece of yellow and green paste. Using a medium-sized blossom plunger cutter, cut out five of each colour (see page 88) and leave to dry. Roll out the white flower paste thinly. Using a small five petal cutter, cut out two shapes and place on a flower pad. Soften the edges with a bone tool and leave to dry.

7 Divide the royal icing into two, colour half yellow and half green to match the flower

paste. Half-fill two greaseproof paper piping bags fitted with a tiny star nozzle each with yellow and green icing. Fold down the tops.

8 Remove the coloured sugar shells and invert the mould. Place one green shell on the mould so it sits firmly and pipe a line of green icing around the edge. Place the second green shell on top to fit together. Pipe a row of stars around the outside edge to cover the join. Secure a semi-circle of yellow blossoms on the egg and the white flower in the centre. Pipe a coil of yellow icing in the centre of the white flower. Repeat to make and decorate the yellow egg using yellow icing and green blossoms and the remaining white flower.

9 Measure and fit the ribbon around the base of the cake and finish with some ribbon loops secured with a stainless steel pin. Arrange the eggs on top of the cake, secured with a little icing.

> **HINT**
> These eggs are lovely keepsakes; make extra eggs in various pastel shades and decorate as gifts for Easter.

FOOD COLOURINGS

T here has been quite a revolution in the food colouring industry. Gone are the watery liquids which simply diluted the mediums we were trying to colour rather than tint them. These have now been replaced with a range of vibrant coloured pastes, powders and concentrated liquid food colourings and pens.

The slightest hint of these colours will transform icings, sugar paste and marzipan into pastel shades or rich vibrant colours.

Research into these food colourings has improved greatly, taking into consideration the effects of food additives (prevalent in food colourings) on our health. Good quality food colourings are carefully balanced and blended, so they are expensive.

When using these colourings, only the smallest amount is required so they certainly last a long time and are a good investment. There is often no need to blend and mix colours now as the shades and colours required are already available in an extensive range of colour shades.

WHICH FORM OF FOOD COLOURING TO USE

Liquid colours – these concentrated liquid food colourings are generally used for colouring royal icing, butter cream or frosting. Add them drop by drop using a cocktail stick and they will tint the icing from a pale to a deep shade. They readily mix in giving an even colour throughout and are available in the normal range of everyday colours. To obtain a much deeper colour, there is also a high strength liquid range to obtain bright colours.

Paste colours – this very concentrated range of colourings come as a moist paste in every possible colour you can imagine. They are ideal for colouring sugar paste, flower paste or marzipan and will not affect the consistency of the mixture regardless of the depth of colour required. Tint from a pastel shade to deep ruby red or black; they are vibrant and keep their colour without fading.

When added to mixtures, these colours are inclined to deepen on standing. As some dry a deeper shade and other colours sometimes dry a lighter shade, always test the colours a few days before the sugar paste or icing is being used, to ensure the correct colour or shade is obtained.

Food colour dust – these are edible powder food colourings suitable for kneading into sugar paste, brushing to add colour to finished decorations, or for shading and colouring base icings on cakes to introduce a mixture of colours and patterns.

This useful coloured dust will add instant colour to any iced cake with just the use of a colour mixing palette and a fine brush. The colour choice is vast; the shades vary from pale pastels to rich warm colours. They are clean and easy to use, and do not leak or run. They readily mix together by dipping the brush into one colour then another, and brushing and working the dust into the icing.

Using food colour dust, last-minute colour may be added to a cake if the colour scheme has not been finalised.

Lustre colours – these food colourings come in different powdered finishes – pearl, iridescent, metallic and sparkle lustre dust. All these dust colours are non-edible and should only be used to colour special decorations. These are generally sugar flowers, and plaques which are removed from the cake before cutting and kept as a keepsake.

The real advantage of all these coloured dusts is that they may be brushed on to decorations which have been made out of white sugar or flower paste and left to dry. Shades of coloured dust may be applied to flowers with a fine brush and blended to give a realistic look.

The different finishes apply to the type of decorations you are colouring; pearl finishes look pretty on wedding cakes, whereas iridescent shades are more suitable for a novelty cake. Metallic dust such as silver, gold or bronze are ideal for festive or anniversary cakes. There are many colours and shades to choose from so start with a few basic colours plus the white powder or dust, which will tone down the bright colours by mixing.

Pollen dust – these tiny coloured granules are often used on flower centres instead of stamens to give a

more realistic look. Brush the flower centres with gum arabic glaze and dip into the chosen coloured pollen dust to colour evenly. Being edible, these dusts are better used on unwired flowers.

Glitter flakes – these are the latest range of food colourings made from paper thin flakes of sugar and are edible. They come in a range of vibrant primary colours and add a sparkle to iced cakes. Sprinkle the flakes directly onto iced cakes or use to highlight sugar pieces (see page 117).

Pure gold and silver leaf – these are very fine flakes or sheets of real gold and silver leaf. They look absolutely stunning when applied to cakes for decoration, especially for gold or silver wedding anniversary cakes. They are very expensive and must be applied with great care. Clear alcohol is brushed on to the surface and fine tweezers are used to transfer the gold or silver flakes.

When using all food colouring, add them using a cocktail stick. This will ensure the icing is not over-coloured. Leave the icing to see if the colour deepens, and carefully match icing colours to fabric or flowers in the daylight, not in artificial light. If large quantities of coloured icing are required, always keep some of the coloured icing to match.

Food colouring pens – working just like fibre tip pens, these pens are filled with various liquid food colourings. The pens come plain or with an italic nib. This gives the advantage of writing or drawing directly on to sugar plaques or cake surfaces.

SUGAR PASTE

ugar paste has now become the most popular way of covering and decorating a celebration cake, mainly because of its versatility and ease of use. It originated in Australia and is now widely used in many countries including America, South Africa, Canada, New Zealand and Japan.

Celebration cakes are now often seen as softly rounded, smooth shapes, instead of the sharp, crisp, classical lines of the traditionally royal iced cake and with this delicate visual appearance needs the minimum of decoration.

The main reason for this surge in popularity is that sugar paste is quick, easy and instant to use, saving a lot of time and producing quick results. Sugar paste, being soft and pliable, is easily tinted and may be rolled out and used to cover even the most unusual shaped cake, which could not be achieved with royal icing.

Even the least experienced cake decorator can achieve a smooth well covered cake with a professional finish. This in turn needs only the simplest finishing touch of flowers or ribbons to produce a well presented cake.

Although there is a recipe for sugar paste, there are certainly times when the ready-made sugar paste is better and more convenient to use. There are several types of sugar paste available and basically with a similar kind of recipe but packaged under different names. Textures may vary and some are certainly much better to handle than others. It is a good idea to try a small quantity of sugar paste first to see if it is suitable for the cake you are decorating, before purchasing a large quantity.

Sugar paste may be purchased in 250 g (8 oz) and 500 g (1 lb) packs from many supermarkets and shops, or up to 5 kg (11 lb) boxes from cake icing specialists. It is better to buy a large quantity, knowing that the sugar paste comes from one batch ensuring the colour and texture is even and smooth. Sugar paste will keep for several months as long as the air is completely excluded.

Sugar paste is now available in many colours – white, champagne, pink, blue, peach and many others. This is worth considering if you need a large quantity for a wedding cake as it ensures the colour is even throughout. Kneading food colouring into large quantities of sugar paste is hard work and time-consuming, and it is sometimes quite difficult to obtain an evenly blended colour without incorporating air bubbles into the sugar paste.

This versatile icing may be used to cover all types of cakes from light sponge cakes to marzipan-covered celebration cakes. It may also be used for making decorations such as sugar flowers, leaves, cut-out sugar pieces or for modelling animals or figures.

HOW TO COLOUR SUGAR PASTE

When tinting sugar paste at home, knead the food colouring into a small piece of sugar paste, darker than the colour required. Then knead the coloured piece into the remaining sugar paste until the colour is even throughout the sugar paste, and the correct shade has been obtained (see page 89).

SPECIAL EQUIPMENT FOR SUGAR PASTE

Sugar paste is a very modern aspect of cake decorating and requires a completely different technique to royal icing. Being smooth, pliable and easy to use, high standards are achieved quickly with the help of special equipment. Sets of tools, cutters, crimpers and embossers are all made to produce different designs, patterns, flowers and finishes on cakes covered with sugar paste.

Large acrylic board and rolling pin – these are essential for rolling out large quantities of sugar paste. The acrylic surfaces are non-stick, clean and hygienic to use.

Cake smoother – helps to smooth the surface of sugar paste to obtain a satin smooth finish and eliminate any cracks or imperfections.

Small palette knife – cranked or straight handles are ideal for neatening the edges of sugar paste and lifting decorations.

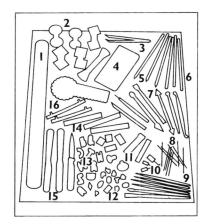

1. *Acrylic rolling pin*   2. *Cake pillars*   3. *Tweezers*   4. *Cake smoother*   5. *Wooden dowel*   6. *Acrylic Skewers*   7. *Modelling tools*   8. *Cocktail sticks*   9. *Brushes*   10. *Blossom plunger cutter*   11. *Crimpers*   12. *Flower and leaf cutters*   13. *Aspic and small cutters*   14. *Embossing stamps*   15. *Palette knives*   16. *Garrett frill cutters*

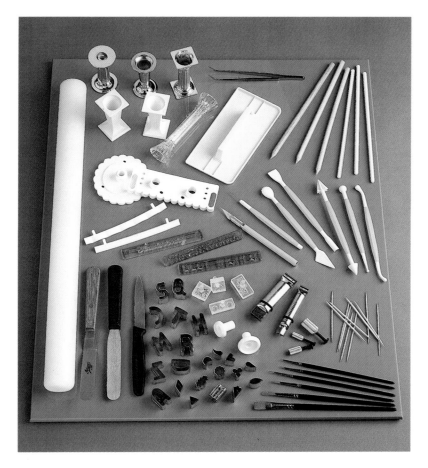

Small knife – for cutting out pieces and shapes.

Crimpers – these tweezer-styled tools have decorative end pieces which imprint various designs on to the surface of the sugar paste.

Embossing stamps – small stamps which each have a raised design of flowers, motifs, letters and seasonal emblems which are printed on to the surface of the sugar paste.

Sugar paste modelling tools – cone tool, cutting knife, bone tool, ball tool – all these tools have a purpose when working with sugar paste, and are well worth buying.

Ribbon slotters – these set of three different sized ribbon insertion cutters are wonderful for making neat slits into the surface of sugar paste ready for inserting the ribbon.

Ribbon insertion blade – a small sharp blade for cutting the ribbon insertion slits cleanly and neatly.

Tweezers – sharp straight-edged tweezers for holding the ribbons in position for ribbon insertion.

Garrett frill cutters – round and straight frill cutters of different sizes for making frills and flounces to fit on to sugar paste cakes.

Cocktail sticks – these are necessary to use for frilling the edge of sugar paste, and adding food colourings to icing.

Acrylic skewers – used to insert into sugar paste cakes to support the upper tiers. They are hygienic and may be cut to the level of each cake.

Hollow cake pillars – these cover the acrylic skewers that support the cake tiers. They are made in plastic in a variety of colours.

Wooden dowel – used to support sugar paste leaves and flowers so they dry in a more realistic curved shape.

Flower and leaf cutters – a selection of simple flower and leaf cutters for making sugar paste flowers and leaves.

Blossom plunger cutter – blossom cutters with a spring plunger which ejects the blossoms and helps to form the shapes.

Aspic and small cutters – used to make designs in sugar paste and marzipan.

Brushes – fine artists' brushes are available in many different shapes and sizes for painting on food colouring dusts and liquids.

SUGAR PASTE

Although sugar paste is more convenient to buy ready-made, it is useful to have a recipe which is quick and easy to make. Always warm the jar of liquid glucose for easy measuring.

1 egg white
30 ml (2 tbsp) liquid glucose
10 ml (2 tsp) rose water
450 g (1 lb) icing sugar, sifted
icing sugar to dust

....

1 Place the egg white, liquid glucose and rose water into a clean bowl, blending with a wooden spoon to break up the egg white. Add the icing sugar and mix together until the icing begins to bind together. Knead with the fingers until the mixture forms into a rough ball. Place the sugar paste on a surface lightly dusted with sifted icing sugar and knead thoroughly until smooth, pliable and free from cracks.

2 If the sugar paste is too soft to handle and is rather sticky, knead in some more sifted icing sugar until firm and pliable. Likewise if the sugar paste is dry and firm, knead in a little boiled water until the sugar paste becomes soft and pliable.

3 Wrap the sugar paste completely in cling film or store in a polythene bag with all the air excluded.
Makes 550 g (1¼ lb) sugar paste

TECHNIQUES USING SUGAR PASTE

There are a variety of techniques, some very easy indeed, which may be applied to cakes covered with sugar paste which instantly transform their appearance. Edges of cakes may be crimped or embossed giving a simple yet effective decorative border design. This pliable paste may also be turned into frills and flounces, enhancing the side of a celebration cake. It may be cut into sugar paste pieces, moulded into flowers and many more ways as you will see.

TO COVER ANY SHAPED CAKE WITH SUGAR PASTE

1 Place the ready marzipanned cake on its matching shaped cake board on the turntable. Brush the surface evenly with a little sherry or cooled boiled water. When covering a sponge cake with sugar paste, you can spread with butter cream first.

2 Dust the surface and the rolling pin with a little sifted icing sugar to prevent the sugar paste from sticking. Roll out the sugar paste to match the shape of the cake and large enough to cover the top and sides, allowing about 5 mm (¼ inch) thickness. Trim the sugar paste to 5-7.5 cm (2-3 inches) larger than the top of the cake, ensuring it moves freely. Brush off any excess icing sugar.

> **HINT**
> Knead the trimmings, seal them in a polythene bag and keep for decorations.

3 Lift the sugar paste and place centrally over the top of the cake, supported by a rolling pin. Unroll the sugar paste, allowing it to cover the cake loosely. With lightly cornfloured hands, smooth the sugar paste over the top, excluding any air bubbles between the surfaces. Ease gently down the side of the cake so that the excess sugar paste is on the board.

4 Trim off the excess sugar paste at the base of the cake using a small knife. With lightly cornfloured hands or using a cake smoother, gently smooth the surface of the sugar paste in circular movements to make the surface smooth and glossy.

5 If the cake is square, using cupped hands at the base of the corners, smooth the sugar paste up towards the top edge of the cake. This prevents the sugar paste from stretching or tearing.

TO COVER A CAKE BOARD

To cover a cake board with sugar paste simply enhances the appearance of the finished cake.

1 Instead of trimming off the excess sugar paste at the base of the cake, allow it to cover the cake board and trim the sugar paste level with the edge of the board.

2 Alternatively, cover the plain cake board with sugar paste.

3 Neaten the sugar paste at the edge of the board.

> HINT
> Allow the coated board to dry, then place the sugar-pasted cake in the centre.

FRILLS AND FLOUNCES

Layers of fine sugar paste frills cascading down the side of a cake can look absolutely spectacular. They may be attached as a single layer or many more in scalloped or arched designs.

They may be enhanced by crimping the edge of the frill where it is attached to the cake, piping details above and below the frills, or embossing, or inserting ribbon to complete the design.

Sugar paste frills are easily made with the use of a frill cutter. These may be straight or curved depending on the design. When making sugar paste frills it is advisable to work quickly, making one frill at a time so that the frill does not crack or break.

It is often more successful to use equal parts of sugar paste and flower paste (see page 154) kneaded well together. This produces a stronger and more elastic paste which is easier to handle and apply to the cake. Once the frill is in position, it dries quickly giving more definition to the flounces.

Tint the sugar paste to make coloured frills, or apply coloured dust to dry frills for added colour. Always apply sugar paste frills to a cake which has been covered at least a day before so that the cake does not fingermark while applying the frills.

TO MAKE A FRILL

1 Using a small acrylic board and rolling pin, roll out sugar paste very thinly. Lift the sugar paste using a fine palette knife so that it moves freely. If it sticks, rub cornflour over the board. Using a frill cutter, cut out the shape.

2 Dip a cocktail stick into some cornflour, place it on the outer edge of the frill. Roll the stick backwards and forwards along the edge of each flute until the edge begins to frill. Move around the edge of the sugar paste.

3 Cut the ring open with a knife, then gently ease the frill open. Pipe a line of royal icing following the shape where the frill has to be attached, or brush the surface with a little water or egg white. Press the frill gently in position and trim to fit if necessary.

4 Repeat this procedure to attach more frills around the cake (see page 98). Add extra layers above the frills already attached to make a multi-frilled design. If liked, neaten the final frill by using an embossing stamp or a small crimper.

CRIMPING

This technique is unbelievably quick and easy to master. Very effective designs are obtained by the use of a crimper. These tweezer-shaped tools come with different shaped and sized end pieces with curved lines, scallops, ovals, 'V', hearts, diamonds and zig-zags, to name but a few. To obtain an even crimped design, it is always advisable to practise on a spare piece of sugar paste. Then crimp on a cake *freshly covered* with sugar paste, otherwise the surface will crack.

TO CRIMP A DESIGN

1 Cover the cake with sugar paste but do not leave it to dry. Dust the crimper lightly with cornflour to prevent it sticking to the sugar paste.

2 Hold the crimper between your thumb and fingers and place it slightly open on to the edge of the cake. Squeeze firmly to mark the pattern on to the sugar paste.

3 Gently release the crimper and lift off, taking care that it does not spring apart or it will tear and ruin the pattern.

4 Place the crimper next to the marked pattern and repeat all around the top of the cake, dusting the crimper with cornflour occasionally to prevent the sugar paste from sticking. Use on the base and sides of various shaped cakes, or make a crimper design on top of the cake.

EMBOSSING

This is a wonderful technique for an instant way of decorating a cake covered with sugar paste. It is similar to crimping where the cake has to be freshly covered with sugar paste to work the design successfully, otherwise the surface will crack.

There are many embossing stamps which are available from cake icing specialists. These range from seasonal patterns, flowers, novelty designs to motifs suitable for wedding and christening cakes.

Many other tools may be used to impress a pattern on to the surface of a cake covered with sugar paste: spoon handles, piping nozzles, buttons.

Choose an embossing stamp and practise on a piece of sugar paste to create the design.

TO EMBOSS A DESIGN

1 Ensure the cake is freshly covered in sugar paste to give a clean sharp impression, and dust the embossing stamp with cornflour or food colouring dust.

2 Take care to press the embossing tool the same depth and angle each time into the sugar paste, to make an even design.

3 Re-dust with cornflour or colouring dust to prevent sticking, or to imprint evenly.

> **HINT**
> Colour may be added by painting part or all of the embossed design by using a fine paint brush dipped into food colouring pastes or using food colouring pens when the sugar paste is dry. Dipping the embossing stamp into food colouring dust will imprint the pattern in colour which gives the finish a very professional look.

CUT-OUT AND APPLIQUÉD DESIGNS

These inspirational designs can look so stunning on a perfectly iced cake. The shapes and colours of the design are transposed in matching cut-out pieces of sugar paste and re-positioned on the cake. The designs may flow from the top of the cake and continue around the sides, giving the cake a very graphic appearance. (For example, see Appliqué Design Cake on page 93.)

Ideas may be obtained from many sources but the most inspiring designs come from fabric patterns, wallpaper prints, gift wrapping paper, cards and porcelain.

A more realistic way of applying this type of design is to use half flower paste kneaded into half of the sugar paste so that the sugar paste pieces set hard before they are applied to the surface of the cake. The advantage being that the pieces may be applied proud of the cake, or set at an angle and holding their own shape to give a three-dimensional appearance to the design.

NOTE: Accuracy of the designs is all-important to this method as the cake has a very graphic appearance and any mistakes at all are very much more noticeable.

TO MAKE A CUT-OUT DESIGN

1 Coat the cake with icing, preferably sugar paste as the soft line lends itself to a flowing design trailing over the edge and around the side of the cake.

2 When the design has been selected, trace the details on to greaseproof paper making a complete copy of the design and use this as a template.

3 Select the colours for the chosen design and tint the sugar paste pieces to match; alternatively cut out the design in white sugar paste and paint the pieces with food colours when the design has dried.

4 Using an acrylic board and rolling pin, roll out one piece of sugar paste thinly, ensuring that it moves freely. Place the template on top and mark the outline of the shape using a scribing needle or pin.

5 Using a small sharp knife or scalpel, cut out the design pieces using the various coloured sugar paste until all the pieces have been cut out.

6 Assemble the pieces to ensure they fit, then apply them piece by piece on to the cake, taking care not to over-handle or mis-shape the pieces. Press gently in position until all the pieces are in place to make up the design. Secure the design to the cake using a little egg white.

RIBBON INSERTION

This is a technique designed to create the effect that a single piece of ribbon has been threaded at regular intervals through the sugar paste. The design of the ribbon which is inserted can be straight, diagonal or curved. This combined with crimper work or dainty piping can make a special feature of this technique.

The cake should be *freshly covered* with sugar paste and feel firm on the surface, but soft underneath. Therefore, it is advisable to leave the cake for 2 hours after it has been covered before embarking on the design.

It is important to work out the design very accurately using a template to mark the insertion lines into the sugar paste as it is very noticeable if the ribbon insertions are uneven.

TO MAKE A RIBBON INSERTION DESIGN

1 Plan the design on paper first, making sure it is accurate, and combine this design with the width of the ribbon being used. Choose the colour and width of the ribbon required to match the shape and colour of the cake. Use plain edged ribbons which are firm as they are easier to insert. Cut as many pieces of ribbon to complete the design. The ribbon pieces should be slightly longer than the spaces allowed, leaving enough room to tuck in both ends.

2 Place the template on top of the cake and mark the design accurately. The sugar paste should feel firm but not soft so care must be taken not to make any imprints on the surface of the sugar paste. Use a scribing needle or a stainless steel pin to mark out the design.

3 Using ribbon slotters, a knife fitted with a ribbon insertion blade or a scalpel, cut the slits accurately in the icing following the marked lines. Insert one end of the piece of ribbon held with a pair of tweezers into the first slit, guiding the end in with a scribing needle, pin or scalpel blade.

4 Tuck the other end of the ribbon into the second slit; press gently to secure. Leave a space and repeat to insert another piece of ribbon until all the slits are filled.

5 Finish the ribbon insertion design with a tiny bow, a neatly crimped pattern or fine embroidery piping.

EXTENSION SUGAR PIECES

These delicately shaped pieces of sugar paste are very like icing run-outs but without all the intricate time-consuming work that run-outs involve. Once the extension sugar pieces have been made, they may be attached to the side or edge of the cake, extending the edge to form a doyley design or to create the effect of a porcelain edge. They may be coloured with food colour dusts or tinted before they are made.

The edging can also look very pretty with fine ribbon woven in and out of the design.

Designs may be inspired by doyley or embroidery patterns or even antique china which has the edges cut out.

There are so many wonderful shapes which can be created in this way from sugar paste. You can use biscuit cutters for the basic shapes, then use tiny aspic cutters, piping nozzle ends, various crimpers and flower cutters to work the more intricate cut-out design.

You should remember to allow for a larger cake board when fitting extension pieces on to the cake, otherwise the design will look unbalanced and the extension pieces are more likely to get damaged. The cake board must extend at least 2.5 cm (1 inch) beyond the extension pieces so they are contained within the cake board, otherwise breakages will occur when the cake is boxed.

TO MAKE EXTENSION SUGAR PIECES

1 Extension sugar pieces may be made from sugar paste but for extra strength and quick drying use half sugar paste and half flower paste. Roll out the sugar or flower paste in small quantities as the flower paste dries exceptionally quickly. Roll it so thinly that you can almost see through it.

2 Using cutters of varying shapes and sizes, or a template, cut out one or two pieces from the rolled out sugar or flower paste. Cut out the details.

3 Arrange the pieces on a flat surface dusted with cornflour or on a piece of foam sponge in a warm, dry place until hard. Repeat this procedure to make the number of extension or sugar pieces needed to decorate the cake. Always make a few extra pieces to allow for breakages.

4 When they are all dry, tint them with coloured dust if desired. Always arrange extension sugar pieces on the cake first to ensure the design fits the cake. Sometimes it is necessary to make small corner pieces to fit a square cake.

5 Attach the sugar pieces with royal icing and allow the cake to dry overnight in a cardboard cake box in a warm, dry place.

CUT-OUT DECORATIONS

Cut-outs make an instant decoration for any iced cake. Simply colour the sugar paste in the chosen colours, or leave it the original colour.

Roll out the sugar paste thinly on a surface lightly dusted with icing sugar. Cut out small icing shapes using tiny aspic or small cocktail cutters, simple rounds, triangles or squares, and leave them in a warm place to dry. Arrange these shaped on to the top and sides of the cake to make a border design and to decorate the sides, securing them with a little royal icing. On simply decorated cakes, brush the sugar pieces with a little water or glacé icing.

SUGAR PASTE QUANTITY CHART

CAKE SIZES	12.5 cm (5 in) square 15 cm (6 in) round	15 cm (6 in) square 18 cm (7 in) round	18 cm (7 in) square 20.5 cm (8 in) round	20.5 cm (8 in) square 23 cm (9 in) round
SUGAR PASTE	450 g (1 lb)	700 g (1½ lb)	800 g (1¾ lb)	1 kg (2¼ lb)

CAKE SIZES	23 cm (9 in) square 25.5 cm (10 in) round	25.5 cm (10 in) square 28 cm (11 in) round	28 cm (11 in) square 30.5 cm (12 in) round	30.5 cm (12 in) square 33 cm (13 in) round
SUGAR PASTE	1.1 kg (2½ lb)	1.4 kg (3 lb)	1.6 kg (3½ lb)	1.8 kg (4 lb)

SIMPLE SUGAR PASTE FLOWERS

Sugar paste being a soft pliable medium, lends itself to being tinted and moulded into many simple sugar flowers. At one time this skill was only enjoyed by a few who mastered the art of hand moulding sugar flowers which look so realistic. Today we are lucky enough to be able to make all these flowers by hand but with the use of specific flower, petal and leaf cutters, all available from cake icing specialists.

TO MAKE SIMPLE FLOWERS

1 These flowers are made using simple flower cutters with the petals softened. They are not specific blooms but a simple way of introducing sugar flowers as a cake decoration. Tint and colour the sugar paste or make them all white and add colour with coloured dusts.

2 Using an acrylic rolling pin and board, roll out the sugar paste very, very thinly.

3 Cut out several of the chosen flower shapes and place them on to pieces of foam sponge.

4 Using a bone tool, soften the edge of each petal by pressing on to the petals. Press into the centre of each to give a flower shape.

5 Bend the petals if you wish to give a more realistic look and leave the flowers to dry. To add stamens, make a pin hole in each flower and secure with gum glaze or egg white.

6 Brush the dry flowers with coloured dust to shade them and to give them a more realistic look. Use them to make an arrangement on a celebration cake.

BLOSSOM PLUNGER CUTTER FLOWERS

These flowers are so useful and may be cut out in three sizes using special blossom plunger cutters. They may be used for decorating borders, ribbon insertion work, to enhance sugar frills or simply used to infill a floral arrangement. They may be applied directly onto the cake surface.

TO MAKE BLOSSOM PLUNGER CUTTER FLOWERS

1 Tint or colour the sugar paste to the shade you require. Using an acrylic rolling pin and board, roll out the sugar paste very thinly so that you can almost see through the paste.

HINT

When the blossoms are completely dry, store them in a box between tissue paper. Alternatively, wire them together using fine florist's wire to make sprays (see page 156).

2 Cut out the blossom shape using a large, medium or small plunger blossom cutter. Eject the flower by pressing the plunger into a piece of foam sponge to bend the sugar paste to shape the flower.

3 If the blossoms are to have a stamen in the centre, make a pin hole in each blossom as it is made. When dry, brush the back of the stamen with gum glaze (see page 154) or egg white, then thread through the blossom to secure.

MOULDED SUGAR ROSES

The only flower which is essentially moulded by hand is the hybrid rose, each petal being formed from sugar paste and assembled into a realistic rose. Either tint the sugar paste, in several shades of the colour. Otherwise use coloured dust to brush the colour on to the rose when it is dry.

TO MAKE MOULDED SUGAR ROSES

1 Tint the sugar paste the colours you require.

2 Make a cone of sugar paste to use as the centre of the rose and also the base on which to

work. Take a pea-sized piece of the deepest shade of coloured sugar paste and press out a petal, thicker at the base and as fine as possible on the top edge. Smear a little white fat on your fingers to prevent the sugar paste from sticking or drying out. Wrap the first petal completely around the very top so the cone shape is not visible.

3 Make another petal shape and position it so the centre of the second petal is opposite the join of the first petal. Attach the third petal just tucking inside where the second petal finished.

Press gently around the bud at the base and bend the petals over at the top.

4 Continue to add more petals working around the rose using all the shades of sugar paste, using the palest colour for the outer petals.

5 When the rose is the desired size, cut the rose at the base and place on a piece of foam sponge to dry. To make rose buds, just add about four petals to the cone shape.

CUT-OUT LEAVES

1 Colour a piece of sugar paste moss green and roll out very thinly. Cut out the shaped leaf you require with a leaf cutter, or use a real leaf as a pattern to cut around. Alternatively, use white sugar paste and dust with green food colouring dust to give a natural appearance to the leaves.

2 Make the veins by imprinting with a real leaf or a tool.

3 Bend slightly and dry over a piece of dowel. Dust.

4 Cut-out leaves add the realistic look to cakes.

ANNIVERSARY HEART CAKE

*T*he textured appearance of this cake covered in sugar paste is obtained by using food colouring and a piece of sponge or muslin, or coloured dusts and a brush. Hand moulded sugar paste roses and ribbon enhance the design.

20.5 cm (8 inch) round rich or light fruit cake mixture (see page 67)

25.5 cm (10 inch) heart-shaped silver cake board

30 ml (2 tbsp) apricot glaze (see page 70)

800 g (1¾ lb) white marzipan

1.1 kg (2½ lb) champagne coloured sugar paste

peach and moss green food colouring dusts

15 ml (1 tbsp) clear alcohol – gin or vodka

piece of foam sponge or muslin

5 moulded sugar roses (see page 89)

7 cut-out rose leaves (see page 89)

1 metre (1 yard), 4 cm (1½ inch) wide fancy orange ribbon

1 metre (1 yard), 1 cm (½ inch) wide plain cream ribbon

....

1 Prepare a 20.5 cm (8 inch) heart shaped cake tin (see page 11). Make the rich or light fruit cake mixture and place in the tin. Bake according to the cake chart on page 68. Place the cake in the centre of the cake board and brush with apricot glaze. Cover smoothly with marzipan (see page 73). When the marzipan is dry, cover the cake and cake board with sugar paste (see page 82), reserving one-third to make sugar roses and leaves.

2 Mix a little peach food colouring dust with a little alcohol on a plate to make a thin consistency. Roll out a sample piece of sugar paste. Dampen the sponge or muslin and wring out well. Scrunch up the sponge or muslin and dab quickly into the coloured mixture. Lightly dab the surface of the sugar paste to imprint a light touch of colour. Work in a methodical pattern all over the sugar paste, tightening or loosening the material to vary the pattern. Add more peach colour dust if the imprint is too pale.

3 Once you are happy with the colour and the pattern, apply the colour evenly all over the cake and cake board. The sugar paste is better to work on if it is dry, to prevent indenting the sugar paste if the pressure is too great when applying the colour.

4 Using the remaining sugar paste, mould seven roses each varying in size and shape, following the instructions on page 89. Leave them to dry in a warm place. Using a fine paint brush and peach dust, brush the rose petals to tint the edges.

5 Roll out the remaining sugar paste and cut out seven rose leaves (see page 89) and leave to dry. Brush the leaves with moss green dust to colour evenly. Alternatively, first colour the sugar paste green.

6 Measure and fit the fancy ribbon around the base of the cake and tie a large bow. Secure with a stainless steel pin. Measure and fit the plain ribbon around the cake board and secure with a pin. Arrange the roses and leaves over the top of the cake, securing each with a small piece of damp sugar paste. Leave the cake to dry in a cardboard cake box in a warm dry place.

HINT
The pattern achieved on this cake may be varied by using a mixture of different shades to produce a stencilled surface.

APPLIQUÉ DESIGN CAKE

C hoose any design from fabrics, wallpaper or
porcelain and transfer the pattern in sugar paste
pieces on to the cake. Choose your own colour scheme or
copy the design you have chosen.

25.5 cm (10 inch) round rich or
   light fruit cake mixture (see page
   64 or 67)
30.5 cm (12 inch) round silver
   cake board
60 ml (4 tbsp) apricot glaze (see
   page 70)
1 kg (2¼ lb) white marzipan
1.4 kg (3 lb) white sugar paste
claret pink and holly green food
   colourings
1 metre (1 yard), 1 cm (½ inch)
   wide white ribbon
1 metre (1 yard), 5 mm (¼ inch)
   wide turquoise blue ribbon

....

1 Prepare a 25.5 cm (10 inch)
   round cake tin (see page 11).
Make the rich or light fruit cake
mixture and place in the tin. Bake
according to the cake chart on
page 66 or 68. Place the cake in
the centre of the cake board and
brush with apricot glaze. Cover
smoothly with marzipan (see page
73). When the marzipan is dry,
reserve one third sugar paste and
cover the cake and cake board
smoothly with the remaining sugar
paste (see page 82). Place the cake
in the cardboard cake box and
leave until dry in a warm dry place.
Knead the trimmings together.

2 Trace the design on to a
   piece of greaseproof paper
and use as a template. Divide the
sugar paste into four pieces and
colour one piece claret, one piece
pink, another piece pale green and
the last piece holly green. Knead
well so they are evenly coloured.
Lay the template on top of the
cake and lightly outline the design
using a scribing tool as a guide for
fitting the sugar pieces. (See page
208 for this cake design.)

3 Starting with the leaves, roll
   out the dark green sugar
paste thinly. Place the paper design
over the sugar paste and mark the
outline of each leaf shape using a
scribing tool. Remove the paper
design, cut out the leaves using a
sharp knife. Mark the veins on the
leaves using a veiner or real leaf.
Place the leaves on to the paper
pattern to ensure the leaves fit in
position.

4 Repeat this method to cut
   out the flowers using the
light and dark pink sugar paste,
and the stems from the pale green
sugar paste. Arrange the cut out
sugar pieces on top of the cake
following the outline of the design.

5 Using a little water and a fine
   paint brush, brush the
underside of each sugar paste piece
and press gently in position. Cut
out the fine stems from the dark
green sugar paste and position over
the pale green stems. Continue the
design. Fit a strip of dark pink
paste around the base of the cake.

6 Measure and fit the ribbons around the edge of the cake board and secure with a stainless steel pin. Leave the cake to dry in a cardboard cake box in a warm dry place. If desired, cut out a sugar paste plaque and write a message or greeting appropriate to the cake using food colouring pens.

HINT
This pattern has been taken from a furnishing fabric and traced on to a template.

CHRISTMAS FRUIT GARLAND

*C**oloured fruits moulded from marzipan or sugar paste decorate this Christmas fruit cake. Choose festive ribbons to fill the centre, or make more fruits.*

18 cm (7 inch) round light fruit cake mixture (see page 67)

23 cm (9 inch) round gold cake board

45 ml (3 tbsp) apricot glaze (see page 70)

700 g (1½ lb) white marzipan

550 g (1¼ lb) white sugar paste

orange, green, gold and silver food colouring dusts

15 ml (1 tbsp) whole cloves, cut into halves

30 ml (2 tbsp) royal icing (see page 108)

1 metre (1 yard) festive ribbons or gift decoration

....

1   Grease and base line a 23 cm (9 inch), 2.3 litre (4 pint) ring mould. Make the light fruit cake mixture and place in the tin. Bake for 2½-2¾ hours, according to the cake chart on page 68. Place the cake on the cake board and brush with apricot glaze. Cover smoothly with marzipan (see page 73). Knead the trimmings together to use to mould the fruit. When dry,

cover the cake smoothly with sugar paste and reserve the trimmings (see page 82). Leave the cake to dry in a cardboard cake box.

2   To make the marzipan fruits, shape about 22 marble size balls of marzipan. Shape about 100 tiny peas of marzipan to make the grapes. Roll out marzipan thinly and, using a vine leaf cutter, cut out 11 leaves and vein them.

3   Place a little of each of the food colouring dusts into a colouring palette. Coat nine balls with orange dust and roll the balls

in the palm of your hand to colour evenly. Roll each ball on a nutmeg grater to texture the surface. Coat another six balls in green dust and roll to coat evenly like the oranges. Using a modelling tool, make an indentation in each end to make an apple shape.

4   Colour the remaining balls gold and shape into pear shapes in the palm of your hand. Dust all the pea-sized pieces gold and the leaves green. Using the halved cloves, press the tops in the fruit for stalks and the other end of the clove into the base of each fruit. Dust all the fruit with silver dust.

5   Arrange the apples, pears and oranges in three groups on top of the cake and secure with royal icing. Arrange the grapes a few at a time cascading over the edge of the ring cake. Secure with royal icing.

6   Bend the leaves and position each side of the grapes and fruit. Band the front of the cake with two strips of ribbon and fill the centre with festive ribbon or more marzipan fruits.

HINT

Fruits coloured with gold and silver dust are inedible. Use only the coloured dust for edible fruits.

DOMED WEDDING CAKE

This rather unusual cake gives a stunning appearance swathed with paper-thin sugar paste in pastel shades and finished with fine beads of icing.

18 cm (7 inch) round rich fruit cake mixture (see page 64)

25.5 cm (10 inch) round silver cake board

45 ml (3 tbsp) apricot glaze (see page 70)

450 g (1 lb) white marzipan

900 g (2 lb) champagne coloured sugar paste

old gold and cornflower blue food colourings

60 ml (4 tbsp) royal icing (see page 108)

1 metre (1 yard), 1 cm (½ inch) wide champagne ribbon

....

1 Grease and line an 18 cm (7 inch), 1.7 litre (3 pint) bell shaped cake tin; protect the outside with brown paper (see page 11). Make the rich fruit cake mixture and place in the tin, making a deep depression in the centre. Bake the cake for 3-3¼ hours, according to the cake chart on page 66. Cool in the tin. Place the cake on the centre of the cake board and brush with apricot glaze. Cover the cake smoothly with marzipan (see page 73). When the marzipan is dry, cover the cake smoothly with sugar paste and allow the excess sugar paste to cover the board (see page 82).

2 Knead the remaining sugar paste and the trimmings together and cut into three pieces. Tint one-third cream with a drop of old gold food colouring and one-third pale blue with a drop of blue food colouring. Knead well.

3 Roll out a strip of champagne coloured sugar paste so thinly that you can see through it. Using a sharp knife, cut a strip 40.5 × 7.5 cm (16 × 3 inches). Roll the edges of the sugar paste inwards using your fingers, then carefully form the strip into folds, giving a soft folded appearance and pleating one end. Brush the top of the cake with a little water and holding the pleated end of the sugar paste gently, place in position on top of the cake, coiling the end inwards. Press gently.

4 Allow the remaining sugar paste to come around the front of the cake until it is directly

underneath the top coil and only 5 cm (2 inches) above the cake board. Brush the sugar paste with a little water to secure the sugar paste drape in position on the side of the cake and allow the excess folds to fall on to the cake board. Neaten the edge, cutting at an angle with a knife. Make another two strips of folded sugar paste, attaching the cream strip below and the blue strip above the champagne strip already attached to the cake.

5 Using the remaining blue and champagne coloured sugar paste, roll out and trim one thin strip of each 15 × 2.5 cm (6 × 1 inches). Fold and coil the ends and place in position on top of the cake, secured with a little water. Allow the ends to fall naturally into folds.

6 Tint the royal icing
champagne colour with a
drop of old gold food colouring and

place in a greaseproof paper piping
bag fitted with a No. 2 plain writing
nozzle. Fold down the top. Pipe
groups of three beads of icing
evenly spaced apart over the plain
sugar paste surface and also over
the cake board. Measure and fit the
ribbon around the base of the
board and secure with a stainless
steel pin. Place the cake in the
cardboard cake box and keep in a
warm dry place until required.

HINT
It is important to roll out the
sugar paste for the drapes so
thinly that you can see through
it as it gives the very soft folded
effect of a fabric. Ensure the
strips move freely on the board
before pleating the ends.

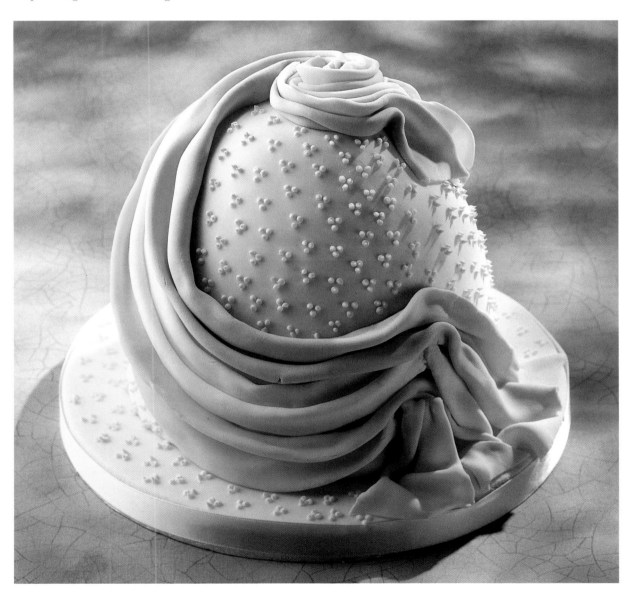

MOTHER'S DAY CAKE

A *pretty shaped Madeira cake cooked in a ring mould and finished with cascading frills and carnations edged with coloured dust.*

3-egg quantity Madeira cake mixture (see page 69)

23 cm (9 inch) round silver cake board

30 ml (2 tbsp) apricot glaze (see page 70)

450 g (1 lb) white marzipan

700 g (1½ lb) white sugar paste

1 metre (1 yard), 1 cm (½ inch) wide plain purple ribbon

6-8 hand made carnations

moss green food colouring

6-8 hand made leaves

violet food colouring dust

1 metre (1 yard), 1 cm (½ inch) wide plain white ribbon

1 metre (1 yard), 5 mm (¼ inch) wide fancy purple ribbon

....

1 Grease and base line a 19 cm (7½ inch), 1.4 litre (2½ pint) fluted ring mould. Make the Madeira cake mixture and place in the tin. Bake for 1-1¼ hours, according to the cake chart on page 70. Place the cake in the centre of the board and brush with apricot glaze. Cover smoothly with marzipan (see page 73).

2 When the marzipan is dry, cover the cake and the cake board using three-quarters of the white sugar paste (see page 82). Knead the trimmings together. Measure and fit the wide purple ribbon around the base of the cake and secure with a stainless steel pin.

3 To make the sugar paste frills, follow the instructions on page 83. Make and apply one frill at a time, securing the top with a little water and allowing the frill to fall in a gentle curve down the side of the cake. Brush the underneath edge of the frill with a little water to secure. Make and fit another four frills from the centre to the base of the cake. Repeat to make another five frills and secure each one just above the first frills.

4 Use a small double curved crimper to pattern the edge as soon as each second frill has been fitted. Repeat with remaining frills. For each carnation, make

one frill as for the cake. Very finely frill the edge. Moisten the straight edge and roll up.

5 Colour 25 g (1 oz) sugar paste with a drop of moss green food colouring. Knead until evenly coloured. Very thinly roll out the sugar paste and using a petal shaped cutter, cut out six to eight leaf shapes. Frill the edges with a cocktail stick and leave to dry. Brush the edge of the frills and the carnations with violet food colouring dust and use a fine brush to tint the edges.

6 Arrange the leaves and flowers in the centre top of the cake in between the frills. Measure and fit the wide white ribbon around the edge of the cake board, then the narrow purple ribbon and secure with a stainless steel pin. Store the cake in a cardboard cake box until required.

TWO-TIER
OVAL WEDDING CAKE

*S*o simple and so effective, this wedding cake could
be made in two days. Simply covered with
champagne coloured sugar paste and decorated with
beautiful ribbons and fresh flowers.

30.5 cm and 20.5 cm (12 inch and
8 inch) round rich fruit cake
mixture (see page 64)

35 cm and 25.5 cm (14 inch and
10 inch) oval silver cake boards

75 ml (5 tbsp) apricot glaze (see
page 70)

1.7 kg (3¾ lb) white marzipan

30.5 cm and 25.5 cm (12 inch and
10 inch) cardboard cake boxes

1.8 kg (4 lb) champagne coloured
sugar paste

4 metres (4 yards), 5 cm (2
inches) wide fancy shaded pink
ribbon

3 metres (3 yards), 1 cm (½ inch)
wide fancy champagne ribbon
fresh flowers to match the ribbons

6 acrylic skewers

....

1 Prepare the 30.5 × 25.5 cm
and 20.5 × 15 cm (12 × 10
inch and 8 × 6 inch) oval cake
tins (see page 11). Make the rich
fruit cake mixtures and place in
the tins. Bake according to the
cake chart on page 66. Place the
cakes in the centre of their
matching cake boards and brush
with apricot glaze. Cover smoothly
with marzipan (see page 73). Store
the cakes in their cardboard boxes
to dry or until required.

2 Cover each cake and cake
board smoothly with
champagne coloured sugar paste
(see page 82). Measure and fit the
fancy pink ribbon around the base
of each cake and secure with a
stainless steel pin.

3 Take the end of the ribbon
and fold into loops to create
a rouched effect. Secure with a
stainless steel pin and cut off the
excess ribbon. Repeat to make a
matching one and attach to one
side of each cake. Measure and fit
the champagne ribbon around the
edge of the cake board. Secure
with a stainless steel pin. Place the
cakes in their boxes until required.

4 To assemble the cakes,
lightly mark six even spaces
4 cm (1½ inches) in from the edge
of the large cake with the aid of a
template.

5 Insert the skewers and mark
the top so they stand 2.5 cm
(1 inch) above the surface of the
cake. Remove the skewers, cut off
the excess and replace them into
the cake. Place the small cake on
top and check that it sits evenly on
the skewers.

6 Just before the cake is needed, make an arrangement in the centre of the top cake in a small vase, or straight on to the surface of the cake. Decorate with the remaining ribbon folded into loops. (The design of this cake depends on the choice of ribbon and flowers. There are many beautiful ribbons available in many vibrant colours but do ensure that the flowers complement the ribbon in colour, shape and size.)

HINT
Using florist tape, bind the end of each fresh flower so the moisture is retained in the stem, preventing the flowers from fading.

RIBBONED WEDDING CAKE

T his elegant three-tier hexagonal wedding cake may be decorated with any shade of ribbon. Finish the tiers with fresh flower blooms to match the occasion.

25.5 cm, 20.5 cm, 15 cm (10 inch, 8 inch, 6 inch) round rich fruit cake mixture (see page 64)

30.5 cm, 25.5 cm, 20.5 cm (12 inch, 10 inch, 8 inch) hexagonal silver cake boards

135 ml (9 tbsp) apricot glaze (see page 70)

2 kg (4½ lb) white marzipan

2.7 kg (6 lb) white sugar paste

3 metres (3 yards), 1 cm (½ inch) wide satin peach ribbon

4 metres (4 yards), 5 mm (¼ inch) wide satin peach ribbon

2 metres (2 yards), 3 mm (⅛ inch) wide satin peach ribbon

3 metres (3 yards), 2 cm (¾ inch) wide organza peach ribbon for the cake boards

1 quantity royal icing (see page 108)

8 white plastic cake pillars

8 acrylic skewers

fresh or silk flowers to decorate the top

....

1 Prepare the 25.5 cm, 20.5 cm, 15 cm (10 inch, 8 inch, 6 inch) hexagonal cake tins (see page 11). Make the rich fruit cake mixtures and place in the tins. Bake according to the cake chart on page 66. Place each cake in the centre of its matching cake board and brush evenly with apricot glaze. Cover the cakes smoothly with marzipan (see page 73). Place them each into a cardboard cake box and leave overnight or until required.

2 Using about 1.6 kg (3½ lb) white sugar paste, smoothly cover the large cake and cake board (see page 82). Knead the sugar paste trimmings together and reserve. Leave the cake to dry for a few hours.

3 Measure and cut out a paper template 5 cm (2 inches) smaller than the top of the large cake. Divide each of the sections into 1 cm (½ inch) spaces and mark with a pencil. These spaces will mark where the ribbon is to be inserted on top of the cake. Measure and cut another template to fit one side section of the cake. Place a cup or rounded object over the top edge so it covers two-thirds of the template. Draw around the shape and cut out neatly to form a scalloped shape, see page 206-207.

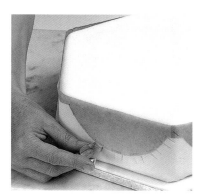

4 Leave a 1 cm (½ inch) space from the top edge of each side of the scallop shape. Divide the remaining shape into seven equal points. Mark a line 5 mm (¼ inch) each side of the points to mark the 1 cm (½ inch) ribbon

insertion lines. Carefully place the side template sections in position around the cake and secure with a pin where each section meets, at the top of the template. Using a set of ribbon slotters, take the large size or use a ribbon insertion knife, mark the lines and cut neatly following the template to the width of the ribbon.

5 Repeat on all the sides of the cake, marking in all the sections. Cut the 2 cm (¾ inch) ribbon into lengths just slightly longer than the insertion cuts. Insert the ribbon neatly into the cuts with the help of a pair of tweezers and a small knife (see page 86), leaving a space in between each piece of ribbon.

6 Using a 1 cm (½ inch) curved crimper, adjust them using an elastic band so they fit the spaces in between the inserted ribbon without squeezing them. Press the crimper on to the surface of the sugar paste in between the ribbon to imprint the pattern in the spaces. Repeat this design of

inserted ribbon and crimper pattern all around the sides of the cake.

7 Using the top template, mark the pattern carefully on to the surface of the sugar paste as above and cut the ribbon insertion lines. Insert the ribbon and crimp the pattern neatly.

8 Using the same width of ribbon, band the base of the cake and secure the ribbon with a stainless steel pin. Measure and cut the organza peach ribbon and fit around the cake board, securing with a pin.

9 Tie six neat bows from the 3 mm (⅛ inch) ribbon. Fit a greaseproof paper piping bag with a No. 1 plain writing nozzle and half-fill with royal icing. Fold down the top. Secure the ribbon bows at the top corner of each side of the cake with a bead of royal icing.

10 Pipe six tiny beads of icing in between the inserted ribbon to form a flower shape, repeat around the side and top of the cake. Pipe a bead and scroll design following the scallop shape on the side of the cake. Place the cake in the cardboard cake box and store in a warm dry place.

11 Repeat to sugar paste the middle sized cake and cake board. Make the top template 5 cm (2 inches) smaller than the top of the cake and mark each section into 1 cm (½ inch) spaces. Cut out the side template and mark with seven sections as before. Using the middle sized ribbon slotter or ribbon insertion knife, mark and cut the ribbon insertion lines to fit the 1 cm (½ inch) peach ribbon. Repeat the design as for the large cake, but using narrower ribbon.

12 Finally, sugar paste the remaining small cake and board. Cut the top template 5 cm (2 inches) smaller than the top of the cake. Cut out the side template and mark as before. Using the smallest ribbon slotter or ribbon insertion knife, mark and cut the ribbon insertion lines following the template. Insert the 5 mm (¼ inch) ribbon and band the base.

13 When the cakes are required, arrange the cake pillars on the base and middle cakes and insert the acrylic skewers. Cut the skewers to size (see page 17). Slip the pillars over the skewers and arrange the cakes on top. Decorate the top of the cakes with matching coloured fresh or silk flowers.

HINT

Celebration cakes are made for special occasions where a great many people are attending and will be tasting the cake. Therefore it is of the utmost importance that certain rules must be observed about hygiene, cleanliness and the use of non-edible cake materials.

Hands should be scrubbed clean, including fingernails.

After the cakes have been baked, make sure they are wrapped well and stored in a clean, dry place to prevent mould growth. Always use boiled, sieved apricot jam before applying the marzipan to prevent any fermentation between the cake and the marzipan. Then, once covered, store the cake on a new cardboard cake board as used ones will harbour bacteria, especially in the cut marks from the previous cake. From then on, keep the cake in a new cardboard cake box in a dry place.

Extra care must be taken when applying sugar paste or royal icing. Any small particles of dirt or cake crumbs can get into the icing and it will always come to the surface.

Wear a white overall or cotton shirt so that wool or fabric particles will not fall into or on to the icing.

Apply all food colourings with a clean cocktail stick and throw away afterwards to prevent any contamination or colour mixing.

If pins are used to secure ribbons to cakes and cake boards, use stainless steel pins with bead heads so they may be easily detected. Ensure the recipient knows that pins have been used.

ROYAL ICING

A royal iced cake is often preferred to a cake covered with sugar paste simply because of the crisp texture and taste of the icing. Although this method of icing is far more time-consuming and takes patience and practice, the end result is a sparkling finish with the classical lines of a traditional English celebration cake.

A different technique of icing requires specialised pieces of equipment to obtain good results. So before even starting royal icing, you must have a turntable, straight edge and side scraper to obtain a smooth flat surface. Other royal icing skills require a variety of piping nozzles to create beautiful piped designs, run-outs and piped flowers.

SPECIAL EQUIPMENT FOR ROYAL ICING

Turntable – this is the most essential piece of equipment for easy movement of cakes while icing and decorating. Although a turntable is expensive, it will last for ever. There are different qualities to choose from, so do make sure the turntable revolves smoothly and evenly as this is essential when royal icing the side of a round cake. Also check that the turntable is stable and does not tip easily.

Straight edge – this is a long metal ruler which is used to obtain a smooth flat finish on the surface of a royal iced cake. The straight edge is made of metal, is quite rigid and will not bend. They are obtainable in different lengths but a 30.5 cm (12 inch) straight edge is easier to handle on cakes up to 25.5 cm (10 inches).

Side scrapers – these are used to smooth butter or royal icing on the sides of round or square cakes. They are made from plastic or stainless steel, each obtaining a good finish, although the plastic variety is more flexible.

Patterned side scrapers – these are made from plastic or stainless steel and come in a variety of cut-out, zig-zag, scalloped and curved designs. They are ideal for finishing the sides of an iced cake in many different patterns and finishes.

Muslin – when it is damp it is ideal for covering a bowl of royal icing to prevent a skin forming on the surface. Being white it will not impart any colour or particles to the icing. Always keep the muslin clean and dry during storage.

Greaseproof paper piping bags – these may be purchased ready-made in a variety of sizes, or they can be easily made (see page 129). Always use a straight-sided metal piping nozzle in a greaseproof paper piping bag.

Fine piping nozzles – straight-sided metal nozzles are the best type to buy as they produce a clean, sharp icing result and they fit into greaseproof paper piping bags. They are available in many different designs and sizes, and it is advisable to buy the best quality. Choose a few simple shapes first.

Nozzle brush – essential for cleaning all piping nozzles without bending or mis-shaping the ends.

Cranked palette knife – this shaped palette knife is ideal for spreading icing on to the top and sides of cakes smoothly, and for peaked icing finishes.

Small straight palette knife – use for removing excess royal icing from corners and top edges.

Flower spinner nail – this looks like a mini turntable and is invaluable when piping sugar flowers, to form the petal at the correct angle while piping.

Run-out film – this fine transparent plastic film is for producing accurate run-outs which slide so easily off the film when they are dry.

Fine wax paper – may be used also for run-out pieces, or for use when piping sugar flowers.

Sheet perspex – small pieces of perspex are ideal for using over designs for run-outs, or for piping lace pieces. Cover the surface with run-out film and leave the items to dry in position.

Scribing needle – used for etching the surface of royal icing to transfer designs from templates.

Paint brushes – a selection of fine paint brushes for use when making run-outs and for tinting dry icing with food colouring dust.

Ruler, pencil, compass, rubber – necessary when working out side and top cake designs.

ROYAL ICING
QUANTITY GUIDE

It is always so difficult to estimate how much royal icing will be used to ice a cake. The quantity varies so much according to how the icing is applied, the thickness and the number of layers applied to the cake. The design also has to be taken into consideration, whether it is just a piping design, or a number of run-outs or piped sugar flowers.

The best guide to follow when icing cakes is to make up the royal icing in small batches using 1 kg (2¼ lb) icing sugar, which is double the quantity of either recipe provided. Each batch of icing made is fresh and free from any impurities which may occur when larger quantities of royal icing are made for one cake. This way you can assess how much more icing you require to finish a cake.

The chart below is just a guide for covering each cake with two or three thin layers of flat royal icing.

QUANTITY OF ROYAL ICING	CAKE SIZE
450 g (1 lb)	12.5 cm (5 inch) square
	15 cm (6 inch) round
700 g (1½ lb)	15 cm (6 inch) square
	18 cm (7 inch) round
900 g (2 lb)	18 cm (7 inch) square
	20.5 cm (8 inch) round
1.1 kg (2½ lb)	20.5 cm (8 inch) square
	23 cm (9 inch) round
1.4 kg (3 lb)	23 cm (9 inch) square
	25.5 cm (10 inch) round
1.6 kg (3½ lb)	25.5 cm (10 inch) square
	28 cm (11 inch) round
1.8 kg (4 lb)	28 cm (11 inch) square
	30.5 cm (12 inch) round
2 kg (4½ lb)	30.5 cm (12 inch) square
	33 cm (13 inch) round

HOW TO OBTAIN
GOOD ROYAL ICING

To produce a beautifully royal iced cake, it is essential to have a well prepared level cake which has been well marzipanned. The lines must be kept sharp, keeping the cake a good shape. The royal icing must be light and glossy in texture and of the correct consistency. If not, it will be impossible to produce a well iced cake. Then with patience, practice and the right tools, a good result will be achieved.

● Everything must be spotlessly clean when making the royal icing; all mixing bowls, sieves and utensils must be clean and dry, and as dust-free a working area as possible. Wear a white overall to cover clothes which may have bits on them, as little fibres can get into the icing and will come to the surface on a flat coat of icing, or even cause the piping nozzles to block.

● Fresh egg whites or egg albumen may be used to make the icing, both producing good results. A little lemon juice helps to strengthen the albumen in fresh egg whites, but care must be taken not to add too much as this will make the icing short, causing it to break during piping, as well as making it difficult to obtain a smooth flat finish. Do not add glycerine to egg albumen as it does not set as hard as fresh egg white icing.

● Adding the icing sugar must be a gradual process, giving plenty of mixing rather than beating during each addition of icing sugar, until the required consistency has been reached, and the icing is light and glossy in texture. A food mixer may be used, especially if large quantities of royal icing are required for a cake. Use the mixture at the lowest speed while gradually adding the icing sugar. Scrape down the bowl to ensure even mixing until the icing is light, glossy and of the correct consistency. Take care not to over-mix or aerate the icing too much. Always allow mixer-made royal icing to stand for 24 hours before using, then stir well to disperse the air bubbles.

● Royal icing made by adding too much icing sugar too quickly will form a dull, heavy icing and be grainy in appearance. It will be difficult to work with, producing bad results. As it sets it will be chalky and dull in appearance instead of sparkling. Also it will be difficult to pipe, soon becoming short and breaking off when the icing is piped.

● The icing must be covered at all times to exclude all the air and to prevent the surface from drying and causing lumps. Damp cling film to seal the surface is fine, or an airtight container as long as it is filled to the top with icing to exclude any air. Covering the icing with a damp piece of muslin is fine during short periods or while in use but if it is left overnight, the icing will absorb all the moisture from the muslin causing the consistency to be diluted. Always check the icing regularly during use to make sure the consistency and texture are correct.

● If the icing is too stiff, add egg white or reconstituted egg albumen to make it softer; also if the icing is too soft, gradually stir in more sifted icing sugar, mixing well until the required consistency has been reached.

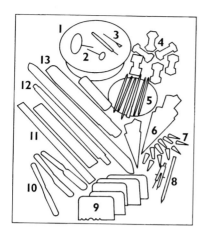

1. *Turntable* 2. *Flower spinner nail* 3. *Nozzle brush*
4. *Pillars* 5. *Paint brushes*
6. *Greaseproof paper piping bags* 7. *Fine piping nozzles*
8. *Compass and pencil* 9. *Side scrapers* 10. *Palette knives*
11. *Straight edge* 12. *Run-out film* 13. *Wax and greaseproof papers*

● Work with a small quantity of icing in a separate bowl taken from the main batch of royal icing, covering it with damp muslin during use. Keep the icing well scraped down in the bowl and if the icing does become dry around the top edges of the bowl, causing hard bits, it will not affect the whole batch of royal icing.

ROYAL ICING CONSISTENCIES
The skill of using royal icing and the results obtained are always determined by the consistency of the icing made. Each technique requires a different consistency, stiff icing which will hold its shape for piping designs, softer icing for spreading and coating cakes to give a flat sparkling finish, or even softer consistencies for filling in run-out pieces and collars.

Piping consistency – stir the icing well with a wooden spoon. When the spoon is drawn out of the icing, it should form a fine, sharp point, termed as 'sharp peak'. This consistency will flow easily for piping and will retain a definite shape produced by the piping nozzle used. When piping from a very fine writing nozzle, the icing will need to be made slightly softer, to prevent aching wrists.

Flat or peaked icing consistency – stir the icing well with a wooden spoon. When the spoon is drawn out of the icing, it should form a fine point which just curves over at the end, termed as 'soft peak'. This consistency spreads smoothly and evenly and creates a flat finish when a straight edge is pulled across the surface. It also pulls up into sharp or soft peaks with a palette knife, producing peaked icing.

Run-out icing consistency – a medium peak consistency icing is used to pipe the outlines which retain the shape of the run-out. Icing the consistency of thick cream is used to fill in the shapes. This icing consistency flows with the help of a fine brush to fill in the run-outs, but holds a rounded shape within the piped lines. Always remember to make the icing for run-outs with double strength pure egg albumen, or use egg whites without glycerine so that they dry hard and are easily handled without breakages.

ROYAL ICING RECIPES

Egg albumen – when buying dried egg white there are two qualities – the pure egg albumen which is equivalent to real egg whites and a fortified powder which is used in place of fresh egg whites for making royal icing. Simply blend the egg albumen with water to reconstitute it as directed on the packet, then just add the icing sugar. It is more convenient to use as there are no egg yolks to dispose of and it produces a good, light, glossy icing which is easy to handle for all types of cake icing and decorating. Used as flat icing for tiered cakes, it sets hard enough to support the weight of the cakes.

ROYAL ICING (EGG ALBUMEN)

This icing is suitable for flat or peaked icing, piping and all decorating. Use double-strength dried egg albumen for run-outs.

15 ml (1 tbsp) dried egg albumen, sieved
90 ml (6 tbsp) tepid water
450 g (1 lb) icing sugar, sifted

1 Place the egg albumen into a clean bowl. Using a clean whisk, gradually whisk in the water and blend well together until the liquid is smooth and free from lumps.

2 Add sufficient icing sugar and mix well using a wooden spoon to form the consistency of unwhipped cream. Continue mixing and adding small quantities of icing sugar every few minutes until the desired consistency has been reached, mixing well and gently beating after each addition of icing sugar. The icing should be smooth, glossy and light, almost like a cold meringue in texture, but not aerated. Do not add too much icing sugar too quickly as this will produce a dull, heavy icing which is difficult to work with.

3 Alternatively, for large quantities of royal icing use a food mixer on the lowest speed following the same instructions as before.

4 Allow the icing to settle for several hours before using it; cover the surface with a piece of damp cling film and seal well, excluding all air.

5 Stir the icing thoroughly before use as this will disperse all the air bubbles, then adjust the consistency if necessary by adding more sifted icing sugar or reconstituted egg albumen.
Makes 450 g (1 lb) royal icing

ROYAL ICING (FRESH EGG WHITES)

This icing is traditionally used to cover celebration cakes. According to the consistency made, it may be used for flat, smooth icing, peaked icing, or piping designs and decorations on cakes. Omit the glycerine when making run-outs.

2 (size 3) egg whites
1.25 ml (¼ tsp) lemon juice
450 g (1 lb) icing sugar, sifted
5 ml (1 tsp) glycerine

1 Place the egg whites and lemon juice into a clean bowl. Stir to break up the egg whites.

2 Add sufficient icing sugar and mix well to form the consistency of unwhipped cream. Continue mixing and adding small quantities of icing sugar every few minutes until the desired consistency has been reached, mixing well and gently beating after each addition of icing sugar. The icing should be smooth, glossy and light, almost like a cold meringue in texture, but not aerated. Do not add the icing sugar too quickly or it will produce a dull, heavy icing. Stir in the glycerine until well blended.

3 Alternatively, for large quantities of royal icing use a food mixer on the lowest speed, following the same instructions as before.

4 Allow the icing to settle before using it; cover the surface with a piece of damp cling film and seal well, excluding all the air.

5 Stir the icing thoroughly before use as this will disperse the air bubbles, then adjust the consistency if necessary by adding more sifted icing sugar.
Makes 450 g (1 lb) royal icing

TO ROYAL ICE A SQUARE CAKE

1 Make a quantity of royal icing to soft peak consistency, then cover the bowl with a piece of clean, damp muslin. Place the marzipanned cake on its cake board on the turntable. Have ready a small cranked and a small straight palette knife, a straight edge, a side scraper and an extra piece of damp muslin.

2 Using the small cranked palette knife, apply the royal icing to the top of the cake to cover the surface evenly. Spread the icing back and forth in lines across the top to help eliminate the air bubbles and to ensure the icing is spread evenly. Smooth the top, spreading lightly in the opposite direction of the lines.

3 Neaten the top edges of the cake by removing the excess icing using a small straight palette knife. Take the cake off the turntable and place on a rigid surface.

4 With the cake directly in front, hold the straight edge comfortably on the top edge and place it at the far side of the cake, just resting on the surface. Steadily pull the straight edge across the top of the cake in one continuous movement to smooth the icing. If the icing is not smooth enough, repeat the movement once again,

using a clean straight edge to smooth the surface or if necessary re-spread the top of the cake with a little more icing as before, neaten the edges and start again. Do not worry about this first layer being perfect; it needs to just evenly cover the cake thinly.

5 Trim away the excess icing from the top edges of the cake using a small clean palette knife to neaten the edges. Leave the icing to dry for about 2 hours or overnight in a warm dry place. Store the cake in a cardboard cake box to prevent any damage.

6 Replace the cake on the turntable and, using a small cranked palette knife, smoothly spread one side of the cake with royal icing to cover evenly. Spread the icing back and forth to eliminate the air bubbles and to ensure the icing is spread evenly. Remove the excess icing from the dry icing edge on the top of the cake and at both corners with a palette knife.

7 Place the cake on to a rigid surface and, with a side scraper at the far corner of the cake resting on the cake board, pull the side scraper across the surface of the cake in one movement to smooth the icing. If the surface is not satisfactory,

repeat the process once again with a clean side scraper to smooth the icing or re-spread the side of the cake with more icing as before; neaten the top edge and the corners and repeat again. This first layer of icing needs only to cover the surface evenly.

8 Trim away the excess icing from the top edge and the corners of the cake using a clean small palette knife to neaten. Ice the opposite side of the cake in the same way. Neaten the edges with a palette knife and ensure the cake board is clean. Leave to dry for at least 2 hours.

9 Repeat to royal ice the remaining two opposite sides of the cake as before so the cake has one complete layer of icing covering it. Trim away the excess icing from the top edge and corners of the cake. Leave the cake to dry overnight in the box.

10 Ice the cake with another two or three thin layers of royal icing, repeating the method as before, until the icing is smooth and flat. For the final coat of icing, to obtain a really smooth finish, use a slightly softer consistency of icing, which will skim the surface leaving it smooth and sparkling. Once the icing is dry, ice the cake board if required.

TO ROYAL ICE A ROUND CAKE

1 The method of royal icing a round cake is the same technique as icing a square cake, but easier and quicker as there are only two sides to royal ice – the top and one side.

2 Make a quantity of royal icing to soft peak consistency, then cover with a clean piece of damp muslin. Place the marzipanned cake on the cake board on a turntable, and collect together the utensils for icing the cake.

3 Using a small cranked palette knife and a small amount of icing, spread the icing back and forth across the top of the cake to eliminate any air bubbles. Spread the icing smoothly over the top of the cake to cover the surface evenly. Remove any excess icing from the top edge of the cake with a small straight palette knife to neaten the edge. Take the cake off the turntable and place it on a rigid surface.

4 With the cake directly in front, hold the straight edge comfortably on the top edge and place at the far side of the cake resting on the edge. Steadily pull the straight edge across the top of the cake in one continuous movement to smooth the icing. If the icing is not smooth enough, repeat the movement once again using a clean straight edge to smooth the surface, or re-spread the top of the cake with a little more icing as before, neaten the edge and start again. Do not worry about this first layer being perfect; it needs to just evenly cover the cake thinly.

5 Trim away the excess icing from the top edge of the cake with a clean small palette knife to neaten, then leave the icing to dry for about 2 hours or overnight in a warm, dry place. Store the cake in a cardboard cake box to prevent the surface from being damaged or marked.

6 Replace the cake on the turntable and using a small cranked palette knife, spread the side evenly with the royal icing, spreading the icing back and forth to eliminate the air bubbles and to ensure the icing is spread evenly. Leave the cake on the turntable and neaten the top edge with a small palette knife.

7 Hold the side scraper firmly on to the side of the cake, resting on the cake board. Hold the edge of the cake board and the edge of the turntable with one hand and the scraper around the back of the cake with the other hand. Slowly turn the cake and turntable continuously in one revolution in one direction and at the same time hold the side scraper firmly against the icing, pulling it towards you in the opposite direction to smooth the surface. Draw the side scraper gradually off the cake, which will leave a slight 'pull off' mark. If the surface is unsatisfactory, repeat the

process once again with a clean side scraper to smooth the icing or re-spread the side of the cake with more icing as before. Neaten the top edge and repeat the process again to obtain a smooth, even finish. Neaten the top edge and clean the cake board. Place the cake in the cardboard box and leave to dry.

8 Leave the cake to dry before repeating the procedure to cover the cake with another two or three thin layers of icing, using a slightly softer consistency icing for the final layer which will skim the surface, leaving it smooth and sparkling. When the icing is dry, ice the board if required.

9 Once you have achieved a perfectly smooth royal icing finish on a cake, it only needs a minimum amount of decoration to complete the cake.

HINT
After each coat of royal icing has dried, use a small palette knife to scrape away the pull-off mark on the side of the cake.

TO ROYAL ICE A SQUARE CAKE BOARD

1 Ensure the icing is completely dry, place the cake on the turntable and make sure the cake board is free from any pieces of dry icing. Spread a thin layer of icing evenly on to one side of the cake board. Neaten the edge of the board with a palette knife.

2 Place the cake on a rigid surface and draw the side scraper across the icing to smooth the surface. Repeat if the finish is not satisfactory. Neaten the edge of the board and ice the opposite side. Leave to dry for 2 hours or overnight. Repeat to royal ice the remaining opposite sides of the cake board. Ensure all the sides of the cake board are clean. Leave the cake board to dry for at least 2 hours. Store the cake in the cardboard cake box in a warm, dry place.

3 Repeat with a second layer of royal icing to give a smooth finish to the cake board.

TO ROYAL ICE A ROUND CAKE BOARD

1 When the icing is completely dry, place the cake on to the turntable and make sure the cake board is free from pieces of dry icing. Spread a thin layer of royal icing evenly on to the cake board, neaten the edge of the board with a palette knife.

2 Hold the outside of the cake board and turntable with one hand, place the side scraper on to the board with the other hand. Turn the cake and turntable in one revolution, pulling the side scraper towards you to smooth the icing on the board. Repeat if the finish is not satisfactory. Neaten the edge of

the cake board, and ensure the side of the cake board is clean. Leave the cake board to dry for at least 2 hours. Store in a cardboard cake box in a warm, dry place.

3 Repeat with a second layer of royal icing to give a smooth finish to the cake board.

PEAKED ROYAL ICING

Royal icing is very versatile and can be smoothed on to a cake to make it a perfectly flat finish for decorating, or peaked to give a textured finish, which is always related to Christmas as it gives a snow scene effect.

The royal icing may be applied and spread evenly over the cake and then peaked, but this gives a rather rough iced appearance. To make beautifully even peaks, the icing must be of *soft peak* consistency and well mixed. Because the icing begins to set quite quickly, for the best results peak the side first, then the top.

1 Spread the top of the marzipanned cake evenly with royal icing using a small palette knife to obtain an even surface. Smooth the top of the cake by using a straight edge to level the icing and covering the surface evenly but not perfectly flat. Spread the sides of the cake with an even coat of royal icing and use a side scraper to smooth the icing on the side of the cake so that it is fairly even and covers completely. Ensure the cake board is perfectly clean.

2 Give the icing a quick stir and make sure the consistency is soft, then cover with a piece of damp muslin. Using a small, clean palette knife, dip one side of the blade into the icing. Start at the base and work to the top edge of the cake in a line, pressing the palette knife with the icing on to the side of the iced cake and pulling sharply away to form a peak. Repeat this to form about two or three peaks, then re-dip the palette knife into the icing and repeat this process to make more peaks until you reach the top edge of the cake. Start the second line of peaks about 1 cm (½ inch) apart from the first line, starting just above the first peak. Continue until the side is completely peaked, then continue to peak the top of the cake, leaving a smooth area for decoration if desired.

3 If the top of the cake is to be flat iced allowing for decorations, and the sides are to be peaked, follow the instructions for flat icing the top of a cake. When the top is completely dry, spread the sides with soft peaked royal icing and smooth as evenly as possible, then peak as above.

CHRISTMAS WREATH CAKE

A *traditionally iced Christmas cake with peaked*
sides and a smooth top. The holly garland is made
from sugar paste or marzipan cut-out leaves.

20.5 cm (8 inch) square rich or
　light fruit cake mixture (see page
　64 or 67)
25.5 cm (10 inch) square silver
　cake board
45 ml (3 tbsp) apricot glaze (see
　page 70)
1 kg (2¼ lb) white marzipan
1.1 kg (2½ lb) quantity royal icing
　(see page 108)
225 g (8 oz) white sugar paste or
　marzipan
holly green and red food
　colourings
1 metre (1 yard), 1 cm (½ inch)
　wide fancy red ribbon
0.25 metre (¼ yard), 5 mm
　(¼ inch) wide red ribbon
1 metre (1 yard), 5 mm (¼ inch)
　wide green ribbon

1　Prepare a 20.5 cm (8 inch)
　square cake tin (see page 11).
Make the rich or light fruit cake
mixture and place in the tin. Bake
according to the cake chart on
page 66 or 68. Place the cake in
the centre of the cake board and
brush with apricot glaze. Cover
smoothly with marzipan (see page
72).

2　When the marzipan is dry,
　cover the top of the cake
with two or three thin coats of
smooth royal icing (see page 109)
and leave to dry. Cover the sides of
the cake with royal icing and form
it into sharp peaks (see page 111).
Ensure the cake board is clean.

3　Using a greaseproof paper
　piping bag fitted with a
medium-sized star nozzle, pipe a
row of stars around the top edge of
the cake. Leave to dry completely
before adding holly and ivy garland
decoration.

4　Colour a quarter of the sugar
　paste or marzipan a light
green and the other quarter a rich
green with green food colouring.
Thinly roll out the sugar paste or
marzipan and, using large holly
and ivy leaf cutters, cut out 15
holly leaves from the rich green
and 11 ivy leaves from the light
green sugar paste or marzipan.
Mark the veins using real holly and

ivy leaves, or use a veining tool.
Bend the leaves and dry over a
piece of wooden dowel. Colour a
piece of sugar paste or marzipan
red and shape the holly berries.
You will need thirty-three berries
to complete the decoration.

5　Roll out the remaining white
　sugar paste or marzipan into
two 38 cm (15 inch) pencil thin
lengths. Twist the pieces together
and join the ends to make a ring.
Place on the centre of the cake.
Pipe 'Noel' in white royal icing
using a No. 1 plain writing nozzle,
then overpipe in red using the
same nozzle. Arrange alternately
seven holly and ivy leaves together
in a circle. Place two holly leaves
at each corner. Secure to the ring
and the corners of the cake with a
little royal icing. Place the
remaining ivy leaves on the board.
Add groups of berries.

6　Tie a bow using the narrow
　red ribbon and place at the
front of the garland, securing with
icing. Measure and fit the
remaining red and narrow green
ribbon around the cake board.

DAISY CAKE

*T*he cream royal icing gives a subtle background to
this daisy-strewn cake which may be made for any
special occasion.

*25.5 cm (10 inch) round rich fruit
cake mixture (see page 64)*

*30.5 cm (12 inch) round silver
cake board*

*60 ml (4 tbsp) apricot glaze (see
page 70)*

1 kg (2¼ lb) white marzipan

*1.4 kg (3 lb) quantity royal icing
(see page 108)*

Cornish cream food colouring

*225 g (8 oz) flower paste (see
page 154)*

*yellow, orange and apple green
food colouring dusts*

*1 metre (1 yard), 2 cm (¾ inch)
wide yellow ribbon*

*1 metre (1 yard), 1 cm (½ inch)
wide green ribbon*

1 Prepare a 25.5 cm (10 inch)
round cake tin (see page 11).
Make the rich fruit cake mixture
and place in the tin. Bake
according to the cake chart on
page 66. Place the cake in the
centre of the cake board and brush
with apricot glaze. Cover smoothly
with marzipan (see page 72). Store
the cake in a cardboard cake box
for at least 24 hours before
covering with royal icing.

2 When the marzipan is dry,
tint the royal icing cream
with a few drops of Cornish cream
food colouring. Cover the top and
side of the cake with three thin
coats of smooth cream royal icing
(see page 110). Smoothly coat the
cake board with royal icing and
leave in the cake box to dry.

3 Roll out a small piece of
flower paste at a time and,
using a set of daisy cutters, cut out
about eight large, six medium and
eight small daisy shapes. Leave
some of them on a flat surface to
dry, and place the remainder on a
piece of foam sponge or a flower
pad. Using a modelling tool, lightly
press the centre and the petals to
shape them.

4 Using the remaining flower
paste, roll out thinly and cut
out 12 leaf shapes using a daisy leaf
cutter. Mark the veins with a real
leaf or a veining tool, bend slightly
and leave to dry. Place a little of
each of the food colouring dusts on

to a palette. Brush the daisy
centres orange and the petals
yellow. Brush all the leaves with
shaded green colouring.

5 Fit a greaseproof paper
piping bag with a No. 3 plain
writing nozzle and fill with a little
royal icing. Pipe a plain shell
border around the top and base of
the cake. Arrange the daisies over
the top of the cake and secure
each with a bead of icing. Secure
the remaining daisies over the edge
and down the side of the cake on
to the cake board.

6 Place the daisy leaves
intermittently between the
daisies, secured with beads of royal
icing. Measure and fit the ribbons
around the cake board and secure
with a stainless steel pin. Store the
cake in the cake box until
required. A message or greeting
may be piped on to a sugar plaque
or directly on to the cake to suit
the occasion.

18TH BIRTHDAY CAKE

A bright triangular-shaped cake, appealing to an eighteen-year-old. Choose a combination of bright glittering colours to decorate this cake with fine strips of sugar paste and cut-out numbers and shapes.

25.5 cm (10 inch) round rich or
  light fruit cake mixture (see page
  64 or 67)
30.5 cm (12 inch) triangular
  silver cake board
90 ml (6 tbsp) apricot glaze (see
  page 70)
1 kg (2¼ lb) white marzipan
1.1 kg (2½ lb) quantity royal icing
  (see page 108)
350 g (12 oz) white sugar paste
gentian, black and poinsettia
  paste food colourings
gentian, poinsettia and silver
  glitter flakes
1 metre (1 yard), 1 cm (½ inch)
  wide black ribbon

1 Prepare a 25.5 cm (10 inch) triangular-shaped cake tin (see page 11). Make the rich or light fruit cake mixture and place in the tin. Bake according to the cake chart on pages 66 or 68. Place the cake in the centre of the cake board and brush with apricot glaze. Cover smoothly with marzipan (see page 72). When the marzipan is dry, cover the top and sides of the triangle with three thin coats of smooth royal icing (see page 109). Place the cake in a cardboard cake box until dry.

2 Cut the sugar paste into three equal pieces. Colour one piece gentian, one piece black and the remaining piece poinsettia. Roll out a piece of poinsettia sugar paste thinly and cut into three 15 cm × 5 mm (6 × ¼ inch) strips.

Pipe a line of royal icing on the back of these strips. Arrange one strip along the top edge of the cake from the right hand top corner to the centre edge of the cake.

3 Place the second strip directly underneath the top strip on to the centre side of the cake. Place the third strip along the base line of the cake from the centre to the left hand corner making a zig-zag line. Repeat making a black line, then a gentian line following the same pattern.

4 Continue this pattern on the remaining two sides but

change the sequence of colours. Start the next side with a black strip, then gentian and poinsettia and on the last side with gentian, then poinsettia, then black.

5 Cut out some extra 1 cm (½ inch) strips of each coloured sugar paste and dust the surface of each using the matching glitter flakes to coat evenly. Cut out 12 × 1 cm (½ inch) triangles from each. Using small numeral cutters, cut out an '18' from each colour. Repeat to cut out about twenty 5 mm (¼ inch) triangles from the poinsettia and gentian sugar paste. Roll out some black sugar paste, dust with silver glitter flakes and, using large 1 and 8 numeral cutters, cut out an '18' and leave to dry flat on a piece of foam sponge. Arrange the small gentian and poinsettia triangles over the large numbers and secure with royal icing.

6 Attach a mixture of the larger coloured triangles on to the right hand side on each side of the cake, with a small '18' on the left hand side. Pipe beads of royal icing on to the back of the larger numbers and arrange the '18' on the centre on the top of the cake. Sprinkle the cake board with the remaining glitter flakes. Band the cake board with black ribbon and secure with a stainless steel pin. Store the cake in a cardboard box until required.

HINT
The design on this cake is obtained by using concentrated paste food colouring and glitter dusts – edible flakes of coloured sugar.

GOLDEN STAR CAKE

Gold Christmas stars adorn this special Christmas cake: gold dust is brushed on to the stars and rubbed in for an even finish. Remove them before cutting the cake and use as attractive Christmas decorations.

20.5 cm (8 inch) round rich or light fruit cake mixture (see pages 64 or 67)

25.5 cm (10 inch) round gold cake board

60 ml (4 tbsp) apricot glaze (see page 70)

1 kg (2¼ lb) white marzipan

900 g (2 lb) quantity royal icing (see page 108)

125 g (4 oz) flower paste (see page 154)

gold food colouring dust

gold dragees

1 metre (1 yard), 2.5 cm (1 inch) wide gold ribbon

1 metre (1 yard), 2 cm (¾ inch) wide fancy gold ribbon

....

1 Prepare a 20.5 cm (8 inch) round cake tin (see page 11). Make the rich or light fruit cake mixture and place in the tin. Bake according to the cake chart on pages 66 or 68. Place the cake in the centre of the cake board and brush with apricot glaze. Cover smoothly with marzipan (see page 72). When the marzipan is dry, cover the top and side of the cake with three thin coats of smooth royal icing (see page 110). Place the cake in a cardboard cake box until dry. Reserve the royal icing for piping.

2 Cut out a template for the star shape (see page 211). Roll out the flower paste on an acrylic board to 3 mm (⅛ inch) thick. Using the template, cut out the star shape and leave to dry.

3 Knead the flower paste trimmings together and roll out thinly. Using a 6.5 cm (2½ inch) star shaped biscuit cutter, cut out three star shapes. Cut out the centres of each using a 4 cm (1½ inch) matching shaped cutter and cut out a further two smaller stars, making five small stars and three star frames. Brush all the star shapes with gold dust.

4 Fit a greaseproof paper piping bag with a No. 2 plain writing nozzle and half-fill with some of the reserved royal icing. Carefully slide the large star on to the top of the cake and position it centrally. Pipe a continuous thread of icing from point to point to outline the star shape. Repeat to pipe around the inside of the star shape. Over-pipe each with a second line of icing.

5 Position a gold dragee at each point of the star and around the top and base of the cake. Secure the five small gold stars on top of the cake with the three star frames in the centre, each with a little royal icing.

6 Using a greaseproof paper piping bag fitted with a medium-sized star nozzle, pipe a row of stars around the top edge in between the star points, and at the base of the cake. Decorate the stars with gold dragees. Measure and fit the ribbons around the cake and cake board, securing with beads of icing. Arrange the remaining gold ribbon into loops and attach the ribbon on the side of the cake with a stainless steel pin. Leave the cake to dry in a cardboard cake box in a warm dry place.

HINT
The golden stars on this cake may be made ahead of time and stored flat in a warm dry place.

REBECCA'S
CHRISTENING CAKE

*T*his delicate cake could be made with pink or blue
accessories and the name changed to suit. The
plain royal icing gives this cake a very classical look.

---

*25.5 cm (10 inch) round rich fruit
cake mixture (see page 64)*

*30.5 cm (12 inch) oval silver cake
board*

*60 ml (4 tbsp) apricot glaze (see
page 70)*

1 kg (2¼ lb) white marzipan

*1.4 kg (3 lb) quantity royal icing
(see page 108)*

*225 g (8 oz) white sugar paste
rose pink food colouring*

pink food colouring pen (optional)

*1.5 metres (1½ yards), 2.5 cm
(1 inch) wide fancy pink ribbon*

*1 metre (1 yard), 1 cm (½ inch)
wide pale pink ribbon*

....

1 Prepare a 25.5 cm (10 inch)
oval cake tin (see page 11).
Make the rich fruit cake mixture
and place in the tin. Bake
according to the cake chart on
page 66. Place the cake in the
centre of the cake board and brush
with apricot glaze. Cover smoothly
with marzipan (see page 72). Store
the cake in a cardboard cake box
in a warm dry place until the
marzipan has set for at least 24
hours before royal icing. When the
marzipan is dry, cover the top and
sides of the cake with three thin
coats of smooth royal icing (see
page 110). Smoothly cover the cake
board with royal icing and leave in
the cake box to dry.

2 Tint the sugar paste pale
pink with a drop of food
colouring. Using the pink sugar
paste, make the shawl. Roll out a
piece of sugar paste so thinly that
you can almost see through it.
Trim to a 10 cm (4 inch) square,
using a straight frill cutter. Using a
medium blossom plunger cutter,
cut out a pattern all around the
edges of the shawl. Eject the
blossoms on to a piece of foam to
shape and reserve for the edge of
the cake. Using the end of a No. 1
plain writing nozzle, make tiny cut-
out holes all over the shawl.
Carefully fold the shawl in half and
arrange in soft folds on the top of
the cake.

3 Cut out a small oblong of
thin sugar paste 6.5 × 5 cm
(2½ × 2 inches) using the straight
frill cutter. Pattern the edge with
the small blossom plunger cutter;
reserve the blossoms for the shoes.
Cut out a round for the neck.
Drape the bib over a piece of dowel
and leave to dry.

4 To make the shoes, roll out
the sugar paste thinly and
cut out two 'soles', two toe pieces
with straps and two shoe 'backs'
(see page 209). Using a paint brush
and a little water, brush the edge
of the shoe 'soles' and position the
'backs'. Press the edges together
and mark with a modelling tool.
Place the toe pieces in position,
press the edges together and mark
with the modelling tool. Press
inside the toe piece of each shoe to
round the shape using a bone tool.
Arrange the strap and secure a
little button-shaped piece of sugar
paste with a little water. Leave to
dry.

5 Shape a round marble-sized
piece of sugar paste for the
rattle and mould a 10 cm (4 inch)
thin piece of sugar paste and shape
into a handle. Secure the ball to
the handle with a little water and
support the handle while the rattle
is drying. Roll out the remaining
pink sugar paste and using a
medium-sized blossom plunger

cutter, cut out and eject the blossoms on to a piece of foam sponge to shape each one. Using a greaseproof paper piping bag fitted with a No. 1 plain piping nozzle, half-fill with royal icing. Pipe beads of icing around the top of the cake to secure the cut-out blossoms. Repeat to secure the blossoms at the base of the cake and the small blossoms on to the baby's shoes.

6 Write the baby's name on to the bib, using a pink food colouring pen or pipe with royal icing and a No. 1 nozzle. Measure

and fit the fancy ribbon around the side of the cake and secure with a bead of icing. Add a bow. Secure the plain ribbon around the cake board with a stainless steel pin. Using a scribing needle or pin, pattern the toes of the shoes, the rattle and the shawl. Position all the accessories neatly on the cake and store in a cake box.

HINT
Make all the accessories in advance and store in a warm dry place until required.

SPECIAL OCCASION CAKE

A beautiful smooth royal iced cake with the minimum amount of decoration could be used for almost any occasion. Choose bright ribbons and flowers to give an instant decoration.

20.5 cm (8 inch) round rich or light fruit cake mixture (see page 64 or 67)

25.5 cm (10 inch) round silver cake board

45 ml (3 tbsp) apricot glaze (see page 70)

700 g (1½ lb) white marzipan

900 g (2 lb) quantity royal icing (see page 108)

purple and yellow food colourings

2 metres (2 yards), 1 cm (½ inch) wide purple ribbon

1 metre (1 yard), 1 cm (½ inch) wide yellow ribbon

fresh flowers

0.5 metre (½ yard), 3 mm (⅛ inch) wide purple ribbon

0.5 metre (½ yard), 3 mm (⅛ inch) wide yellow ribbon

....

1 Prepare a 20.5 cm (8 inch) round cake tin (see page 11). Make the rich or light fruit cake mixture and place in the tin. Bake according to the cake chart on page 66 or 68. Place the cake in the centre of the cake board and brush with apricot glaze. Cover smoothly with marzipan (see page 72). Store the cake in a cardboard cake box in a warm dry place for at least 24 hours before royal icing.

2 When the marzipan is dry, cover the top and side of the cake with three thin coats of smooth royal icing (see page 110). Cover the cake board with royal icing and leave in the cake box to dry. Reserve remaining icing.

3 Using a large greaseproof paper piping bag fitted with a medium sized star nozzle, half-fill with royal icing. Fold down the top. Pipe a shell edging around the top and base of the cake, following the instructions on page 128.

4 Colour 15 ml (1 tbsp) of icing purple and 15 ml (1 tbsp) yellow, using the purple and yellow food colourings. Fit two greaseproof paper piping bags each with a No. 1 plain writing nozzle and place the coloured icing in each bag. Pipe alternate beads of purple and yellow icing in between the shell piping around the top and base of the cake.

5 Measure and fit the wider purple and yellow ribbons around the side of the cake and secure each with a bead of icing. Measure and fit the remaining wide purple ribbon around the cake board.

6 Just before serving, arrange the fresh flowers together and tie them neatly with fine purple and yellow ribbons, curling the ends of the ribbons. Place the flowers on the cake.

21ST BIRTHDAY CAKE

E ye-catching and different, this two-tiered 21st birthday cake is decorated with strips of silver sugar paste. Cover with cut-out 21s and stars or, for a silver wedding anniversary, cut out bells, hearts and 25s.

23 cm (9 inch) square rich fruit cake mixture (see page 64)

25.5 cm (10 inch) square silver cake board

15 cm (6 inch) thin round silver cake board

75 ml (5 tbsp) apricot glaze (see page 70)

1 kg (2¼ lb) white marzipan

1.6 kg (3½ lb) quantity royal icing (see page 108)

450 g (1 lb) white sugar paste

silver food colouring dust

1 metre (1 yard), 1 cm (½ inch) wide white satin ribbon

1 metre (1 yard), 5 mm (¼ inch) wide silver ribbon

2 metres (2 yards), 1 cm (½ inch) wide silver ribbon

....

1 Prepare a 20.5 cm (8 inch) square and a 12.5 cm (5 inch) round cake tin (see page 11). Make the rich fruit cake mixture and place in the tins, so the mixture is the same height in both of the tins. Bake separately according to the cake chart on page 66. Place the cakes in the centre of the cake boards and brush with apricot glaze. Cover smoothly with marzipan (see page 72). When the marzipan is dry, cover the top and sides of the cakes with three thin coats of royal icing (see page 109). Leave in cardboard cake boxes to dry. Reserve the royal icing.

2 Roll out about one-third of the sugar paste to 3 mm (⅛ inch) thick and brush the surface with silver dust. Rub evenly on the surface of the sugar paste to colour evenly. Using large and small 2 and 1 numeral cutters, cut out one large and three small sets of '21'. Cut out 14 star shapes using a small 4 cm (1½ inch) star cutter.

3 Roll out two-thirds of the remaining sugar paste and trim to an oblong about 45.5 × 20.5 cm (18 × 8 inches). Brush the surface with silver dust to cover evenly. Fit a greaseproof paper piping bag with a No. 3 plain writing nozzle. Half-fill with royal icing. Cut the sugar paste into 1 cm (½ inch) strips. Place the longest strips across the centre of the square cake from corner to corner. Pipe a line of icing underneath the end of the strips of sugar paste and press gently on to the cake. Trim off the ends at the base. Repeat to add the strips, positioning them evenly spaced apart across the cake before securing.

4 Knead the trimmings together with the remaining sugar paste and roll out to an oblong 28 × 12.5 cm (11 × 5 inches). Colour silver and cut into 1 cm (½ inch) strips and cover the round cake to match the square cake.

5 Measure and fit the white satin and thin silver ribbons around the edge of the square cake board and secure with a pin. Make four sets of ribbon loops using the wide silver ribbon and attach to each corner of the cake. Leave the cake to dry stored in a cardboard cake box.

the side and on top of the square cake and the small '21's on the side of the round cake; secure each with a bead of royal icing. Using a piece of sugar paste, mould into two pieces to support the large numbers. Arrange on top of the cake and secure with royal icing.

6 Place the small round cake in the centre of the square cake. Arrange the 14 stars around

HINT

This spectacular looking cake may be made in any colour you care to choose. Gold and silver look great, or introduce a vibrant colour such as red, blue, emerald green or black. Highlight the strips with glitter flakes which will make the whole cake sparkle.

Silver food colouring is not edible but when this cake is cut the sugar paste strips separate from the cake.

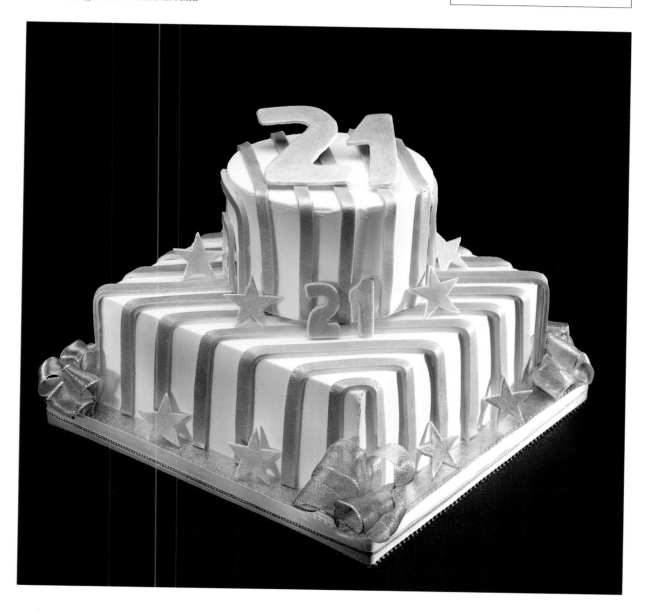

PIPING

Piping is one of the most traditional skills, used to decorate all types of cakes. It is an art in itself and can only be mastered by continual practice and patience. It may look extremely difficult, especially if the designs are piped from very fine piping nozzles, but it is only like using a pen or a paint brush.

The only tools necessary to learn this skill are a piping bag and good quality metal piping nozzles. Equipped with these simple tools, dairy cream, butter cream, royal icing and meringue mixture may be transformed into shells, whirls, stars, scrolls, lines and beads.

Although piping appears to be complicated, the secret is to get used to using and controlling the medium you are piping. Take every opportunity to practice; instead of spreading or spooning mixtures, pipe them. Make up a quantity of royal icing just for practising and pipe around cake tins, plates, boards, anything, to get the practice and you will be amazed how quickly you will become proficient in this skill.

Try simple piping to start with using just one or two piping nozzles then as your skills improve, try more advanced designs using a larger selection of nozzles, contrasting colours and piping techniques.

SPECIALISED PIPING EQUIPMENT

Commercially made piping bags – these are available ready-made in washable fabrics from most cake icing specialists or kitchen shops. They are especially good to use if you are a beginner as they are easy to handle. Sizes vary from small to large and are ideal for piping dairy cream, butter cream and meringue mixtures. Always fit them with a good quality straight-sided metal piping nozzle.

Greaseproof paper piping bags – the great advantage of the greaseproof paper piping bag is that they can be purchased ready-made or made in advance in various sizes and may be used with or without a piping nozzle. If they are used without a nozzle, simply fill the bag with icing, fold down the top and snip off the point to pipe lines or beads, or a 'V' shape to pipe leaves. After use they may be thrown away or when the icing runs out, simply transfer the piping nozzle to a new greaseproof paper piping bag

and refill it with icing. Choose a good quality greaseproof paper or non-stick baking parchment for making the paper piping bags and follow the instructions on page 129.

Piping nozzles – these are available in such a wide variety of shapes and sizes that it is quite daunting to know which ones to choose. As a beginner, it is advisable to start with a small selection of good quality straight-sided metal piping nozzles as they give a clean, sharp icing result. Choose two plain writing nozzles, size 1 and 2, small, medium and large star nozzles and a basket weave nozzle. When you have mastered the use of these nozzles, build up your collection as you try new piping designs. Keep them clean and store them carefully in a box or rigid container so they do not get damaged, then they will never need replacing and are worth the extra expense. Always clean piping nozzles with a nozzle cleaning brush so that the ends do not become bent or damaged.

PIPING TECHNIQUES

Before using any piping equipment, it is essential to have the dairy cream, butter cream or royal icing at the correct consistency. When a wooden spoon is drawn out of royal icing or butter cream, it should form a fine but sharp point. If the icing is too stiff it will be very difficult to pipe; also if too soft the icing will be difficult to control and the piped shapes lose their definition. Always remember the larger the nozzle, the stiffer the icing and for a very fine nozzle, the consistency needs to be slightly softer.

TO PIPE DAIRY CREAM AND BUTTER CREAM

When piping dairy cream, the consistency is much softer; whip the cream until it softly peaks. Once the cream is in the piping bag it may feel too soft but with the warmth of the hands it causes the cream to thicken and the piping result is soft and

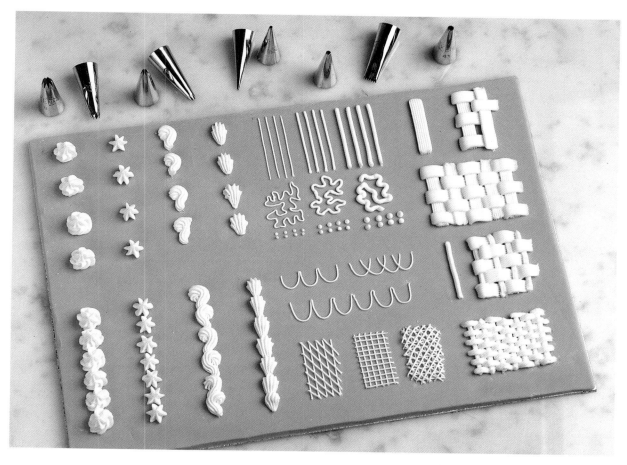

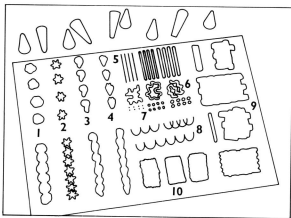

1. *Swirls*   2. *Stars*   3. *Scrolls*   4. *Shells*
5. *Lines*   6. *Filigree or cornelli work*   7. *Beads or*
dots   8. *Dropped loop thread work*   9. *Basket*
weave   10. *Trellis*

smooth. Over-whipping causes the cream to separate and curdle and produces unsightly piping. Only use some of the cream at a time when piping, then if the cream does curdle only some of it is affected.

It is better to use a nylon piping bag fitted with a larger nozzle to pipe whipped cream and butter cream into swirls, shells or stars.

Half-fill the bag with whipped cream or butter cream and twist the top of the bag so the cream or icing comes to the end of the nozzle. Hold the top of the bag with one hand and the nozzle with the other and gently press out the cream into the desired shape, twisting the bag as it empties, keeping a constant flow of cream or icing.

TO PIPE ROYAL ICING

When piping royal icing only quarter- or half-fill the bag with icing, depending on the nozzle size. Do not be tempted to over-fill the bag otherwise as you squeeze the piping bag, it will force the icing to come out of the top and the harder it is to squeeze the icing out of the nozzle. This will only result in aching wrists and hands and poor piping. A good guide to remember is the smaller the end of the piping nozzle, the smaller the piping bag and the less icing you require.

Hold the piping bag comfortably in your hand with the nozzle through the first two fingers and thumb, rather like holding a pencil, and apply the pressure at the top of the bag. The wrists and arms should be relaxed, just ready to guide the nozzle.

SIMPLE PIPING

Piping is the obvious choice when decorating a cake, but it is easy to be discouraged by complicated piping designs. Choose just a simple star piping nozzle and fit it into a greaseproof paper piping bag to pipe swirls, scrolls and shells. Ensure the cake is at the right height for piping – at eye level for piping the sides and at waist level for piping the top of the cake.

To pipe a swirl – half-fill the greaseproof paper piping bag fitted with a star nozzle, fold down the top and squeeze the icing to the end of the nozzle. Place the icing nozzle upright just on to the surface of the cake, press out the icing and pipe a swirl of icing in a circular movement. Stop pressing the bag and pull up sharply to break the icing. Repeat to pipe swirls around the top edge and base of the cake if desired.

To pipe a star – pipe just a star shape also from the same nozzle, holding the bag straight above the cake, with the nozzle just touching the surface. Press the icing out, lift slightly forming a star shape on the top edge of the cake. Stop pressing then pull up sharply to break off the icing; repeat to make a neat border.

To pipe scrolls – hold the piping bag at an angle so that the nozzle is almost on its side in front of you, just touching the surface of the cake. Press out the icing on to the top edge of the cake to secure the beginning of the scroll. Pipe towards the centre of the cake in a circular movement and return the nozzle to the edge of the cake. Stop pressing the bag and break off the icing. Repeat again to pipe a second scroll in the opposite direction but piping the icing away from the centre of the cake in a circular movement, then return the nozzle just to the edge. These are called reverse scrolls, piping scrolls inwards and outwards. To pipe a plain scroll design, pipe the scrolls in one direction only.

To pipe shells – hold the piping bag at an angle to the cake so that the piping nozzle is almost on its side in front of you, just touching the surface of the cake. Press out some icing and secure the shell to the surface of the cake, pressing gently. Move the nozzle forward, then move it slowly up, over and down almost like a rocking movement. Stop pressing and break off the icing by pulling the nozzle towards you. Repeat piping the icing on to the end of the first shell to make a shell edging.

To pipe lines – fit a small piping bag with a plain writing nozzle, the smaller the hole the finer the lines, and only quarter- to half-fill the piping bag with icing. Holding the piping bag almost upright, pipe a thread of icing, securing the end to the surface of the cake. Continue to pipe lifting the thread of icing just above the surface of the cake, allowing the thread of icing to fall in a straight or curved line or following the marked design on the cake. Stop pressing just before the end of the line, to prevent the icing running on, and break off the thread neatly.

To pipe a trellis design – fit a small piping bag with a No. 0 or No. 1 plain writing nozzle and half-fill with icing. Pipe parallel lines about 5 mm (¼ inch) apart, keeping the lines very even. Then over-pipe lines of icing in the opposite direction, keeping the spacing the same. A third line of icing piping may be piped diagonally across the trellis to give a better finish.

To pipe dropped loop thread work – using a plain writing nozzle, pipe a thread of icing, securing the end to the side of the cake. Continue to pipe the icing just away from the side of the cake so the thread forms a loop. Stop pressing the icing when the loop is almost long enough, and press the thread of icing gently on to the side of the cake to secure the loop and break off the icing. Repeat piping more loops until the loops have been piped all around the side of the cake. It is possible to repeat the procedure and to over-pipe each loop in white icing or a different colour, making them double in width and slightly stronger. There are endless designs with this dropped thread work which look very attractive on the side of a cake.

To pipe filigree or cornelli work – fit a small piping bag with a plain writing nozzle and half-fill with icing. Hold the piping bag in your hand with the nozzle like a pen between the thumb and forefinger. Pipe a thread of icing on to the surface of the cake and start piping into rounded 'w' and 'm' shapes. Keep the flow of the icing constant and work in all directions without breaking the thread for as long as possible. Re-join the icing where the break finished to keep the design constant.

To pipe beads or dots – to pipe beads of icing is quite simple but the icing has to be of a softer consistency so there is not a sharp point on the end of the bead of icing which has been piped. Fit a grease-proof paper piping bag with a No. 3 plain nozzle. Half-fill with icing and fold down the top. Hold the nozzle directly above the surface of the cake in an upright position and press the icing out on to the surface of the cake to form a rounded bulb of icing. Pull upwards sharply to break off the icing. Repeat to make a border of nicely rounded beads of icing. The size of the beads of icing are determined by the size of the nozzle and the pressure applied when piping them.

To pipe basket weave – fit a greaseproof paper piping bag with a ribbon nozzle. Pipe a vertical line from the top of the cake to the bottom. Start at the top of the cake and pipe 2 cm (¾ inch) lines of icing across the vertical line at 1 cm (½ inch) intervals. Pipe another vertical line of icing on the edge of the horizontal lines, then pipe short lines of icing in between the spaces across the vertical line to form a basket weave. Repeat all around the cake (see also Basket Weave Heart on page 28 – the basket weave is piped in butter cream).

TO MAKE A GREASEPROOF PAPER PIPING BAG

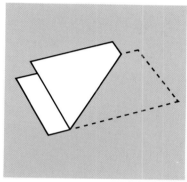

1 Cut out a 38 × 25.5 cm (15 × 10 inch) rectangle of greaseproof paper or non-stick baking parchment. Fold diagonally in half to form two triangular shapes, each with a blunt end. Cut along the fold line.

2 Fold the blunt end of the triangle over into a sharp cone and hold in position in the centre.

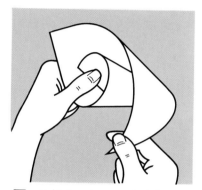

3 Fold the sharp end of the triangle over the cone shape.

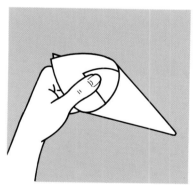

4 Hold all the points together at the back of the cone, ensuring the point of the cone is sharp.

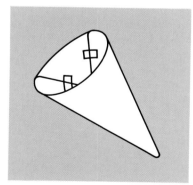

5 Turn the points inside the top edge of the cone and crease firmly. Secure with sticky tape or staple if desired.

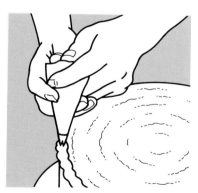

6 For piping, fill the piping bag with sharp peak or piping consistency royal icing (see page 107).

WRITING

Writing on a cake can often be daunting for most people, simply because they are worried about making a mistake on a finished cake or because they have not developed a distinctive style of writing and feel it looks untidy.

It is often very disappointing when you try to pipe freehand writing or lettering on to a cake and find the lettering is cramped, or too spaced out, going up- or downhill and generally looks untidy.

When you start writing with a piping bag you will have no particular style of your own, although with some practice you will soon develop a style suited to your own hand. Keep on practising the style that suits you letter by letter.

First look at lettering and writing samples in cake decorating or calligraphy books, then copy a style you like. Study this style in depth, draw it on to a piece of plain paper and cover with a piece of perspex. Using a No. 1 plain writing nozzle and royal icing, pipe the letters over and over again in the chosen style. Write the style on a pad while on the telephone 'doodling', or even use it to write a letter so that it becomes second nature to write freehand in this chosen style, you will then feel confident about piping it.

Keep practising on the perspex and wiping it clean. Pipe 'Happy Birthday', 'Congratulations', 'Good Luck' and family names. Always calculate the number of letters in each word and learn how much space the letters take up so that you can space them evenly apart on the surface of the cake, keeping them all level.

TO PIPE WRITING

1 If you still feel unsure about the spacing of the letters, trace them on to a piece of greaseproof paper and mark the letters on to the cake with a scribing needle or pin.

2 Pipe the letters in white or base colour royal icing first, then over-pipe in coloured icing if wished to finish the letters. Never pipe a different colour icing directly on to the surface of the cake because if you make a mistake, the surface of the cake will be stained when the icing is removed.

3 Another way to apply writing to a cake is to pipe or stencil on to a ready-made sugar plaque (see also page 121). This gives you the opportunity of several attempts and having the confined space to work on is often easier. Also food colouring pens are good to use, but you cannot afford any mistakes.

If using a lettering stencil, which are available in words or the alphabet, first place in position on the cake. Colour in the stencil shape using a food colouring pen or print in with colouring dust or food colouring. Take care not to move the stencil while working. Lift off cleanly.

> **HINT**
> Cut out the template to fit the top of the cake you wish to write on. Measure accurately where the letters have to be positioned using free hand writing or stencils. Always choose a style you feel comfortable about piping.

LACE WORK

Lace work designs are copied in piped icing to produce intricate sugar pieces. These delicate lace designs look so dainty and seem a natural choice for a wedding cake as lace work is often used in making wedding dresses and veils.

Once the designs have been worked out and piped, they may be applied to the cake as an edging border or side design, or to enhance extension work, frills or ribbon insertion. Designing lace pieces is quite easy by using lace patterns from a book or copying a lace ribbon edging or lace inserts from a dress.

TO PIPE LACE WORK

1 Once you have chosen or designed the shape you require, draw the designs boldly on to a piece of paper. Repeat the design several times, so that once you start piping you can continue.

2 Place the design on a flat surface and cover it with a piece of run-out film, waxed paper or non-stick baking parchment. Secure the edges with tape or beads of icing.

3 Ensure the royal icing is of the correct consistency and that double strength egg albumen is used (see page 108); no glycerine should be added to egg white royal icing. Quarter-fill a greaseproof paper piping bag fitted with a No. 0 plain writing nozzle, fold down the top. This is to ensure the bag is held comfortably like a pen and only a small amount of icing is used to pipe these fine pieces; and it prevents the wrists and hands aching which can be a problem if there is lots of lace to pipe.

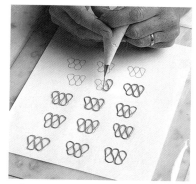

4 Most lace work consists of small curves and lines so the nozzle is used very close to the surface, and even pressure should be applied while piping. Uneven pressure will cause uneven lines and too little pressure will produce weak spots which will easily break.

It is important that all the lines of lace pieces must touch as any gap causes a weakness and the pieces may break. Lace pieces may also be overpiped to give double strength to them.

5 Pipe more pieces than required to allow for breakages. Allow the pieces to dry flat in a warm place. To release each piece, run a fine palette knife underneath the lace.

6 Apply them to the cake with beads of royal icing. If the lace pieces need to be stored, leave them on the run-out film or waxed paper and keep them flat in a cardboard box in a warm dry place.

7 To enhance the pieces, especially on the side of a cake, pipe embroidery to complete the design.

TUBE EMBROIDERY

This is a fascinating way of decorating a cake; the embroidery design is worked in many different shades of royal icing. Piped in the traditional embroidery stitch shapes, the threads of icing build up a pattern, floral design or picture.

Before embarking on any embroidery design, it is essential to practise each of the embroidery stitches first, which are made up of tiny loops, curved lines, dots and crosses. Once these basic stitches have been mastered, make up simple designs to pipe on to a sugar plaque and see how effective it is. Designs may be inspired obviously by paper embroidery patterns, fabrics, porcelain and china patterns or antique embroidered table linen.

TO PIPE TUBE EMBROIDERY

1 Once the design has been established, trace or draw it on to greaseproof paper as accurately as possible, then transfer the design on to the surface of the cake using a scribing needle or pin. Mark only the main outline of the design as too much detail may be confusing.

2 When the colour scheme has been worked out, divide the royal icing into the number of colours or shades required. Tint or colour the icing according to the

pattern, making sure the icing is soft enough to flow easily from the nozzle. Place a small amount of each colour into a greaseproof paper piping bag fitted with a No. 0 plain writing nozzle. Small quantities in the bag are comfortable to hold and allow more freedom of movement for piping close to the surface to obtain an accurate design.

3 Start piping with the nozzle gently scraping the surface as the icing is pressed out using an even pressure and holding the piping bag like a pen. Pipe the background of the designs first and work towards the front. Complete one section at a time, changing the shades where necessary, piping lighter colours over darker shades while it is still wet, before moving on to the next part of the design. This way you produce a smooth result and the shades will blend well.

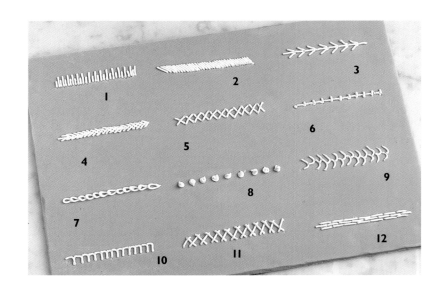

4 If the stitches appear rather uneven or little tails are showing, draw a fine damp paint brush through the stitches to flatten them slightly.

1. Long and short   2. Satin
3. Fish bone   4. Stem
5. Cross   6. Couching
7. Chain   8. French knot
9. Feather   10. Button hole
11. Herring bone   12. Running

EXTENSION WORK

Spectacular extension work is an extremely delicate form of cake decoration and requires an enormous amount of time and patience to obtain a satisfactory result.

It is a method of decorating the sides of a cake with vertical lines of icing which stand away from the side of the cake. These lines of icing are supported by a series of dropped loops piped exactly on top of each other to form a solid bridge.

The piping must be extremely neat and straight, and must be piped accurately to produce a high standard. Extension work must always be retained within the width of the cake board to prevent breakages, so always allow for extra width. The extension work should always be designed carefully and accurately to complement the shape of the cake and any other decorations included in the design. Other decorations that will complement this beautiful decoration are lace pieces, tube embroidery, sugar flowers and ribbon insertion.

When piping extension work, the cake base being decorated must have straight sides, smooth icing or

sugar paste, and free from any blemishes or major faults as this work will not hide any flaws on the base covering of the cake.

Before piping extension work, the icing must be well made using pure egg albumen, of medium peak consistency, smooth and of a good texture. It should also be free from any air bubbles or tiny lumps which may block the piping nozzle. The addition of liquid glucose will give the icing a greater elasticity, which is an advantage when piping vertical lines. Use 1.25 ml (¼ tsp) liquid glucose to each 225 g (8 oz) icing sugar. Leave the medium peak royal icing at room temperature for 24 hours before using.

Decide on the design of the extension work and make a template accordingly. Fit a strip of greaseproof paper the exact length and depth of the side of the cake. Mark the base scalloped design for the bridge work and measure the template to the depth of the vertical lines. The template should now be cut to the shape and depth required for the design. Secure the template around the side of the cake with sticky tape and, using a pin, mark the top edge and the base shape of the design around the cake.

At this stage, pipe or decorate a border around the base of the cake, or any other decoration like ribbon insertion, as this cannot be achieved after the extension work has been piped.

TO PIPE EXTENSION WORK

1 To pipe the bridge, place the cake on a turntable so that it is at eye level. Support the base with a piece of card or something small to tilt the cake away from you. Using a scribing needle or a pin, re-mark the high points of the scallop design so that you are in no doubt where the loops should start and finish.

marked line. Touch the scallop at the next highest point on the design to secure the thread.

piping to dry completely before piping the vertical lines.

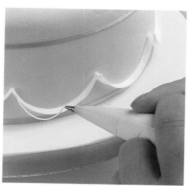

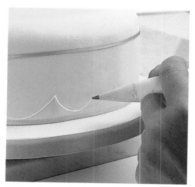

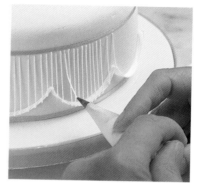

2 To work the bridge, touch the cake at the highest point of the scallop with the nozzle and press out a little icing to attach a thread. Pull the nozzle away from the cake and maintain an even pressure of icing to pipe the thread, allowing it to follow the

3 Continue piping these dropped loops of icing and work around the cake, making sure the first row of bridge work is dry before starting on the second row. There should be no gaps in between the dropped loops, which form the scallops, on the cake as this can cause a weak bridge. Pipe each loop exactly over the preceding loop, just finishing the thread slightly shorter on each so they fit neatly together. Pipe approximately six loops or more to build up the bridge. Allow the

4 To pipe the extension work, this time tilt the cake towards you so that the lines fall straight as they are piped. Touch the cake with the nozzle at the top of the design to attach the thread of icing, pull away immediately, taking care not to form a bulb of icing at the top. Pipe vertical lines just beyond the bridge, then break the thread of icing. Remove any icing ends with a fine damp paint brush. The lines should be parallel and so close together that you cannot pipe a line in between the strands. When the extension work is dry, pipe on any details.

ICING RUN-OUTS

Icing run-outs are one of the most exacting forms of cake decoration. They can be made in any shape or form by simply tracing over a design or pattern.

Run-outs are made from royal icing and are very fragile. Therefore, it is wise to choose a small solid shape at first, and make more than required to allow for breakages. When you are confident at making the simple, small, solid shapes, practise making finer corner pieces or collars. Accuracy, not speed, is important when making run-outs, so always allow plenty of time, not only for making them, but also for completely drying them.

Once made, small run-outs can be kept successfully between layers of waxed paper in a box stored in a dry place. This means if a quantity of run-outs are needed to decorate a cake, they can be made in advance. Large run-outs and collars are more difficult to store as they may warp in storage; they are better made, dried completely and applied directly to the cake.

The consistency and texture of the royal icing must be right or the run-outs will be difficult to make and handle. Use double strength dried pure egg albumen or egg whites with no additives such as glycerine or lemon juice. The icing should be light and glossy, not heavy and dull. Use a medium peak consistency icing for piping the outline of the run-outs, as these are piped with a fine plain writing nozzle.

Icing to fill in the run-out must be like softly whipped cream, soft enough to flow with the help of a paint brush but holding its shape until tapped, then becoming smooth and rounded. Dilute the royal icing with reconstituted double strength egg albumen. Test a little on a flat surface to ensure the consistency is correct.

Leave the icing to stand overnight if possible, covered with damp muslin in a polythene bag, allowing any air bubbles to come to the surface, then stir until smooth.

TO MAKE AN ICING RUN-OUT

1 Draw or trace the chosen design several times on a piece of plain paper, well spaced apart. Place the paper on a flat surface and cover with a piece of thin perspex or glass. Cover the perspex or glass with a piece of run-out film or waxed paper and secure with tape or four or six beads of icing to the perspex or glass.

2 Fit a small greaseproof paper piping bag with a No. 0 or 1 writing nozzle and half-fill with icing to pipe the outline. Fill several greaseproof paper piping bags with the soft icing. Fold down the tops and leave.

3 Pipe carefully around the outline of the design with a continuous thread of icing or with as few breaks as possible. Squeeze out a little icing at the least focal point of the run-out and secure the icing thread. Lift the thread of icing just above the surface and squeeze the bag gently following the outline of the tracing. Allow the thread to fall on the marked line around the shape of the run-out. Stop squeezing to prevent the icing thread from running on, and join the icing where it started.

4 Snip the pointed end off one of the soft icing bags and start to fill in the run-out, working in small areas at a time. Start by piping around the inside edge at one end of the run-out to keep the outline soft, otherwise it may break. Work towards the centre, filling the shape so that the icing looks rounded and over-filled, not flat as the icing shrinks as it dries.

5 Use a fine paint brush to coax the icing into small areas to ensure the whole run-out is completely filled, and the icing is smooth and rounded. Gently tap the board so that any bubbles rise to the surface; if so, burst these with a pin. Repeat to pipe more run-outs on the same surface if necessary. Carefully lift the perspex or glass off the design and leave the run-outs to dry. Replace another piece of perspex or glass to cover the drawing design with more run-out film or waxed paper and repeat to make as many run-outs as required.

6 Leave the run-outs under a spotlight if possible to dry the surface as quickly as possible, then dry them for at least 24 hours in a warm, dry place, or even longer if the weather is damp, until they have set hard. The more quickly they dry, the glossier the run-outs will be. Pipe any details on the run-outs at this stage and allow to dry. Carefully release the run-outs from the film using an extra fine-bladed palette knife and use to decorate the cake. Otherwise store them flat on the film in a box between layers of waxed paper in a warm dry place until required.

7 Arrange the run-outs on the cake and secure with small beads or a line of royal icing.

PIPED FLOWERS

With the use of a petal nozzle, many simple flower shapes may be piped using royal icing. The nozzles come in a range of sizes, each suited to piping different sized flowers. They are also available for the left or right hand.

Fit the nozzle into a greaseproof paper piping bag and half-fill with sharp peak royal icing (see pages 107 and 129). Fold down the top and hold the bag comfortably in your hand with the thick end of the nozzle towards the centre. It is much easier to use a flower spinner nail, like a miniature turntable, with a square of waxed paper secured with icing.

TO PIPE A BASIC BLOSSOM SHAPE

1   Start by piping the petal shapes to get the feel of the icing. Keep an even pressure and pipe a close horseshoe shape. Rotate the spinner nail slowly as you pipe the second petal.

2   By the time you have piped the third petal, two-thirds of the flower should be piped; if not, the petals are too fat or too thin.

3   Keep rotating to pipe the remaining two petals. Pipe a contrasting bead of icing in the centre. Colour the royal icing pale pink or blue, or leave the icing white and brush the dry blossoms with coloured dust.

TO PIPE A DAISY

1   Using a flower spinner nail, secure a square of waxed paper to the surface with a bead of icing. Using a greaseproof paper piping bag fitted with a petal nozzle, half-fill with white or yellow royal icing. Hold the nozzle on its side with the broad end towards the centre.

2   Pipe the petal shapes in an up and down movement whilst turning the flower nail, to make the petals larger and thinner. Pipe 10 petals with beads of yellow or green icing in the centre.

TO PIPE LEAVES

1   Fill a greaseproof paper piping bag with icing and press the icing to the end point of the bag. Cut the end of the piping bag into an inverted 'v'.

2   Place the end of the piping bag on to the surface of the cake. Press out the icing to form a leaf shape, then sharply break off the icing.

3   Repeat to make a pretty border, leaves to decorate flowers, or to make a design. Alternatively, pipe individual leaves on to squares of waxed paper and leave to dry.

CHRISTMAS GREETING CAKE

*F*inely piped holly and ivy leaves cascade around
this elliptical shaped cake trimmed with bright
berries and ribbon.

20.5 cm (8 inch) round rich fruit
cake mixture (see page 64)
25.5 cm (10 inch) oval silver cake
board
45 ml (3 tbsp) apricot glaze (see
page 70)
700 g (1½ lb) white marzipan
700 g (1½ lb) white sugar paste
1 quantity royal icing, made with
pure egg albumen (see page 108)
red and green food colourings
1 metre (1 yard), 5 mm (¼ inch)
wide red ribbon
2 metres (2 yards), 5 mm (¼
inch) wide green ribbon
1 metre (1 yard), 1 cm (½ inch)
wide red ribbon

1 Prepare a 20.5 cm (8 inch)
oval cake tin (see page 11).
Make the rich fruit cake mixture
and place in the tin. Bake
according to the cake chart on
page 66. Place the cake in the
centre of the cake board and brush
with apricot glaze. Cover smoothly
with marzipan (see page 73). Place
in a cardboard cake box overnight
to dry. Cover the cake smoothly
with white sugar paste (see page
82).

2 Using holly and ivy leaf
cutters, draw around each
shape several times on a piece of
paper, spacing each one apart.
Place the paper on a board and
cover with run-out film or non-
stick baking parchment. Reserve
30 ml (2 tbsp) white royal icing;
colour one-third of the remaining
royal icing red and the remaining
two-thirds bright green, using the
red and green food colourings.

3 Fit two greaseproof paper
piping bags each with a No. 1
plain writing nozzle and half-fill
one bag with green icing and place
the white icing in the remaining
bag. Fold down the tops. Using the
green icing, pipe around the holly
and ivy leaves, following the
marked lines on the paper. Pipe in
the veins. Move the paper as the
designs are filled until you have
piped 30 holly and 12 ivy leaves,
allowing a few extra for breakages.
Leave in a warm place to dry.

4 Measure and fit the narrow
red and green ribbons
around the cake. Start at the top of
the cake at the back, sweeping the
ribbon down and across the front.
Secure to the back of the cake
with a stainless steel pin. Measure
and fit the wide red and narrow
green ribbon around the cake
board and secure with a stainless
steel pin. Using the white royal
icing, pipe the letters CHRISTMAS
GREETING across the top of the
cake on the left hand side.

5 Carefully release the piped
leaves from the paper using a
fine palette knife. Secure groups of
three holly leaves just above the
ribbon at intervals around and on
top of the cake with beads of white
royal icing. Place the ivy leaves in
between the holly leaves and
secure with icing. Pipe three white
berries in between the holly leaves.

6 Place the red icing in a greaseproof paper piping bag fitted with a No. 1 nozzle and over-pipe the letters and the berries with red icing. Leave in a cardboard cake box in a warm place to dry.

HINT
If an oval cake tin is not available, the design looks just as eye-catching on a round cake. Pipe a different message on the cake if desired.

CORNELLI CAKE

This elegant cake would suit so many occasions – a wedding anniversary, coming-of-age or a christening. A lemon Madeira cake mixture is simply covered with champagne sugar paste and piped with one plain nozzle. Fresh or sugar flowers may be used.

28 cm (11 inch) and a 15 cm (6 inch) round lemon-flavoured Madeira cake mixture (see page 69)

30.5 cm (12 inch) petal-shaped silver cake board

15 cm (6 inch) thin silver cake board

1.5 kg (3¼ lb) white marzipan

1.6 kg (3½ lb) champagne coloured sugar paste

75 ml (5 tbsp) apricot glaze (see page 70)

old gold, yellow food colouring

1 quantity royal icing (see page 108)

25 simple blossom flowers (see page 155)

3 hand moulded yellow roses (see page 89) or fresh flowers

2 metres (2 yards), 2.5 cm (1 inch) wide fine organza cream ribbon

1.5 metres (1½ yards), 1 cm (½ inch) wide fancy cream ribbon

0.5 metre (½ yard), 3 mm (⅛ inch) wide yellow ribbon

....

> **HINT**
> This distinctive cake may be made using a rich, light or Madeira cake mixture. To change the decoration, cover the cakes in a pastel coloured sugar paste and use a contrasting coloured royal icing to pipe the cornelli work. Fresh flowers may also be used.

1 Prepare a 27 cm (10½ inch) petal shaped tin (see page 11) and grease and base line a 15 cm (6 inch), 900 ml (1½ pint) ovenproof glass pudding basin. Make each quantity of the Madeira cake mixture and flavour them lemon. Place each mixture into its prepared tin and pudding basin. Bake according to the cake chart on page 70. Place the petal cake on its matching cake board and the domed cake on the small round cake board, then brush with apricot glaze. Cover each cake smoothly with marzipan (see page 73). Place each into a cardboard cake box to dry overnight.

2 Using three-quarters of the champagne coloured sugar paste, cover each of the cakes smoothly (see page 82), then store in the cake boxes until dry. Knead the trimmings together with the remaining piece of sugar paste. Divide the sugar paste into three pieces. Colour one piece pale yellow and another piece creamy yellow, giving three graduating shades of colour.

3 Using the cream sugar paste, follow the instructions for making Mexican hat flowers (see page 155). Using a five-petalled flower cutter, cut out the shape. Using a cone shaped modelling tool, shape the centre and soften the petals on a flower mat, using a bone modelling tool to give a realistic shape. Add a few pearl stamens to the centre of the flowers, cutting them to size and inserting into the centre. Make 25 flowers and leave them to dry in a warm place. Using the remaining three colours of sugar paste, mould three roses starting with the deeper colour and working out to the palest shade (see page 89). Leave to dry.

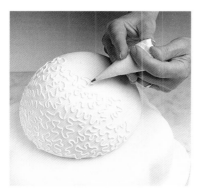

royal icing and fold down the top. Carefully position the domed cake in the centre of the petal-shaped cake. Start piping cornelli work from the top of the domed cake (see page 128). Pipe in rounded 'm' and 'w' shapes working in all directions, always joining on to the thread where you stopped piping to start the design again so that the thread looks continuous.

4 Tint the royal icing with a few drops of old gold food colouring so it matches the sugar paste on the cake. Fit a grease-proof paper piping bag with a No. 2 plain writing nozzle, half-fill with

5 Pipe the petal-shaped cake after the dome shape is complete until both cakes have been piped. Pipe the cake board. Arrange groups of three sugar flowers around the base of the

domed cake and secure with royal icing. Arrange the remaining flowers and roses on top of the cake and at the base, securing with royal icing.

6 Take the organza ribbon, cut in half and fold two ends into pretty loops. Secure on top of the cake using a stainless steel pin. Coil the remaining ribbon tails around the side of the cake and secure the ends to the board using stainless steel pins. Band the cake board with the fancy cream ribbon and secure with a pin. Tie six tiny bows from the fine ribbon and pin in position around the cake board.

EMBROIDERY CAKE

A clever way to decorate a cake using an embroidery pattern and different shades of icing to fill in the chosen design.

20.5 cm (8 inch) round rich fruit cake mixture (see page 64)

25.5 cm (10 inch) round silver cake board

45 ml (3 tbsp) apricot glaze (see page 70)

700 g (1½ lb) white marzipan

700 g (1½ lb) champagne coloured sugar paste

1 quantity royal icing (see page 108)

coral, yellow and green food colourings

1 metre (1 yard), 1 cm (½ inch) wide orange ribbon

1 metre (1 yard), 1 cm (½ inch) wide champagne ribbon

....

1 Prepare a 20.5 cm (8 inch) round cake tin (see page 11). Make the rich fruit cake mixture and place in the tin. Bake according to the cake chart on page 66. Place the cake in the centre of the cake board and brush with apricot glaze. Cover the cake smoothly with marzipan (see page 73). Leave overnight to dry in a cardboard cake box. Cover the cake and cake board smoothly with sugar paste (see page 82). Leave to dry.

2 Make the royal icing and divide into six parts. Colour each part pale and dark coral, pale and dark yellow and pale and dark green using the food colourings. Using six greaseproof paper piping bags, fill each with the coloured icing. Fold down the tops. Place the chosen embroidery pattern on to the cake and pin in position (see page 210). Mark out the main shape of the design on the top and side of the cake, using a pin or scribing needle. Do not over-mark or the design becomes confused.

3 Snip the point off the ends of the light and dark green icing bags. Pipe the stems on the top

and side of the cake in stem stitch using the dark green icing. Pipe long stitch with dark green and short stitch with the light green icing to fill in the leaves on the top and side of the cake.

4 Using the light coral icing, fill in the petals of the large flowers with satin stitch. Outline each petal with running stitch or using a lazy daisy stitch. Fill in the remaining matching flowers using dark coral to fill in the petals and base of the flowers, and the light coral to outline the petal shapes.

5 Work the daisy shaped flowers using dark yellow satin stitch and outlined in pale yellow. Fill in the large flower centres with pale yellow outlined with dark yellow.

6 Pipe the chosen name in light coral and over-pipe with dark coral. Measure and fit the ribbons around the cake board. Secure each with a stainless steel pin. Place the cake in a cardboard cake box in a warm dry place.

GOOD LUCK CAKE

A simple graphic design piped on to a square royal iced cake. Choose any colour of royal icing for the base or the piping.

23 cm (9 inch) square rich fruit
  cake mixture (see page 64)
28 cm (11 inch) square silver cake
  board
60 ml (4 tbsp) apricot glaze (see
  page 70)
1 kg (2¼ lb) white marzipan
1.6 kg (3½ lb) quantity royal icing
  (see page 108)
blue and green food colourings
1 metre (1 yard), 1 cm (½ inch)
  wide green ribbon
1 metre (1 yard), 1 cm (½ inch)
  wide blue ribbon

....

1 Prepare a 23 cm (9 inch)
  square deep cake tin (see
page 11). Make the rich fruit cake
mixture and place in the tin. Bake
according to the cake chart on
page 66. Place the cake in the
centre of the cake board and brush
with apricot glaze. Cover the cake
smoothly with marzipan (see page
72). Place the cake in a cardboard
cake box for at least 24 hours
before royal icing.

2 Make the royal icing and ice
  the cake with three coats of
smooth royal icing (see page 109).
Cover the cake board smoothly
with royal icing and leave in the
cake box to dry. Colour one third
of the remaining royal icing royal
blue and one third emerald green
with the food colourings. Fit three
greaseproof paper piping bags each
with a No. 1 plain writing nozzle
and half-fill one with blue, one
with green and one with white
icing.

3 Measure 12.5 cm (5 inches)
  in from the top left hand
corner of the cake. From this point
on the top edge of the cake, mark
twelve 5 mm (¼ inch) points using
a scribing needle or beads of royal
icing. Repeat to mark the same
points on opposite edge of the cake
using a ruler to align the points. It
is important to carefully mark out
the graphic design accurately, so
that the lines of piping will look
perfect when completed.

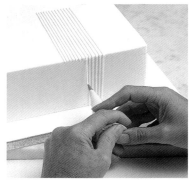

4 Using the white royal icing,
  start at the marked points on
top edge of the cake and pipe a
parallel line of icing across the top
of the cake, to match up with the
marked points on the opposite
side. Repeat until all the lines have
been piped. Tilt the cake away
from you and pipe matching lines
of icing from the top edge to the
base of the cake and from the base
of the cake to the edge of the cake
board. Repeat on the opposite side
of the cake. Measure 5 cm (2
inches) in from the opposite side
of the piped lines on the top edges
of the cake.

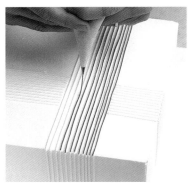

5 Mark another twelve 5 mm
  (¼ inch) points from each
side of the lines. Repeat to pipe the
parallel lines, piping from the
centre lines to edge of the cake
and on both sides. Pipe matching
lines on both sides of the cake and
the board. Over-pipe all lines in
blue and green, in three lines of
each colour. (The choice of icing
colours for this over-piping will
change the look of the cake.)

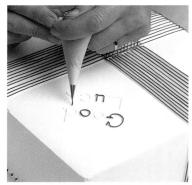

6 Pipe beads around base with
  a No. 3 writing nozzle and
white icing. Pipe alternate diagonal
lines of blue and green, where lines
meet. Over-pipe white beads with
blue and green.

LATTICE GARDEN CAKE

P *iped trellis work over a backcloth of coloured*
butter cream gives this cake a three-dimensional
appearance. The trailing apple blossom, simple flowers
and leaves make this cake suitable for almost any
occasion. Make additional tiers for a wedding cake.

30.5 cm (12 inch) round orange-
flavoured Madeira cake mixture
(see page 69)

35.5 cm (14 inch) hexagonal silver
cake board

700 g (1½ lb) butter cream (see
page 25)

green, pink and violet food
colourings

1 quantity royal icing (see page
108)

2 metres (2 yards), 2 cm (¾ inch)
wide yellow ribbon

2 metres (2 yards), 5 mm (¼
inch) wide green ribbon

....

1 Prepare a 30.5 cm (12 inch) hexagonal shaped cake tin (see page 11). Make the Madeira cake mixture, flavour it orange and place in the tin. Bake according to the cake chart on page 70. Place the cake on the centre of the cake board. Make the butter cream and colour one-third green with a few drops of green food colouring. Spread the top and sides of the cake evenly with green butter cream using a large palette knife. Place a straight edge on top of the cake and pull across to smooth the butter cream and to make a level top. Using a side scraper, smooth each side section of the cake to give a fairly smooth and even surface. Reserve the green butter cream for piping the leaves.

2 Make several large greaseproof paper piping bags and fit one with a basket weave or ribbon nozzle. Half-fill with plain butter cream and fold down the top. Place the cake on a turntable and place a cloth underneath the cake to tilt the cake away from you. Pipe diagonal lines of butter cream across one section of the cake leaving a 1 cm (½ inch) space in between each line. Repeat to over-pipe these lines of butter cream in the opposite direction to make a lattice pattern. Continue to pipe each side section all around the cake. Remove the cake from the turntable.

3 To pipe the top, start in the centre of the cake and pipe across the top from side to side with long continuous lines of icing. Continue to pipe evenly spaced lines in one direction, then pipe diagonally in the opposite direction.

4 Half-fill a greaseproof paper piping bag with plain butter cream, snip off the end to form an inverted 'V' shape. Pipe a leaf edging around the top and base edges and down each side section (see page 135). Place the cake in a cardboard cake box and leave in a cool place to set.

5 Make the royal icing and divide into thirds. Colour one-third pale pink and one-third mauve using the pink and violet food colourings. Pipe about 40 apple blossom flowers following the instructions on page 135, using the

green butter cream to pipe the stamens. Leave overnight to dry in a warm place. Using a greaseproof paper piping bag, half-fill with mauve icing, fold down the top and snip off the end into a 'V' shape. Cut out about 40 squares of waxed paper and on to each pipe a circle of three leaves and one in the centre. Repeat to pipe about 40 simple flowers. Leave to dry.

6 When the flowers are dry, peel them away from the paper squares. Attach five apple blossoms in a semi-circle on to one side section of the cake with five mauve flowers in between. Using a greaseproof paper piping bag half-filled with green butter cream, snip off the end into a 'V' shape and

pipe pairs of leaves in between each flower. Repeat all around the side of the cake. Arrange the remaining flowers on top of the cake in a circle with some in the centre. Pipe in the leaves. Place the cake in the box in a cool place until required.

DOILY CELEBRATION CAKE

overed in a pastel sugar paste, the soft lines of this trefoil cake lends itself to the dainty embroidery design and extension work.

25.5 cm (10 inch) round rich fruit cake mixture (see page 64)

30.5 cm (12 inch) trefoil silver cake board

75 ml (5 tbsp) apricot glaze (see page 70)

1 kg (2¼ lb) white marzipan

1.1 kg (2½ lb) peach coloured sugar paste

15 cm (6 inch) thin round silver cake board

450 g (1 lb) quantity royal icing, made with pure egg albumen (see page 108)

3 metres (3 yards), 5 mm (¼ inch) wide peach ribbon

2 metres (2 yards), 1 cm (½ inch) wide peach ribbon

2 metres (2 yards), 5 mm (¼ inch) wide white ribbon

fresh flowers to match the cake

....

HINT
The extension work on this cake is very time-consuming so allow plenty of time. Pipe the in-fill lines over a period of several days instead of trying to finish it all at once. Remember to tilt the cake towards you and pipe the lines at intervals around the cake.

1 Prepare a 25.5 cm (10 inch) trefoil shaped cake tin (see page 11). Make the rich fruit cake mixture and place in the tin. Bake according to the cake chart on page 66. Place the cake in the centre of the trefoil cake board and brush with apricot glaze. Cover smoothly with marzipan (see page 73). Cover the cake and cake board smoothly with sugar paste (see page 82). Place in a cardboard cake box until the sugar paste is dry.

2 Knead the sugar paste trimmings together and roll out into a round, 5 mm (¼ inch) thick. Cut out a 20.5 cm (8 inch) circle and place on a small acrylic board. On greaseproof paper, cut out a circle measuring 20.5 cm (8 inches) and fold into 12 sections. Using a rounded object, place at the wide end and draw around the shape and cut out to make a 12-scalloped circle (see page 210). Place the template on the sugar paste circle and cut around the shape using a sharp knife. Place on the thin round silver cake board.

3 Use the end of a fine paint brush or knitting needle and mark 12 daisy shapes, one in each scallop shape with six petal shapes and a round centre. Mark groups of three rounds in between the marked daisy shapes and a circle of rounds 5 cm (2 inches) from the centre. (For the design, hold the paint brush or knitting needle at an angle to mark the oval shaped petals and straight upright to make the holes.)

4 Make the template to fit around the cake for the extension work (see page 209).

Cut a strip of greaseproof paper to fit exactly around one side section of the cake and to measure two-thirds of the depth. Fold the template into six equal folds and using a rounded object, place within the edge of the template. Draw around the shape and cut out neatly. Pin the template in position allowing a gap of 5 mm (¼ inch) at the base. Mark with a scribing needle along the top and around the scallop shape at the base. Mark this design accurately on all sides of the cake.

5 Fit the fine peach ribbon around the base of the cake. Fit fine ribbon around the cake side just on the marked template line.

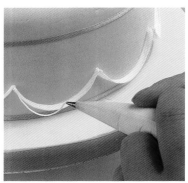

6 Make the royal icing and half-fill a greaseproof paper piping bag with a No. 1 plain writing nozzle. Fold down the top. Pipe the bridge for the extension work, following the scalloped line (see page 133). Leave to dry.

HINT
Make the doily in advance and store in a warm dry place so it sets hard.

7 Pipe the vertical lines from the ribbon to the bridge taking great care. Do not pipe one line after another; pipe at intervals all around the cake and gradually fill in. Place carefully in a box and leave to dry.

8 Pipe around the doily design using the same piping nozzle. Outline the holes with circles of icing and the oval petals with lazy daisy or chain stitch (see page 132). Pipe a tiny shell edging around the edge of the doily. Pipe a daisy, scroll and bead design in each section on top of the cake.

9 Position a piece of sugar paste about 1 cm (½ inch) thick and 5 cm (2 inches) round in the centre of the cake. Carefully slide the sugar paste doily off the thin cake board and place on top of the sugar paste round. Position the flowers on the centre of the doily at the last minute.

10 Band the cake board with the remaining wide and narrow ribbons and secure with stainless steel pins. Tie six tiny bows and secure on to ribbon around the cake board.

WEDDING FAN CAKE

*T*rellis fan-shaped run-outs adorn the sides of this elegant cake with piped lace work on the top and side to enhance the design. Use a colour to suit the occasion to infill the fans and to over-pipe the lace.

30.5, 23, 15 cm (12, 9, 6 inch) square rich fruit cake mixtures (see page 64)

38, 28, 20.5 cm (15, 11, 8 inch) square silver cake boards

200 ml (7 fl oz) apricot glaze (see page 70)

3.2 kg (7 lb) white marzipan

5.5 kg (12 lb) quantity royal icing (see page 108)

24 run-out fan shapes (see page 134) made with pure egg albumen royal icing

ice blue food colouring

8 metres (8 yards), 1 cm (½ inch) wide blue ribbon

6 metres (6 yards), 2 cm (¾ inch) white ribbon

8 white plaster cake pillars

....

> **HINT**
> Ensure the templates for making the run-out fans are drawn accurately, so they fit neatly on each cake. When piping the lattice in-fill, make sure the royal icing is of sharp peak consistency so that the threads will not bend but keep straight.

1 Prepare 30.5, 23 and 15 cm (12, 9 and 6 inch) square cake tins (see page 11). Make the rich fruit cake mixtures and place into their appropriate sized tins. Bake according to the cake chart on page 66. Store until required (see page 13). Place the cakes in the centre of each of their matching cake boards and brush with apricot glaze. Cover the cakes smoothly with marzipan (see page 72). Place each cake into a cardboard cake box and leave for at least 24 hours.

2 Make up small quantities of royal icing at a time for icing the cakes smoothly. Royal ice each cake with three thin smooth coats (see page 109). Cover the cake boards smoothly with royal icing. Leave the cakes to dry in their boxes in a warm dry place. Reserve the remaining royal icing.

3 Make the royal icing for the run-outs using pure egg albumen, adjusting the consistency for piping the outline and filling in the run-outs (see page 134). To make the run-out fan shapes, trace the given fan shapes from page 206 which come in three sizes to fit the large, medium and small sized cakes. Trace one size of each shape of fan accurately on a separate piece of paper and cut out neatly. Repeat turning the template over and cut out another three shapes which will give you a left and right template for each corner.

Place the largest size fan shape on a piece of glass, perspex or a baking sheet and cover with eezioff, run-out film or waxed paper, then secure.

4 Pipe the outline and fill in the shape according to the instructions on page 134. Carefully slide the template along to reveal the shape and repeat to pipe another fan shape. Each cake requires four left and four right hand fan-shaped run-outs, except the small cake which requires two extra shapes to decorate the top. It is advisable to make two extra shapes in each size in case of breakages. These run-outs may be made well in advance. When the run-out shapes are completely dry, release them from the paper using a fine palette knife and invert each shape.

11 Complete the small cake in the same way, cutting the ribbon lengths to 7.5 cm (3 inches) and pipe three dropped loops at 2 cm (¾ inch) intervals. Join the two top fan shape pieces with royal icing and leave to set standing up.

5 Ensure the consistency of the icing is sharp peak for piping. Tint the icing pale blue with a little ice blue food colouring or to the colour you have chosen. Half-fill a greaseproof paper piping bag fitted with a No. 1 plain writing nozzle with pale blue royal icing. Fold down the top. Pipe parallel lines of icing in one direction across each section of the fan shape. Over-pipe in the opposite direction to make a trellis pattern to fill in the fan shape neatly (see page 128). Leave to dry.

6 Using the 1 cm (½ inch) blue ribbon, cut four 15 cm (6 inch) lengths. Secure these lengths of ribbon in the centre at the base on each side of the large cake with beads of blue royal icing.

7 Fit a greaseproof paper piping bag with a No. 3 plain writing nozzle and half-fill with white royal icing. Pipe a line on both sides of each corner and along the base to the ribbon to secure the run-out forms. Taking great care, with the cake placed in the centre of a flat surface away from the edges, carefully attach each large fan shape to the corners of the large cake, pressing the corners very gently in position and leaving the ends slightly away from the cake. Ensure there is enough icing to hold them firmly in position.

8 In between the fan shapes along the top edge of each side, measure and mark three 2.5 cm (1 inch) spaces. Using a No. 1 plain writing nozzle and white royal icing, pipe from the top edge three dropped loops following the marked points. From the centre loop, pipe another two dropped loops to finish underneath the first loops and finally one loop to create the design. Pipe three beads of icing underneath the centre loop and two side loops. Pipe on top of the cake to mirror the same design. Over-pipe the whole design in pale blue royal icing.

9 Repeat this design on the remaining three sides of the cake. Band the cake board with white and blue ribbon and secure with a stainless steel pin. Place in a cardboard cake box in a warm dry place until required.

10 Repeat the same designs on the middle sized cake but cutting shorter lengths of ribbon, 11 cm (4½ inches) to fit in between the fan shapes. Pipe the top and side design smaller, marking four 2.5 cm (1 inch) points to pipe the three dropped loops and graduating the design.

12 To assemble the cakes, space the cake pillars evenly apart on the large cake and place the middle-sized cake centrally on top. Arrange the remaining pillars on the middle cake and centrally position the small cake. Arrange the top decoration in position on top of the cake.

HINT
Fan-shaped run-outs are time consuming, so make them in advance and store them flat in a warm dry place.

FLOWER PASTE

This remarkable medium is used mostly for modelling very fine sugar flowers, sugar plaques and intricate items. When the paste is made, it is exceptionally easy to work with as it can be rolled out so thinly that you can see through the paste.

It may be moulded or cut into flower shapes, which dries so quickly that the flowers set in such a way that they look almost real. Once dry, the paste is exceptionally strong and the flowers may be wired on to stems and shaped into sprays or bouquets.

Flower paste is also wonderful for making sugar plaques and cards. They may be made in any shape or size, with the edges patterned, frilled or crimped, making their uses endless. When the paste is dry, it is as hard as a ceramic tile, which makes it a good working base for a cake design. Flowers may be applied, run-outs, piping or free hand pictures drawn using food colouring pens, or designs painted on the plaques with a fine paint brush and paste food colourings.

This paste may be purchased from any cake decorating specialist as petal paste, and is sold in 250 g (8 oz) packets or 500 g (1 lb) packets, but it is very expensive to buy if a large quantity is required. Flower paste may also be purchased in a ready-to-mix powder form, which is very convenient for small quantities but again rather expensive for large quantities. To make the flower paste, you just add water.

The recipe for flower paste is easy and very reliable. Once made it must be kept sealed in a polythene bag and used within a month or it will become hard and unusable. Always knead well before using. It is better to make up the flower paste 24 hours before you need it so that it is fresh and pliable to work. Flower paste may be coloured or tinted in the usual way with concentrated food colourings, or used naturally and brushed with coloured dust once the paste has dried. Either colouring method produces excellent results.

Items made with flower paste are not edible because of the hardness of the paste. Also with flowers, wire, stems, stamens and tape are used so it is better to keep these beautiful items as personal keepsakes.

SPECIAL EQUIPMENT FOR FLOWER MAKING

The skill of making sugar flowers has become so much easier these days. This is due to the supply of specialist equipment which enables anyone to obtain a very high standard. Start with a few basic tools and cutters and see how sugar flowers spring to life making the technique of flower making so much simpler.

Small acrylic rolling pin and board – being non-stick, the miniature rolling pin and board are ideal for rolling out tiny pieces of flower paste.

Flower cutters – these metal or plastic cutters are available in every shape and size of flower species imaginable. They come either as complete flower shapes or a set of individual petals.

Calyx cutters – these are sometimes included with the specific set of petal or flower cutters; otherwise they may be purchased individually as small, medium or large.

Leaf cutters and veins – cutters for many different leaves are available as sized sets often including the veins to mark the details on to the leaves. Other varieties of leaves and veins are sold individually.

Flower pad – a solid foam type for pressing and forming cut-out flowers into realistic shapes. The holes in the pad are for placing the cone end of Mexican hat flowers into while shaping the edge of the flowers.

Mini acrylic stick rolling pin – used to roll out the edges of Mexican hat flowers paper thinly while retaining the cone shape in the centre. Also for modelling the centre of flowers into a hollow cone shape.

Floppy mat – keep cut-out shapes of flowers or sugar paste underneath the mat to prevent the shapes from drying.

Bone tool – this is the most useful tool for pressing sugar frills in position, for softening or frilling the edge of petals or leaves and rounding the shape.

Plain and ridge cone tool – use this to shape the

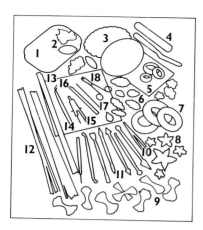

1. *Flower pad*   2. *Leaf veins*
3. *Plaque cutters*   4. *Small acrylic rolling pin*   5. *Small acrylic board*   6. *Leaf cutters*
7. *Tape*   8. *Flower cutters*
9. *Stamens*   10. *Tweezers*
11. *Tools*   12. *Floristry wire*
13. *Floppy mat*   14. *Flower tweezers*   15. *Compass*
16. *Modelling knife*   17. *Mini acrylic stick rolling pin*
18. *Wire-cutting scissors*

inside of flowers to give a smooth or ridged centre.
Scribing needle – to make pin holes in the centre of flowers to insert stamens or wire.
Modelling knife – to cut out shapes of flower paste cleanly and sharply.
Tweezers – round-ended tweezers for bending flower wire when arranging sugar flowers.
Wire-cutting scissors – short-bladed scissors suitable for cutting floral wire.
Floristry wire – available from 24-33 gauge from very fine to thick, coated in white, green or brown tape.
Tape – for taping wired flowers together, available in white or green plastic or paper finish.
Stamens – every colour, size and finish to choose from to suit all varieties of flowers.

CARE OF EQUIPMENT

Flower paste equipment is very specialised and expensive to buy, so great care should be taken in looking after and storing it.

All acrylic equipment should be stored in a cool place and boards particularly stored flat to prevent warping. Flower and floppy mats should be kept separately in polythene bags to prevent any scratching and to keep them spotlessly clean.

All metal and non-metal cutters should be stored in rigid containers or boxes to prevent damage or bending of the shapes, keeping them warm and dry to prevent rusting. The tools particularly should only be used for flower making. Keeping all this specialist equipment safe means it need never be replaced.

FLOWER PASTE

Flower paste is used for making very special non-edible cake decorations, simply because these specialised sugar pieces are kept as a keepsake. The paste, being very pliable and almost elastic, will mould into very fine but strong sugar pieces. Liquid glucose and gum tragacanth are available from all cake icing and decorating specialists.

225 g (8 oz) icing sugar, sifted
15 ml (1 tbsp) gum tragacanth, sieved
7.5 ml (1 rounded tsp) liquid glucose
15-30 ml (1-2 tbsp) cold water

....

1 Sift the icing sugar and gum tragacanth into a bowl. Make a well in the centre and add the liquid glucose and 15 ml (1 tbsp) water. Mix together with the fingers to form a soft paste, adding more water if necessary. Knead on a work surface dusted well with icing sugar until smooth, white and free from cracks.

2 Place in a polythene bag or wrap in cling film and seal well to exclude all the air. Leave for 2 hours before use, then re-knead. Use small pieces at a time, leaving the remaining flower paste well sealed.

3 Use a little white vegetable fat instead of icing sugar when kneading, rolling out or moulding to prevent the paste from becoming dry and brittle, and making it easier to handle. Good flower paste will make the most realistic and attractive flower decorations.
Makes 350 g (12 oz) flower paste

GUM ARABIC GLAZE

This is much better than egg white for sticking flower petals together, or sugar paste items. It dries very quickly and sets the flower paste.

15 ml (1 tbsp) gum arabic
45 ml (3 tbsp) warm water

....

1 Blend the gum arabic with the water until smooth and free from lumps.

2 Place the glaze in a tiny screw top jar or container and use when needed. Apply with a fine paint brush.

WIRED SUGAR FLOWERS

Sugar flowers are certainly fascinating – their life-like qualities are stunning. Each petal is paper thin and finely formed with stamens, calyx stems and leaves. The colours are pale or vibrant, blended to enhance their appearance.

At one time each flower had to be moulded and crafted by hand but now almost every type of flower cutter is available from cake icing specialists. This now enables anyone to cut out and make these sugar flowers by just using a few basic pieces of equipment and following a few guide lines. Once these skills have been mastered, this hobby can become quite addictive. Always study a real flower form when making them out of sugar; this is the very best visual aid to copy, not only for shape but for detail and colour.

MEXICAN HAT FLOWERS

These flowers are given this name simply because the method used to make the basic flower shape looks like a Mexican hat with a wide brim as a centre cone. Once the cone shape with the brim has been formed, any flower cutter may be used to cut out the flower. Simply place the cutter over the cone, cutting out the brim shape. With a bone modelling tool, the flower may be made extremely realistic. This type of flower can easily have wire or stamens inserted, see opposite. It is one method you can use to produce everyday flowers such as primroses, fuchsia, freesia, periwinkle.

TO MAKE MEXICAN HAT FLOWERS

1 Mould a piece of flower paste into a cone shape, press out the thick end like a brim of a hat, keeping the centre cone thin. Carefully place the flat side down on to a flower mat.

the brim to make the circle very thin with a fine cone shape in the centre. Using a shaped flower cutter, place it over the top of the cone so the cutter sits on the paste, then cut out the shape.

ridged side into the centre of the cone to form the shape of the flower. Place the cone end of the flower in the hole in the flower mat and soften each petal with a bone modelling tool. Leave upside down on foam to dry.

2 Using a thin modelling tool, lightly roll from the centre cone outwards all the way around

3 Remove the cutter, hold the cone and press a pointed modelling tool with a smooth or

4 If you are inserting wire or stamens, insert the hooked wire with the stamens dipped into a little gum arabic glaze and pull through the centre of the flower. If the flowers are very delicate, mould a tiny piece of paste around the wire hook before inserting. Leave the flower upside down to dry, then colour with coloured dust.

TO MAKE A FUCHSIA

1 Roll out a piece of paste very thinly and cut out five petal shapes using a small rose or petal shaped cutter. Brush the edges of each with gum arabic glaze and arrange them in a line, overlapping each petal slightly.

2 Loosely roll up the petals, pressing the pointed ends together to make a petal cone.

3 Take four stamens and fold them in half to make eight. Add one long stamen and wire them together using 28 gauge wire. Cover the base of the stamens with a small piece of sugar paste. Thread the stamens through the centre of the petal cone, brushing the neck of the stamens with a little gum glaze. Press the cone to fit around the wire. Hang upside down to dry for 10 minutes.

4 Shape a piece of flower paste into a cone. Make the Mexican hat shape as above. Cut out the cone shape with the fuchsia cutter. Make a cavity in the centre of the cone with the thin modelling tool.

5 Place the cone end into the hole on the flower mat, then soften and widen the petals using a bone tool. Brush the centre with gum arabic glaze and thread the stamen wire through the centre of the cone petals to fit firmly.

6 Bend each petal slightly backwards to give a realistic appearance. Hang upside down to dry, then dust the fuchsia with pink and purple coloured dusts.

> ### HINT
> These flowers are instantly recognisable by their beautiful shape and colours. Care must be taken when drying these flowers as the individually curled petals are very fragile. Fuchsias are best applied to a cake so they may hang freely.

TO MAKE A FREESIA SPRAY

1 Mould a tiny piece of paste into an elongated shape to make the closed buds. Repeat to make three more buds, each larger than the one before. Make a hole in the base of each bud, dip four stamens into gum glaze and insert one into each of the buds. Leave them to dry.

2 To make the freesia flowers, take two stamens, bend them in half and attach them to a piece of 26 gauge green wire. Secure them with florist tape and cut off the stamen ends.

3 Use a small ball of paste shaped into a cone and make the Mexican hat shape (see page 155). Place the freesia cutter over the cone and cut out the shape neatly. Using a thin modelling tool, press it into the centre of the flower to make a hollow cone shape.

4 Roll out another small piece of flower paste thinly and cut out a flat petal shape using the same cutter. Place the shapes on a flower mat with the cone shape end in the hole so the cone does not get damaged while working on the petals. Soften the edge and centre of each petal using a bone modelling tool to gently curl, enlarge and cup the petal shape.

5 Take the cone shaped petals and brush the centre with a little gum glaze. Place the remaining flat petal on top of the cone shaped petals so the petals fit in between each other.

6 Thread the prepared stamens carefully through the centre, brushing the neck of the stamens with gum arabic glaze. Pull through carefully so the wire does not show inside the freesia.

7 Bend the petals carefully and hang the flower upside down to dry. Repeat to make more individual freesia. Cut out a tiny star calyx from green flower paste and place over the end of each bud and flower.

8 To wire into a spray, use a piece of 30 gauge wire. Start with the tiniest buds and attach together on to the end of the wire with tape. Add the remaining buds, positioning them apart and securing them as the tape is twisted down the stem. Continue adding the flowers, bending the wire to its natural shape.

TO WIRE PLUNGER BLOSSOMS INTO SPRAYS

1 To make blossom plunger flowers (see page 88) into sprays, for each you will need about a 10 cm (4 inch) length of 28-30 gauge florist wire and tape. It balances well to make the sprays up of three large blossoms, four medium blossoms or five small ones. They may be mixed, wiring the small blossoms at the end of the spray with the medium and large blossoms mixed in.

2 Make a hook at the end of the wire, place the stamen through the hook and squeeze together to secure. Attach the tape just next to the back of the blossom and twist in the fingers to cover about 1 cm (½ inch) of the wire and the stamen. Attach another blossom and continue to wrap the tape around the stems to join the blossoms securely together. When you have added the number of blossoms required, continue to wrap the tape around the remaining stem to neaten.

3 Make as many assorted sprays of blossom flowers as required. Store them in a dry, warm place in a box in between tissue paper until required. These fine sprays of blossom are good for filling in flower sprays and arrangements.

CUT-OUT SUGAR FLOWERS

These flowers may be made with the use of a cutter which cuts out the complete flower instead of the individual petal shape. This makes cut-out flowers very simple and quick to make.

The cutters are available from all cake icing specialist shops and come in a variety of shapes and sizes. The most popular flowers are daisy, sweet pea, buttercups, roses, bluebell and Doris pink.

All these flowers are made with flower paste so the petals are paper thin and look so delicate. Leaf cutters and calyx cutters may also be purchased to match the particular flowers. Flower paste and food colouring, 26-28 gauge wire and florist tape are all needed to make these flowers. However, the flowers may also be made without the addition of wires so they may be applied directly to the cake.

TO MAKE A DAISY

1 Using an acrylic rolling pin and board, roll out some white flower paste thinly using a little white fat if necessary. Cut out the shape using a daisy cutter. Use a modelling knife to cut each petal in half to double the number of petals. Ensure the daisy moves freely and, using a cocktail stick, frill all the petals. Place the daisy on a piece of foam. Press the centre with a bone tool to cup the daisy.

2 Using a piece of 26 gauge wire, make a hook at the end. Dip the end in gum glaze and cover the hook with a small bead of yellow flower paste. Dip into gum glaze and yellow pollen dust.

3 Thread the yellow centre through the middle of the daisy and brush the underside with gum glaze. Attach the centre to the daisy. Using the cutter provided, cut out the calyx from thinly rolled green flower paste. Thread on to the back of the daisy and secure with gum glaze. When the daisy is dry, dust lightly around the base of the petals with moss green coloured dust.

TO MAKE A SWEET PEA

1 Using 26 gauge green wire, hook the end and dip into gum glaze. Cover with a tiny piece of flower paste. Shape the centre with a flat back and a sharp front to match the length of the centre of the small cutter. Leave to dry. Make several centre pieces.

2 Using an acrylic rolling pin and board and a little white fat if necessary, roll out a piece of paste thinly and cut out a petal using the small round cutter. Soften the edges on a flower mat using a bone tool. Brush the back of the wired centre with a little gum glaze, fold the petal around the centre and press together to form a flat, semi-circular petal shape.

3 Cut out a second petal using the medium-sized cutter. Place on the flower mat and soften the edges like the previous petal. Cup each side with a modelling tool and attach to the previous petal with a little gum glaze so that it looks like a butterfly. Cut a larger petal, soften the edges, mark the veins with a modelling tool and attach with gum glaze.

HINT
Twist a thin piece of green tape around a needle to make a spiral. Slide the spiral off the needle and attach to the wire stem to make 'tendrils', twisting to secure.

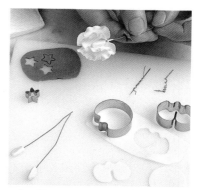

4 Cut out a green calyx using a sweet pea calyx cutter and moss green flower paste. Thread the wire through and attach to the sweet pea with gum glaze. Hook the end and hang upside down to dry.

TO MAKE A DORIS PINK

1. Make a hook at the end of a piece of 26 gauge wire, tape the end of the hook with green florist tape and continue to cover the stem.

2. Roll out a piece of coloured paste thinly on an acrylic board. Cut out the shape using a Doris pink cutter. Using a cocktail stick, frill the edge, turning the paste while working and applying lots of pressure to obtain the very fine edge.

3. Carefully place the wire through the centre of the petal. Very lightly brush half the circle with gum glaze and fold up to make a semi-circle. Brush half the petal again with gum glaze and fold over the right-hand third. Turn the petal over and repeat on the other side. Press the neck of the petal very gently on to the wire, hook the end and hang up to dry.

4. Cut and frill two more petals. Brush the centre of each with gum glaze and thread them separately on to the wire so that they fall into a natural shape. Gently press the bases and leaves to dry upside down.

TO MAKE A FLOWER CALYX

1. There are three sizes of calyx cutters, so just match the sizes to the size of the flower you are making. Sometimes small blossom cutters are more suitable for calyx on the back of tiny flowers, or the star cutter included in the sweet pea set is often used.

2. Thinly roll out moss green flower paste. Cut out the calyx shapes. Soften the edges with a bone tool on a flower mat. Thread the calyx on to the back of the flower, secured with a little gum glaze.

TO WIRE LEAVES

1. Using moss green flower paste, roll out very thinly from each side of the centre, leaving a thick centre ridge. Place the leaf cutter so that the ridge runs down the centre of the back of the leaf, then cut out the shape.

2. Make a vein impression on the front of the flower paste leaf by using a real leaf or a veiner. Dip the end of a 7.5 cm (3 inch) piece of 28 gauge green wire into gum glaze and insert into the ridge on the back of the leaf.

3. Bend the leaf to soften the edges and leave to dry. Brush with coloured dust to give the leaf a realistic look.

FLOWER PASTE PLAQUE OR CARD

As flower paste is so strong and dries so hard, it can often be mistaken for fine porcelain. Rolling out the paste finely and cutting very accurately, the paste can be made into fine plaques, cards, boxes and shaped items. Plaque cutters are useful. They may be purchased from a cake specialist shop; they are available in many different shapes and sizes.

All the sugarcraft skills can be combined to make the finished flower paste plaque. Once the shape has been established and cut out, the edges may be frilled, crimped, piped with embroidery or worked as a cut-out edging. Once the shape has been cut, it must not be moved until it is dry or it could distort the overall shape.

The plaque can then be designed to include hand-made sugar flowers, small run-out pieces, appliquéd work or hand painted. Inscriptions may be written, or even modelled items included. Once the plaque has been completed and dried, it can sit on the centre of a cake as the main decoration; otherwise it may be used as a gift and packaged in a pretty box.

TO MAKE A FLOWER PASTE PLAQUE

1 Using an acrylic rolling pin and board, roll out the flower paste thinly dusting with cornflour to enable the shape to move easily. Roll out the plaque shape on the surface on which it is to be dried.

2 To cut out the shape, use a plaque cutter. Alternatively, use a knife to cut out squares or rectangles, or use round and oval cutters. Always cut the shape out cleanly using cornflour to dip the cutter or knife into. Never stretch or pull the shape.

3 Choose the finish required for the edge of the plaque – leave it plain and smooth the edges with the fingers, or crimp a design around the edge. Use a cocktail stick to frill the edge or cut out a broderie anglaise design. Allow the plaque to dry in a warm place for at least 12 hours.

4 Plan the design for the plaque and decide how you are going to decorate it. Make all the items such as flowers, ribbon loops, run-out pieces or pencil out painting designs. Arrange all the items as they are to go on to the plaque, then attach with icing.

WIRING A FLOWER SPRAY

This type of decoration can be invaluable for a last-minute decoration to transform a plain cake.

All the flowers may be made in stages as and when you feel like making them, then stored in rigid boxes. They will last like this for ever if they are kept dry; the slightest form of moisture will cause the petals to soften and collapse.

Make a selection of flowers in shades of colour which will set the scene for the type of cake you are making. Make blooms which sit well together. Remember roses, freesia and carnations are lovely but you must have sprays of small blossoms and ribbons to infill. All arrangements look much better if they are open and loose with a feeling of freedom.

TO WIRE A FLOWER SPRAY

1 Once all the flowers, leaves, blossoms and ribbons are made and wired, arrange them together loosely into the size and shape of the arrangement you require.

2 Take a piece of 30 gauge wire and make a small loop at the end. Attach the first flower within the loop and start to wrap the tape around the top just under the head of the flower to secure. Twist the tape to cover one quarter of the flower stem and the wire. Add the next flower underneath the first and continue to cover with the tape twisting down the stem to secure.

3 Continue in this way adding leaves, flowers and ribbon loops, making sure they all sit on top of the wire stem and not underneath, to make the shape. Bend the stems just underneath the flower heads using only tweezers, otherwise the flowers will break. Use wire cutting scissors to cut away the excess wire stems, but not the main stem.

4 Once all the flowers have been wired together, finish covering the stem with tape to make a neat end. Bend the end of the arrangement into a coil or a loop. Do ensure all the arrangement sits flat on the surface and the spine is flat. Bend the blossom sprays and flowers at various angles.

HARVEST CAKE

*W*heat fields and blackberries all indicate the end of
the summer and the start of harvest. This cake will
appeal to the artist; if you do not feel confident to apply
the design directly to the cake, make a flower and sugar
paste plaque first.

20.5 cm (8 inch) round rich fruit
cake mixture (see page 64)

25.5 cm (10 inch) round silver
cake board

45 ml (3 tbsp) apricot glaze (see
page 70)

700 g (1½ lb) white marzipan

700 g (1½ lb) champagne sugar
paste

1 quantity flower paste (see page
154)

12.5 cm (5 inch) thin round silver
cake board

old gold, purple and green food
colourings

gum arabic glaze (see page 154)

green, violet and beige food
colouring dusts

black food colouring pen

26 gauge floral wire

1 metre (1 yard), 1 cm (½ inch)
wide purple ribbon

1 metre (1 yard), 1 cm (½ inch)
wide green ribbon

1 metre (1 yard), 2 cm (¾ inch)
wide cream ribbon

1 metre (1 yard), 5 mm (¼ inch)
wide purple ribbon

1 Prepare a 20.5 cm (8 inch)
round cake tin (see page 11).
Make the rich fruit cake mixture
and place in the tin. Bake
according to the cake chart on
page 66. Place the cake at the back
edge of the cake board and brush
with apricot glaze. Cover the cake
smoothly with marzipan (see page
73). Place the cake in a cardboard
cake box in a warm dry place
overnight. Cover the cake and cake
board smoothly with sugar paste
following the instructions on page
82. Knead the trimmings together.
Store the cake in the cake box to
dry.

2 Make the flower paste and
colour one-third champagne
with a few drops of old gold food
colouring. Thinly roll out a piece
and place over the thin cake board
dusted with cornflour. Cut around
the edge of the board to remove
the excess flower paste. Knead the
trimmings together and return
them to the polythene bag. Using a
small pair of crimpers, crimp the
edge of the plaque. Leave in a
warm place to dry completely.

3 Colour the remaining flower
paste a quarter purple and a
quarter green using the food
colourings. Make 11 green leaves,
using a rose leaf cutter or a real
blackberry leaf. Insert flower wire
into several leaves following the
instructions on page 158.

4 Make five stems of wheat by
rolling thin tube pieces of
white flower paste 5 cm (2 inches)
in length. Cut five pieces of wire
half the size of the sugar paste.
Bend over the top and cover the
hook shape with a bead of flower
paste. Dip the end into gum glaze
and insert into the tubes of flower
paste. Using a small pair of
scissors, snip the paste from side
to side from the base to the top to
form the top of the wheat. Leave to
dry.

5 Make the seven blackberries by moulding seven tiny balls of white paste about the size of a pea. Bend the tops of seven pieces of wire. Dip the end into gum glaze and insert each into the balls of paste. Shape lots of tiny beads from the purple flower paste. Brush one wired ball at a time with gum glaze and cover with beads of paste. Repeat to complete seven blackberries. Cut out three white blossom shapes using a large blossom plunger cutter and wire each separately (see page 156).

6 Using a small star cutter, cut out seven shapes of green flower paste and thread into the blackberries. Press in position and secure with gum glaze. Brush the stems and leaves with gum glaze and green dust, the blackberries with gum glaze and violet dust, the calyx and stems green, and the wheat and stems with beige dust.

7 Using a fine pencil or black food colouring pen, lightly sketch the design on to the plaque. If you make a mistake, use a damp cotton bud very lightly to clean the surface. Sprinkle a little of each coloured dust on to a palette using a fine paint brush and glaze, complete one colour at a time – dipping the brush into the gum glaze then into the colourings. Clean the brush in water before using the next colour. Paint the surface design following the outlines; add more depth of colour with extra dust and less glaze. Allow the design to dry.

8 Measure and fit the purple and green ribbons around the base of the cake and cream and remaining narrow purple ribbon around the cake board.

9 Place the plaque in the centre of the cake and raise it with a small piece of flower paste.

10 Press a small piece of flower paste at the base of the cake and insert five blackberries, wheat, flowers, wired and unwired leaves to make an arrangement. Secure a small piece of flower paste at the base of the plaque and arrange the remaining blackberries, flowers and leaves. Use tweezers to bend the wires so the sugar items do not get broken. Keep in a cake box until required.

HINT
Use food colouring pens to colour in the design if you prefer. To give the blackberries and leaves a sheen, quickly pass each piece through steam from the spout of a boiling kettle.

WOODLAND CAKE

Spring flowers all made from flower paste look so
realistic standing up in a woodland arrangement.
There is no need for other decorations, just a simple
shaped cake covered with sugar paste and tinted with
food colouring dust.

20.5 cm (8 inch) square rich or
light fruit cake mixture (see page
64 or 67)

25.5 cm (10 inch) square silver
cake board

45 ml (3 tbsp) apricot glaze (see
page 70)

700 g (1½ lb) white marzipan

700 g (1½ lb) white sugar paste

1 quantity flower paste (see page
154)

yellow, blue, violet and green food
colourings

28 gauge green coloured floral
wire

gum arabic glaze (see page 154)

yellow, thrift pink, brown and
moss green food colouring dusts

green stemtex floral tape

pale green pollen dust

cream stamens

1 metre (1 yard), 1 cm (½ inch)
wide blue ribbon

1 metre (1 yard), 1 cm (½ inch)
wide green ribbon

1.5 metres (1½ yards), 2 cm (¾
inch) wide green ribbon

....

1 Prepare a 20.5 cm (8 inch)
square cake tin (see page 11).
Make the rich or light fruit cake
mixture and place in the tin. Bake
according to the cake chart on
page 66 or 68. Place the cake in
the centre of the cake board and
brush with apricot glaze. Cover the
cake smoothly with marzipan (see
page 73). Place the cake in a
cardboard cake box in a warm dry

place overnight. Cover the cake
and cake board smoothly with
sugar paste following the
instructions on page 82. Knead the
trimmings together and reserve.

2 Divide the flower paste into
four pieces, colour one piece
pale yellow, one piece bluebell blue
and another piece moss green,
using the yellow, blue and violet,
and green food colourings.

3 Make 15 primroses using the
yellow flower paste, following
the instructions to make Mexican
hat flowers on page 155. Use a
primrose cutter to cut out the
shape, soften the petals on a flower
mat using a bone tool. Mark the
centres using a serrated cone tool.
Cut a piece of wire 10 cm (4
inches) in length and bend the top
over. Dip this hook end into the
gum glaze. Thread the wire
through the centre of the primrose
and pull to the base of the flower.
Stick the flowers in a piece of
polystyrene to dry upright or
upside down on a piece of foam
sponge. Brush the centres with
yellow food colouring dust. Repeat
to make another 14 flowers.

4 Make 11 wood anemones
using the white flower paste.
Roll out a small piece very thinly
until you can almost see through
it. Using a wood anemone cutter,
cut out six petal shapes. Place the
petals on a flower mat, soften and
cup the petals with a bone tool.

5 Cut a piece of wire 10 cm
(4 inches) in length and bend
over the top. Dip the hooked end
into the gum glaze and secure a
small piece of white flower paste
on the end to cover the hook.
Press the top flat, brush with gum

glaze and dip into the green pollen dust. Arrange the flower petals in a circle and secure each with gum glaze, just overlapping the base of each petal. Take the wired bead of white flower paste and thread through the centre of the flower and secure with gum glaze. Leave the flower to dry in the polystyrene. Repeat to make another ten anemones. When the flowers are dry, brush the back and edges of the petals with thrift pink food colouring dust.

6   Make six stems of bluebells, using the blue and violet food colourings, following the instructions for making Mexican hat flowers (see page 155). Make the centre cone very thin to ensure the cutter fits over the top with just a short brim. Using a bluebell cutter, cut out the petal shape. Press a thin acrylic skewer into the centre to make the bell shape, soften and curl the petals on a flower mat using a bone tool. Make a hole at the end of the cone with a scribing needle. Dip a cream stamen into the gum glaze and insert into the bluebell, pulling it carefully to the end of the cone shape. Leave upside down to dry and repeat to make another 17 bell shapes with stamens. Shape 15 tiny bud shapes and insert a stamen dipped in gum glaze into each. Leave to dry.

7   Using a piece of wire, bend over the top and secure a bluebell bud in position. Take a piece of green tape and twist around the wire and the stamen to secure. Attach another two buds. Wind the tape 5 mm (¼ inch) down the wire and secure a bluebell, twisting the tape around the stamen and the wire stem. Repeat to attach three bells to the stem. Neaten the stem with the tape. Stick in polystyrene to dry. Make another four.

8   Using the green flower paste and wire, make the wood anemone leaves, using the appropriate two cutters provided. The leaves are made up of three or five leaf shapes and need to be wired together to form a spray when they are dry. Make the leaves for the primroses using real leaves or a cutter and a veiner. Dry them over a piece of dowel to give a realistic appearance. Bluebell leaves are very long and thin, so cut out these free hand, using

thicker flower paste. Insert the wire at the base and bend to dry. Brush the leaves with a mixture of brown and moss green food colouring dusts.

9   Using the reserved trimmings, shape a mound of sugar paste and position in the centre of the cake. Brush with green food colouring dust and extend the colour over the top of the cake. Arrange the flowers in the sugar paste, cutting the wire stems as required and bending the stems with a pair of tweezers to prevent breaking the flowers. Start with the leaves and wood anemones, then the bluebells. Infill with primroses and leaves.

10   Measure the blue and green ribbons to fit around the base of the cake and the wide green ribbon around the cake board. Secure with stainless steel pins. Leave the cake in the cake box to dry.

> **HINT**
> To give the flowers a natural sheen, pass the flowers and leaves quickly through the steam from the spout of a boiling kettle. Leave to dry before arranging them.

BUTTERCUPS AND DAISIES

*B**uttercups and daisies give this cake a summery feel
and would be suitable for an anniversary,
birthday, wedding or summer celebration. Make the
flowers ahead of time.*

20.5 cm (8 inch) round rich fruit
  cake mixture (see page 64)

25.5 cm (10 inch) trefoil shaped
  silver cake board

60 ml (4 tbsp) apricot glaze (see
  page 70)

700 g (1½ lb) white marzipan

700 g (1½ lb) champagne coloured
  sugar paste

1 quantity flower paste (see page
  154)

yellow and green food colourings

28 gauge green covered floral wire

yellow pollen dust

yellow and green food colouring
  dusts

30 ml (2 tbsp) royal icing (see
  page 108)

1 metre (1 yard), 2 cm (¾ inch)
  wide champagne ribbon

2 metres (2 yards), 3 mm (⅛
  inch) wide yellow ribbon

....

1 Prepare a 20.5 cm (8 inch)
   trefoil shaped cake tin (see
page 11). Make the rich fruit cake
mixture and place in the tin. Bake
according to the cake chart on
page 66. Place the cake in the
centre of the cake board and brush
with apricot glaze. Cover the cake
smoothly with marzipan (see page
73). Leave in a cake box overnight.

2 Cover the cake and the cake
   board smoothly with sugar
paste following the instructions on
page 82, then leave to dry. Make
the flower paste and colour one-
third yellow and one-third green
using yellow and green colourings.

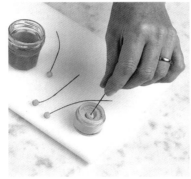

3 Make 12 buttercups using
   yellow and green flower paste
and a set of buttercup cutters. Cut
a 10 cm (4 inch) length of wire and
hook the end. Dip the end into
gum glaze and mould a round of
yellow paste on to the end. Brush
with gum glaze and dip into yellow
pollen dust. Roll out a small piece
of green paste very thinly and cut
out a calyx using the cutter
provided. Place on a piece of foam
sponge.

4 Roll out a small piece of
   yellow paste very thinly and
cut out five buttercup petals, using
the petal shaped cutter. Place the

petals on a flower pad, soften and
cup the petals using a bone tool.
Brush the centre of the calyx with
gum glaze and position each petal,
so they all meet neatly and press
into the centre of the calyx using a
bone tool.

5 Take the centre bead of
   flower paste on the wire and
brush the underneath with gum
glaze. Place in the centre of the
buttercup, pulling the wire gently
through. Leave to dry. Dust the
centre and the petals with yellow
food colouring dust; gold lustre
may be used to give a sheen to the
petals. Make another five wired
buttercups and make nine unwired
buttercups. Make nine unwired
daisies and ten wired daisies, using
white, green and yellow flower
paste, following the instructions on
page 157. Leave to dry. Using the
remaining green flower paste, roll
out thinly and cut out three
buttercup leaves and 12 daisy
leaves, using the cutters provided
in the set. Dust with green food
colouring dust.

6 Arrange a chain of unwired buttercups, daisies and daisy leaves around the side of the cake, securing with royal icing.

7 Measure and fit both ribbons around the cake board. Secure with stainless steel pins. Tie three tiny bows and secure to the cake board at each scalloped shape. Arrange three small posies using two daisies and one buttercup, tied together with yellow ribbon. Position on each side of the cake, pressing into the sugar paste on the board. Arrange the remaining daisies and buttercups into a posy and tie with ribbon. Place on top of the cake with the buttercup leaves. Store the cake in the cake box.

HINT
These tiny buttercups and daisies are very pretty but time-consuming to make. Allow plenty of time to make wired and unwired flowers, making them over a period of time instead of all together. They store well in a dry warm place.

FLORAL CASCADE

T̲his pretty arrangement of fuchsias, freesias, pinks and sweet peas is all that is needed to decorate this fluted domed cake. Tiny beads of royal icing are piped all over the white sugar paste.

---

18 cm (7 inch) round rich fruit cake mixture (see page 64)

20.5 cm (8 inch) scalloped silver cake board

45 ml (3 tbsp) apricot glaze (see page 70)

550 g (1¼ lb) white marzipan

550 g (1¼ lb) white sugar paste

½ quantity royal icing (see page 108)

1 quantity flower paste (see page 154)

pink, green and purple food colourings

fuchsia pink, pearl pink and purple food colouring dusts

28 gauge green covered floral wire

pink stamens

1 metre (1 yard), 2 cm (¾ inch) wide deep pink ribbon

1 metre (1 yard), 1 cm (½ inch) wide pink ribbon

0.5 metre (½ yard), 3 mm (⅛ inch) wide pink ribbon

....

1 Grease and base line an 18 cm (7 inch), 2 litre (3 pint) fluted mould. Make the rich fruit cake mixture and place in the tin. Bake according to the cake chart on page 66. Place the cake in the centre of the cake board and brush with apricot glaze. Cover smoothly with marzipan (see page 73). Place in a cardboard cake box in a warm dry place overnight.

2 Cover the cake smoothly with sugar paste, following the instructions on page 82. Measure and fit the 1 cm (½ inch) wide ribbon around the base of the cake and the 2 cm (¾ inch) ribbon around the cake board. Secure with stainless steel pins. Tie six tiny bows from the narrow ribbon and secure with stainless steel pins around the board.

3 Fit a greaseproof paper piping bag with a No. 1 plain writing nozzle, half-fill with royal icing and pipe groups of three beads of icing all over the cake and cake board. Leave the icing to dry thoroughly.

4 Make the flower paste and colour one-quarter pale pink, one-quarter green and one-quarter purple with pink, green and purple food colourings. Make two white and four pink and purple fuchsias using the white, pink, purple and green flower paste, stamens and wire, following the instructions on page 155. Dust the coloured fuchsia petals with fuchsia pink and purple food colouring dusts. Lightly dust the white fuchsias with pink dust. Using the pink and green flower paste and wire, make seven Doris pinks (see page 158). Make six sweet peas using white and green flower paste and wire (see page 157). Dust the sweet pea petals with pearl pink dust when dry.

5 Using the remaining pink flower paste, make two freesia sprays and two open blossoms (see page 156). Arrange the flowers on the work surface. Wire and tape them together (see page 159).

6 Using a pair of tweezers, bend the spray to fit.

FLOWERS

*F*resh *flowers seem to be the most obvious choice for decorating a beautifully iced cake. They offer all the assets: colour, shape, size, natural charm and appearance, and look so perfect positioned at the last minute. They can also be preserved by sugar frosting. Good silk flowers also make an attractive decoration.*

*W*ith the minimum amount of fuss, a cake may be completed in a matter of minutes using fresh flowers. Simply choose various blooms for shape, size and mutual colourings, tie them into sprays with pretty ribbons, or style in a more formal arrangement.

Small sprays of fresh flowers or posies are often requested for wedding cakes to match the bridal bouquets. These may be ordered through the florist, but with time and patience these pretty arrangements can be made at home. Choose small firm flowers such as freesia, Doris pinks, rose buds, tiny orchids, gypsophilia and miniature daisies. Use florist wire and tape if the flower arrangement needs to form a definite shape. The individual flowers will need to be wired so they can be arranged together before being secured with more wire and tape.

Ribbons also play an important part in making sprays and posies, and offer pretty shades of colour and texture (see page 176). Ribbon loops look so pretty wired into fresh flower arrangements. Loops may be formed as single, double or treble loops with or without tails.

TO SUGAR-FROST FLOWERS AND LEAVES

1 egg white, lightly beaten
caster sugar

....

1 Cover a wire rack with absorbent kitchen paper and insert a skewer to make plenty of holes for the stems to go through.

2 Dry the flowers and leaves with absorbent kitchen paper only if necessary, and leave a small stem intact if possible. Place the egg white in a bowl and the sugar on a plate or in a bowl. Using a fine paint brush, paint both sides of the flower petals, leaves and the stems with egg white.

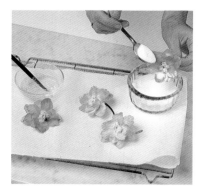

3 Spoon the sugar over the flower petals and leaves to coat evenly on both sides. Carefully shake to remove the excess sugar.

4 Place the flower stems through the paper on the wire rack in a warm, dry place until the sugar has set and is dry. To help keep their shape, some trumpet shaped flowers are better dried with their stems upwards and the petals flat on the paper. Once they have been coated with sugar, see how the petals fall into place as this is the best indication of how they will dry.

5 When the flowers are completely dry, store them separately on absorbent kitchen paper in a cardboard box, taking care not to damage them. When the flowers are required, carefully arrange them on the cake; only secure them with royal icing if necessary.

Fresh flowers make a simple yet beautiful adornment to a cake. Choose various blooms for shape, size and mutual colourings. They can be tied with ribbons or wired and taped for more formal arrangements.

SUGAR-FROSTED FLOWERS

These are even better to use as the fresh flowers of your choice are preserved by egg white and sugar. Once they are completely dry, they will last for several weeks. Teamed with fine coloured ribbons tied into pretty bows, loops and tails, sugar frosted flowers are ideal for decorating a cake for almost any occasion.

Choose fresh, simple, small flowers with fairly flat petals such as violets, primroses, tiny daffodils, delphiniums and freesia. Choose firm herb leaves or fruit leaves. If possible, pick or buy the flowers and leaves freshly just before you need to frost them. Ensure they are young blooms and not wilting.

The individual fresh flowers may also be wired and taped before frosting. Once they have been frosted and dried, they can then be formed into spray arrangements or posies, which gives extra time for assembling the cake on the day. To store

these flowers it is essential not to crush them in any way. If they are placed on a wire rack in a box in a warm dry place, this will ensure that they keep their shape. A posy or arrangement should be supported in a small vase. Always keep sugar-frosted flowers out of a damp atmosphere in a dry place to prevent spoiling.

SILK FLOWERS

Carefully selected and arranged, good silk flowers can look most elegant as an instant decoration on a celebration cake. They are available from cake decorating specialists, departmental stores and florists in a wide selection of blooms, offering vibrant colours and shapes. Teamed with ribbons of matching colour tones, they make instant re-usable decorations. Ensure that the silk flowers are arranged and secured together so they may be removed from the cake.

FLOWER SPRAY CAKE

A beautifully arranged fresh spray of flowers not only enhances a celebration cake but also produces such an instant decoration.

20.5 cm (8 inch) round rich fruit
cake mixture (see page 64)
25.5 cm (10 inch) round silver
cake board
45 ml (3 tbsp) apricot glaze (see
page 70)
700 g (1½ lb) white marzipan
900 g (2 lb) peach coloured sugar
paste
28 gauge floral wire
green florist tape
2 metres (2 yards), 5 mm (¼
inch) wide amber ribbon
1 metre (1 yard), 5 mm (¼ inch)
wide pale peach ribbon
1 metre (1 yard), 2 cm (¾ inch)
wide pale peach ribbon
fresh flowers to decorate

....

1 Prepare a 20.5 cm (8 inch) round cake tin (see page 11). Make the rich fruit cake mixture and place in the tin. Bake according to the cake chart on page 66. Place the cake in the centre of the cake board and brush with apricot glaze. Cover smoothly with marzipan (see page 73). Place the cake in a cardboard cake box in a warm dry place overnight. Cover the cake and cake board smoothly using about two-thirds of the sugar paste (see page 82). Place the cake in the cake box in a warm dry place until required.

2 Select the fresh flowers on the day the cake is required or the day before; choose fresh firm blooms, which have not opened fully.

3 Cut the stems off each flower, leaving 1 cm (½ inch) at the top. Insert a 10 cm (4 inch) piece of 28 gauge wire into the neck of the flower, bend over the top. Twist the wire and the stem. Take a piece of green tape and secure underneath the head of the flower. Twist to cover the wire. Repeat to wire all the flowers required.

4 Arrange the flowers loosely into the shape required. Using a piece of wire, make a hook and attach the neck of the first flower. Attach the tape and twist, securing the flower to the wire. Repeat adding the flowers and

taping; cut away the stems if too many are together at a time making the main stem too thick.

5 Finish the stems with tape, trim to neaten and bend the end into a coil or loop. Sit the flowers in a shallow dish of water until needed. Drain them well on a tea towel before using.

6 If an informal arrangement is required, simply tape the ends of each flower to keep the moisture in, then arrange together and loosely tie with the narrow ribbons. Position the flowers in the centre of the cake adding a few ribbon tails if desired. Alternatively, arrange the chosen flowers in a small piece of oasis contained in a plastic container to hold the water so the flowers will last longer. Band the base of the cake with narrow amber ribbon. Measure and fit the wider pale peach and narrow amber ribbon around the cake board, securing with stainless steel pins.

SUGAR-FROSTED HEART

T his stunning cake is so simple to make. Simply cover the cake with marbled sugar paste and colour match fresh sugar-frosted flowers to add the finishing touches.

20.5 cm (8 inch) round rich fruit cake mixture (see page 64)

25.5 cm (10 inch) heart-shaped silver cake board

45 ml (3 tbsp) apricot glaze (see page 70)

700 g (1½ lb) white marzipan

700 g (1½ lb) white sugar paste blue food colouring

1 metre (1 yard), 2 cm (¾ inch) wide blue ribbon

1 metre (1 yard), 1 cm (½ inch) wide mauve ribbon

fresh flowers to sugar frost (see Hint)

1 egg white

caster sugar

....

HINT
The soft marble effect of this sugar paste may be made in any colour and in a number of shades. Ensure you have the flower colours available before covering the cake with sugar paste to avoid disappointment.

1 Prepare a 20.5 cm (8 inch) heart-shaped tin. Make the rich fruit cake mixture and place in the tin. Bake according to the cake chart on page 66. Place the cake in the centre of the cake board and brush with apricot glaze. Cover the cake smoothly with marzipan following the instructions on page 73. Place the cake in a cardboard cake box in a warm dry place overnight.

2 To marble the sugar paste, colour one third of the sugar paste blue. Divide the white and blue sugar paste each into three pieces. Press alternate coloured pieces together and knead the sugar paste lightly into a ball. Roll out thinly revealing the marbled pattern. If the pattern looks too uneven, fold the sugar paste over, then in half again and roll out.

3 Cover the cake and the cake board smoothly, positioning the sugar paste over the cake to incorporate the best pattern on the top edges and side of the cake, following the instructions on page 82. Place the cake in the cardboard cake box until required.

4 Measure and fit the blue and mauve ribbons around the cake board, securing with stainless steel pins.

5 To sugar-frost the flowers, follow the instructions on page 170, then allow the flowers to dry.

6 On a work surface, arrange the flowers in an attractive arrangement. Transfer the flowers, one by one, to the top of the cake just before the cake is required. Keep the cake in a dry atmosphere.

RIBBONS

R ibbons are invaluable when decorating any type of celebration or everyday cake. It is the one non-edible decoration which transforms the simplest cake into something quite special.

There are many types of ribbons to choose from, and cake specialist shops have a wide variety of widths, colours and textures suitable for all types of cake. There are over 100 colours available in ribbons ranging from 2 mm to 7.5 cm ($\frac{1}{16}$ inch to 3 inch) widths in plain and fancy edges. All these ribbons may be incorporated in many cake designs, adding colour and texture.

If you are planning a very special cake, there are ribbon shops which specialise in many beautiful designs and textures. They are expensive but occasionally it is just the finishing touch the cake needs.

The most popular ribbon is the double-faced polyester satin and is used to make bows, loops and tails for cake decorations and flower sprays. It is also used to band the edge of cake boards and to fit around the sides of cakes to match the cake colour.

Velvet, nylon, paper and synthetic fabric ribbons found in gift wrap departments and florists can also be used to give a different effect. These ribbons look pretty around cake boards or used for posies and sprays, or shaped and tied into bows and loops.

Ribbons may be used to make simple designs or collages to decorate a cake. Cut the ribbons to different shapes and sizes to form the picture or pattern and apply them directly to the cake. Paint in the ends with royal icing to fix the ribbons to the cake surface. Use ribbons of different textures, widths and colours to make pictures and designs.

Ribbons insertion is another way of using ribbon to decorate a cake. Short lengths of ribbon inserted at regular intervals into the surface of a cake freshly covered with sugar paste gives the illusion of a single piece of ribbon threaded through the icing. Different textures, widths and lengths of ribbon may be used to give this effect, and finished with bows or piping, makes a stunning decoration.

RIBBON BOWS

These are best made from the finer ribbons to produce tiny well shaped bows which may be attached to the side or top of the cake to trim a border design or edging. They may be teamed with the ribbons used to band the cake board or side of the cake, in matching colours or contrasting shades.

Double bows may be tied using two colours or the same colour to give a little more impact. Cut the ends at an angle to neaten or cut into 'V' shapes.

Ribbons may also be made with long tail ends which may be curled by pulling the ends over a pair of scissors. This encourages the ends to softly curl and trail which looks so pretty cascading over the edge of a cake.

RIBBON LOOPS

These look so pretty wired into fresh or sugar flower arrangements, especially if the colours tone to match the flowers. Loops may be formed as single, double or treble loops with or without tails.

When making ribbon loops the ends of the ribbon must all face in the same direction and the loops must be even in size. Secure the base of the loops with a small piece of fine wire and neaten with a piece of tape. To make ribbon loops with tails, after bending the size and number of loops required, make one or two loops twice the length. Wire the bases securely and cut the large loops in half to make the tails. Curl the ends over a pair of scissors. Use these loops and tails for filling in flower arrangements.

TULLE

This has many uses in cake decorating: use finely frilled as an edging to a cake or cut-out into designs and finely piped to form delicate decorations. Bridal tulle or veiling is the best type to use as it is soft and fine, not like nylon netting which is coarse and stiff.

Copy lace designs on to the edge of tulle to trim a wedding cake. Piped with a very fine writing nozzle, very delicate and effective designs may be achieved.

Tulle extension work looks so dainty around a cake, fitting scallop shaped pieces of tulle over-piped with cornelli work or fine piping to the cake.

Other decorations may be formed out of tulle; cut out butterfly wings and lace pieces. When the icing is dry, apply the pieces and pipe in the detail.

RIBBONS AND LOOPS

*T*ake any shade of ribbon, different textures, designs
and widths and apply them to a plain iced cake.
This gives an eye-catching instant decoration with the
minimum of fuss.

20.5 cm (8 inch) round rich fruit
cake mixture (see page 64)

25.5 cm (10 inch) oval silver cake
board

45 ml (3 tbsp) apricot glaze (see
page 70)

700 g (1½ lb) white marzipan

700 g (1½ lb) champagne coloured
sugar paste

1 metre (1 yard), 2 cm (¾ inch)
wide pink ribbon

2 metres (2 yards), 7.5 cm (3
inch) wide fancy green and pink
ribbon

....

HINT
To vary the design of this cake,
the edges may be patterned with
a crimping tool. Team different
shades of ribbons together of
varying widths and apply the
ribbons to make your own
designs.

1 Prepare a 20.5 cm (8 inch)
oval cake tin (see page 11).
Make the rich fruit cake mixture
and place in the tin. Bake
according to the cake chart on
page 66. Place the cake in the
centre of the cake board and brush
with apricot glaze. Cover smoothly
with marzipan (see page 73). Place
in a cardboard cake box overnight
in a warm dry place.

2 Cover the cake and cake
board smoothly with sugar
paste following the instructions on
page 82. Knead the trimmings
together. Place the cake in the
cake box to dry.

3 Measure and fit the narrow
pink ribbon around the cake
board and secure with a stainless
steel pin.

4 Measure a length of green
and pink ribbon to go around
the base of the cake. Fold the
ribbon in half and fit the ribbon
around the base. Secure with a
stainless steel pin.

5 Fold the end of the ribbon
into five loops. Cut off the
remaining ribbon and turn the end
piece under. Secure the loops with
a stainless steel pin.

6 Fold the remaining length of
ribbon in half and cut off the
ends at an angle to neaten. Arrange
the ribbon loops and tails on the
top of the cake. Secure with a
stainless steel pin.

7 Store the cake in a
cardboard cake box until
required.

NOVELTY CAKES

NOVELTY CAKES

*N*ovelty cakes are all about having fun! They should
be easy to make and delicious to eat – the highlight
of a party. Simple, graphic designs are effective, light on
icings and requiring the minimum amount of work – the
result is a temptingly edible cake.

*V*ictoria sandwich and one stage quick mix cake (see pages 20 and 21) make the most suitable bases for novelty cakes. Their firm texture is best for cutting and shaping. The traditionally made Victoria sandwich is light but the quick mix cake tends to be firmer and is ideal for cakes such as the Toadstool which requires more shaping.

Freshly made sponge is crumby, crumbly and difficult to work with. Bake the cake base at least a day in advance. Sponge cake freezes well and, once thawed, is even better for shaping and cutting.

The baking of large or deep cakes can be tricky. A low oven temperature and longer time is needed in order to bake the cake through to the centre (refer to How to bake the perfect cake (see page 12) and To test cooked cakes (see page 13)). Most of the cakes included in this section can be baked to shape. However, any scraps of sponge left from cutting can be made into a trifle.

FILLINGS

Most recipes can be made with any flavour combination of sponge and filling. Chocolate is very good with vanilla or coffee flavoured butter cream, and lemon curd is delicious mixed with butter cream. A filling of whipped cream and fresh fruit turns a cake into a dessert. Remember if the cake has a fresh cream filling, it must be kept cool and eaten on the same day.

Strawberry jam tends to be quite a 'slippery' filling. It is fine used for a simple cake base (like the Muncher) but if you need to fill a special shape like the Dinosaur Egg, the top tends to slip askew and spoil the shape. This shape of cake is better filled with butter cream. After filling, cakes can be chilled together in the refrigerator so that they hold their shape well and are easy to handle.

WHICH CAKE TO CHOOSE

Select a recipe to suit your ability. None of the cakes included here are difficult but some require more skill with manipulating the icing, piping and making moulded figures. Some recipes are literally a 'piece of cake' and could be perfectly achieved by the most inexperienced cake maker. Do be sure to read and understand the recipe well in advance. Some need preparation before the day. The meringue for the Kitten Castle and Carousel is best made the day before. Moulded figures also need attention in advance.

ICINGS

The availability of ready-to-roll icing or sugar paste has revolutionised novelty cake making. It is so smooth, malleable and effective that even complicated shapes can be perfectly covered. Different makes do vary. It is well worth trying a few different kinds. Some are firm, others soft and pliable. Choose which one best suits the particular cake that is being made.

The surface of the icing dries quickly and then can wrinkle when shaping around difficult corners. Keep it well covered at all times, even after rolling. Don't roll it out until the cake is shaped and brushed with honey. Use a rolling pin to lift large pieces on to the cake. Once it is on the cake, work quickly using the warmth of the hands to shape and ease it into shape. Cornflour is excellent for dusting when rolling out as it is fine and dry. However, if a cake is to be kept for more than a couple of days, cornflour can cause the icing to ferment. If keeping a cake, it is better to use icing sugar. Apricot glaze (see page 70) can be used to stick the icing to the cake but honey is equally sticky and ready from the jar. Make sure it has a good boil just before using.

CRUMBS

These are the curse of the cake decorator. They somehow creep all over the place and, if they invade the icing, can spoil the finished look of a cake. Be sure to keep a separate work area for cake bases and icings. Wash and dry your hands well when working between one and the other. Brush the cake base down, using a large pastry brush, to make sure loose edges and crumbs are removed before icing.

COLOURS

There is a dazzling array of colours available from specialist cake decorating shops (see also page 78). It is well worth investing in paste food colourings. With these, depth of colour can be achieved without causing the icing to become sticky. Test the colour on a scrap of icing first as the intensity varies a great deal. Some require only a drop to create a glowing hue while others use much more for a pastel shade. Knead the colouring carefully into the icing and check that there are no streaks before using. Ready-to-roll icing or sugar paste can be bought in a variety of colours. This is particularly useful when using deep colours like black and red as the colouring is very even. As colouring can be quite time-consuming, it is a good idea to colour the icing in advance, then store it covered tightly in cling film and in an airtight container.

Other interesting finishes are available. The glitter dust used on the Haunted Castle is great fun and can also be used to give a sparkle to moulded figures or enhance details such as the edge of the star on the Wrestling Ring.

KEEPING CAKES

Finished cakes cannot be frozen. The icing does not survive well and the colours run on thawing. The Novelty cakes in this section will survive well overnight if stored in a cool airy place. But any meringue or figures must be added at the last minute.

ROYAL ICING

Many recipes require a small amount of royal icing. Although making this for a minute piece of detail may seem a chore, no other icing medium has the same qualities. To make a very small amount use part of an egg white and mix in a small bowl with a single beater in an electric hand whisk. Even though it is only a small amount, always sift the icing sugar as lumps may block fine piping nozzles. If making the royal icing in advance, store in an airtight container with a damp piece of absorbent kitchen paper or cling film placed directly on top of the icing. Beat again before using.

Novelty cakes don't always have an obvious place to put candles or write a greeting message. They can always be positioned directly on to the cake board. Make candle holders out of balls of ready-to-roll icing or sugar paste and attach to the board with

water. Candles with or without holders can be fixed in. Light them up and stand back for your masterpiece to be admired. Novelty cakes are always much appreciated by children and adults alike.

NOTE: Cake board sizes are included with the cake recipes, however, you can use a serving plate instead if preferred.

MOULDING FIGURES

Moulding figures requires care and patience. They need two key factors to make them come alive. One is proportion and the other is facial expression.

With experience you will learn the feel of the moulding material — to work it until it is soft and perfectly smooth before shaping. You will learn how to handle it, which finger to use and how much pressure to apply to form the right shapes.

Marzipan is used for figures that need to be sturdy and stand upright. It is firm and easy to work with although the texture is slightly grainy. Ready-to-roll icing or sugar paste is used for delicate figures and finer work. It can be made wafer thin without cracking and dries quickly. It is pure white, smooth and colours easily. The animals in this section can be easily made with either material. However, figures like the wrestlers must be made from marzipan.

It is a good idea to allow at least twenty four hours for figures to dry. They will be easier to handle and, in the case of marzipan, the oil will not soak into the iced cake. But assemble them when they are soft, as heads and limbs can be eased into a natural position.

Most moulded figures are made from three basic shapes; a ball, a sausage and a pear. They take between 25 g (1 oz) and 75 g (3 oz) of moulding material, depending on the size needed. It is important to gauge that the figures are in proportion with each other and with the cake.

Modelling tools are available to shape and mark patterns. However, they are costly and, unless you are very keen on modelling, there are usually kitchen utensils to hand that will do a similar job. Wooden skewers, small spatulas and sharp knives are all useful. It is worth buying a fine sable brush for painting features and patterns using food colourings.

Eyes are usually piped and are an essential part of the character. You will find that with practice you can spot the right angle of a head, quiver of a lip or flash of an eyeball that simply brings the character you have modelled to life.

SUGAR MOUSE

1 Roll the white icing into a pear shape for the body. Roll two small balls and flatten for ears. Snip whiskers using scissors.

2 Roll two small balls of pink icing and flatten them. Attach to the white ears with a little water. Pinch the base together and press into the mouse at either side of the head using a cocktail stick.

3 Attach the tail with a little water. Pipe the eyes.

RABBIT

1 Roll the icing into a pear shape. Using a small pair of scissors, snip two ears from the pointed end.

2 Using a little royal icing, pipe eyes and a big round tail.

DUCK

1 Roll orange marzipan or icing into a small pear shape with a long thin end. Take a marble sized piece of yellow or white, roll it into a ball, then press between the thumb and forefinger to make the head. Roll the head on to the beak.

2 Use the rest of the yellow or white to make an elongated pear shape. Tip the pointed end of the pear upwards to make a duck's tail.

3 Attach the head to the body with a little royal icing and pipe eyes on the head.

STANDING KITTEN

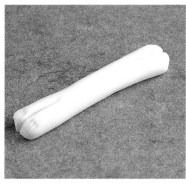

1 Reserve a marble-sized piece of marzipan or icing for the head, roll the rest of the paste into a sausage about 7.5 cm (3 inches) long. Make a 2 cm (¾ inch) cut at each end of the sausage to form the front and back legs. Mark claws with a sharp knife. Arch the sausage so that it will stand up. Snip a tail from the back.

2 Make the head in the same way as the Sitting Kitten and attach the head with royal icing. Pipe eyes and a pink nose.

SITTING KITTEN

1 Roll a marble sized piece of marzipan or icing into a ball. Flatten a little. Make a cut one third of the way through the top and ease each side into ears. Snip whiskers each side of the face.

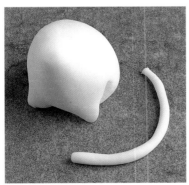

2 Roll a length for the tail and the rest into a pear shape for

the body. Stand it on end and cut two front paws from the bottom slightly tipping the body forward.

3 Use a little royal icing to attach the tail to the back, curling it around. Attach the head to the body and pipe eyes and a pink nose.

WRESTLING FIGURE

Use 50 g (2 oz) flesh coloured marzipan and 50 g (2 oz) coloured marzipan for each figure. Dry for 3-4 days.

1 Roll a ball for the head. Roll a long sausage for the arms. Use the little finger to mark indentations for muscles and flatten each end for hands. Roll two legs, marking muscles.

2 Cut the coloured marzipan in half. Shape one half into the trunk of the body making it 'V' shaped where the legs will join.

Reserve a small piece of coloured marzipan for the straps of the outfit, wrap lightly and store in an airtight container. Cut the rest in half and shape into two boots. They need to match the width of the legs where they will join, and be quite thin and flat so that the figure will stand.

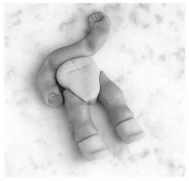

3 Firmly press the arms to the top of the body. Cut the top of the legs at an angle and press to the base of the body. Press the boots to the legs. Carefully place on baking parchment to dry. Secure with royal icing, if liked.

4 To assemble: thinly roll out the reserved coloured marzipan, and cut strips for the straps of the wrestler's suit. Place over the shoulders. Paint the eyes and a mouth. Use yellow royal icing to pipe hair and moustaches. (Hair can also be made by pressing marzipan or ready-to-roll icing through a sieve and on to the head.) Attach the head with icing.

KITTEN CASTLE

he perfect cake for a little girl. The combination of meringue and sponge will be most popular. The kitten could be substituted with any favourite animal.

350 g (12 oz) cake mixture, using
  350 g (12 oz) flour etc. (see page
  20 or 21)
1½ quantities butter cream (see
  page 25)
pink food colouring
strawberry jam for filling
25.5-28 cm (10-11 inch) cake
  board (optional)

TURRETS
2 egg whites
100 g (4 oz) caster sugar
100s and 1000s

DECORATION
flat sweets for windows
1 sitting kitten (see page 185)

....

1 Collect three empty food cans
   to bake the turrets in – one
450 g (1 lb) size, one 225 g (8 oz)
size, and one 150 g (5 oz) size. Use
a 20.5 cm (8 inch) round cake tin
for the castle base. Grease and
base line all the tins.

2 Make the cake mixture. Half
   fill the food cans with the
mixture and use the rest to fill the
large tin. Bake in the oven at 180°C
(350°F) mark 4. Bake the small
cakes for 20-30 minutes and the
large cake for 1 hour. Turn out and
leave to cool on a wire rack.

3 To make the meringue
   turrets: reduce the oven
temperature to 110°C (225°F) mark
¼. Line a baking sheet with non-
stick baking parchment. Draw
three circles on the parchment
using the food cans as a guide.
Whisk the egg whites until stiff.
Gradually whisk in half the sugar,
whisking after each addition until
thoroughly incorporated. Fold in
the remaining sugar very lightly,
with a metal spoon.

4 Spoon the meringue into a
   piping bag fitted with a large
star nozzle. Pipe three large whirls
of meringue, starting outside the
circles so that the meringue will
overlap the edge of the turrets.
Sprinkle the tops with 100s and
1000s. Pipe the remaining
meringue into tiny stars. Bake the
small meringues for 1-1½ hours
and the large for 3 hours until firm
and crisp. Cool on a wire rack.
Store in an airtight container until
ready to use.

5 To assemble the cake, first
   colour the butter cream pink.
Slice the large cake in half and
sandwich together with the
strawberry jam. Set the cake on
the board or a serving plate and
cover the top and sides with butter
cream. Carefully coat each turret
with butter cream, inserting a fork
into the base so that the cake can
be iced more easily. Set each
turret on top of the cake.

6 Push sweets into the sides of
   the turrets for windows and
arrange the small meringue stars
around the side of the larger cake.
Set a large meringue on top of
each turret. Put the kitten in place.

ROBOT CAKE

quick and easy cake to make for a young boy. The
children will enjoy the colourful decoration of
sweets too!

---

*175 g (6 oz) cake mixture, using
175 g (6 oz) flour etc. (see page
20 or 21)*

*½ quantity butter cream (see page
25)*

*jam or butter cream for filling
(optional)*

*20.5 cm (8 inch) round cake
board (optional)*

black and yellow food colourings

1 round biscuit (any sort will do)

*25 g (1 oz) ready-to-roll icing or
sugar paste*

tube of Smarties

packet of Jelly Tots

1 packet fruit Polos

3 lollipops

....

HINT
The birthday child's favourite
sweets may be used to decorate
the cake.

1 Grease and base line a 1.1
litre (2 pint) pudding basin, a
300 ml (½ pint) pudding basin and
a bun tin (or use a paper fairy cake
case). Prepare the cake mixture
and spoon into the prepared basins
and bun tin. Bake in the oven at
190°C (375°F) mark 5. Bake the
small cakes for 20-30 minutes and
the large one for 45-60 minutes.
Turn out and leave to cool on a
wire rack.

2 Slice the large cake in half
and sandwich together with
jam or some of the butter cream.
Set the large cake on the cake
board or serving plate. Attach the
small cake to the top with a little
butter cream. Colour the rest of
the butter cream pale grey and use
to completely cover the cake.

3 Attach the bun to the biscuit
with butter cream, then
spread butter cream on top of the
bun. Colour the ready-to-roll icing
yellow and roll out thinly. Use to
completely cover the bun and
biscuit.

4 Arrange rows of Smarties on
the lower half of the cake
and two for the eyes. Arrange the
Jelly Tots around the join between
the head and base of the robot. Put
the yellow covered bun on top.
Thread three fruit Polos onto a
lolly stick and push into the top of
the robot. Do the same with the
other two lollies and push into the
cake at the front of the robot.

HAUNTED CASTLE

A creepy cake to let your imagination run wild! Add as many spiders and snakes as you like. Definitely not for the faint-hearted!

275 g (10 oz) cake mixture, using
  275 g (10 oz) flour etc. (see page
  20 or 21)
30.5 × 20.5 cm (12 × 8 inch)
  cake board (optional)
jam or chocolate spread for filling
900 g (2 lb) ready-to-roll icing or
  sugar paste
purple, black and green food
  colourings
30 ml (2 tbsp) clear honey
12 red jelly diamonds
silver glitter dust
black candles

....

1 Grease and base line a 30.5 × 25.5 cm (12 × 10 inch) roasting tin and a 150 g (5 oz) food can. Make the cake mixture. Half fill the food tin and put the rest of the cake mixture into the roasting tin. Bake in the oven at 190°C (375°F) mark 5 for about 20 minutes for the food tin and the large cake for 45 minutes-1 hour. Cool on a wire rack.

2 Cut the large cake in half widthways and set on the cake board or a serving plate. Spread with jam or chocolate spread. Break or cut the remaining sponge into pieces and pile on top of the base, fixing with filling as you go. The result should be a lumpy mound of cake! Fix the small cake on top as a tower. Make a semi circular hollow at the front as a gateway.

3 Colour 50 g (2 oz) of the ready-to-roll icing purple, 25 g (1 oz) black and the rest grey. Roll out the grey icing thinly. Add 15 ml (1 tbsp) water to the honey and heat until boiling. Brush the honey all over the cake and drape the rolled out icing over, pressing it into the hollow at the front. Trim the icing at the base of the cake.

4 Roll out the purple icing and cut out to fill the hollow 'mouth'. Attach with the honey. Press the jelly diamonds into the edge of the mouth. Using diluted green colour, paint streaks of green slime. Dust with the silver glitter.

5 With the icing trimmings, make spiders and snakes to crawl over the castle. Roll balls for candle holders and fix on top of the tower with hot honey.

TIGER CAKE

This stunning tiger's face cake is suitable for children and adults alike. The tiger mouth candle holders make the perfect finishing touch.

100 g (4 oz) cake mixture, using
  100 g (4 oz) flour etc. (see page
  20 or 21)
15 g (½ oz) cocoa powder, sifted
chocolate and hazelnut spread for
  filling
225 g (8 oz) ready-to-roll icing or
  sugar paste
yellow, black and pink food
  colourings
25.5 cm (10 inch) round cake
  board (optional)
2 green jelly diamonds
2 sticks of white spaghetti
FROSTING
1 egg white
225 g (8 oz) caster sugar
pinch of salt
pinch of cream of tartar
30 ml (2 tbsp) water

HINT
Other flavours of sponge cake may be used, such as coffee or citrus (see page 20).

1 Grease and base line an 18 cm (7 inch) round cake tin. Make the cake mixture and divide in half. Fold the cocoa powder into one half. Drop spoonfuls of the white cake mixture into the tin. Drop spoonfuls of chocolate mixture to fill the gaps. Smooth the top of the cake. Bake in the oven at 190°C (375°F) mark 5 for about 40 minutes or until well risen and firm to touch. Turn out and leave to cool on a wire rack.

2 Slice the cake in half and sandwich together with the chocolate and hazelnut spread. Set on the cake board or a serving plate.

3 To make the frosting, put all the ingredients together into a bowl and whisk lightly. Place the bowl over a pan of hot water and heat, whisking continuously, until the mixture thickens sufficiently to stand in peaks. This will take about 7 minutes. Colour the icing yellow and pour over the top of the cake. Using a palette knife, spread the frosting to cover the top and sides of the cake, leaving it slightly 'fluffed' up to give a furry effect.

4 Colour 75 g (3 oz) of the ready-to-roll icing black, 25 g (1 oz) pink and 25 g (1 oz) yellow, then leave the remaining 75 g (3 oz) white. Roll out the pink, yellow and a third of the white icing. Cut three 2 cm (¾ inch) rounds of pink, two 5 cm (2 inch) rounds of yellow and two 2.5 cm (1 inch) of white. Gently pull the yellow round to make them pointed at one end. Dampen them with a little water in the centre and attach two of the pink circles. Pinch them together at the bottom to make them curve like ears. Leave to dry over a rolling pin, with the pink side down, for about 30 minutes.

5 Put the white circles in place as eyes. Dampen with a little water and attach the jelly diamonds for pupils. Place the remaining pink circle as a tongue. Divide the unrolled out white icing in half and roll into two flattish balls. Place them to cover the top of the pink tongue to form the

tiger's cheeks. Mark them with a skewer. Break the spaghetti into 10 cm (4 inch) lengths and insert these 'whiskers' into the side of the cheeks.

6 Roll a nut of the black icing into a nose, mark two nostrils and place on top of the two white cheeks. Dust the work surface with cornflour and roll out

the black icing thinly. Using a small and large round, fluted pastry cutter, cut out a variety of curved stripes as shown. Arrange them on the work surface to make sure they form a nice tiger pattern, then put in place on the cake.

7 To make the tiger mouth candle holders, use the trimmings from the pink and white icing. For each candle needed, make two pea sized balls of white icing and cut one 5 mm (¼ inch) round of pink. Dampen the side of the cake board or plate with a little water and press on the pink circles. Mark the white balls with a skewer and press them on top of the pink rounds. Fix the candles into the centre of the white balls.

MUNCHER

 imple yet effective graphic design from a popular computer game which is easily achieved. Use icing of any colour, the brighter the better!

350 g (12 oz) cake mixture, using
   350 g (12 oz) flour etc. (see page
   20 or 21)
jam, butter cream (see page 25) or
   chocolate spread for filling
900 g (2 lb) ready-to-roll icing or
   sugar paste
bright green, yellow and black
   food colourings
30 ml (2 tbsp) clear honey
¼ quantity royal icing (see page
   108)

....

1 Grease and base line a 25.5 cm (10 inch) and a 12.5 cm (5 inch) round cake tin. (If you do not have such a small tin, bake a slightly larger cake and cut it to size.) Make the cake mixture and divide between the two tins. The cakes should be quite shallow. Bake in the oven at 190°C (375°F) mark 5 for 25 minutes for the small one and the large one for about ½ hour. Cool on a wire rack.

2 This cake requires a board approximately 28 × 51 cm (11 × 20 inches) or a serving plate. It may be a good idea to use a chopping board covered with foil. Slice both cakes in half and fill. Cut a wedge (about one eighth) from the large cake.

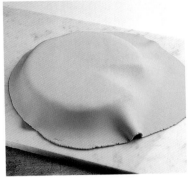

3 Reserve 25 g (1 oz) of the ready-to-roll icing and colour the rest the most fluorescent green possible. Divide into two pieces, one for the small and one for the large cake, and roll out into rounds. Cover to prevent drying out. Add 15 ml (1 tbsp) water to the honey and heat until boiling. Brush over the cakes and cover with icing.

4 As the larger cake has a wedge cut out, the icing will need to be cut and trimmed to fit. Trim the base edges. Lift the cakes on to the board and arrange as though the large one is about to gobble up the smaller one.

5 Prepare a greaseproof paper piping bag fitted with a medium writing nozzle. Colour the royal icing a lively yellow. Pipe small bulbs of icing around the base and top edges of the cakes. On the small cake, pipe a wide open mouth.

6 Colour a marble sized piece of the reserved white icing black. Roll out the white icing and cut out two rounds. Position for an eye on each cake and attach with a dab of water. Roll out the black icing and cut small rounds for the pupils. Attach to the white eyes with water.

DINOSAUR EGG

ver popular with boys and girls, this prehistoric look cake needs a little time and trouble – but well worth the effort.

700 g (1 ½ lb) ready-to-roll icing
  or sugar paste
purple, blue, yellow and black
  food colourings
175 g (6 oz) cake mixture, using
  175 g (6 oz) flour etc. (see page
  20 or 21)
½ quantity butter cream (see page
  25)
30 ml (2 tbsp) clear honey
little royal icing
30.5 × 20.5 cm (12 × 8 inch)
  cake board (optional)

....

1 Make the dinosaur at least three days in advance and leave to dry. Colour 100 g (4 oz) of the ready-to-roll icing purple. Roll it into a large sausage and a small one about the size of the little finger. Curl them round and pull spikes of icing up on the back. Make the small one pointed at one end for a tail. With a sharp knife, cut a slit in one end of the large one for a mouth.

2 It is possible to hire egg shaped cake moulds, if not use two 1.1 litre (2 pint) pudding basins; the egg will be more dumpy. The egg mould only needs greasing but the pudding basins should be greased and base lined. Make the cake mixture and divide equally between the two tins or basins. Bake in the oven at 190°C (375°F) mark 5 for 35-40 minutes. Cool on a wire rack.

3 Colour 100 g (4 oz) of the remaining ready-to-roll icing yellow and the rest turquoise (if you can't buy a suitable blue, mix blue and yellow together). Only partly mix the colouring in so that the icing is marbled.

4 The finished egg will lay on its side. Slice off a small piece of cake from one side to prevent the egg wobbling about on the cake board. Halve the cake, then sandwich the two pieces together with the butter cream.

5 Roll out the turquoise icing. Add 15 ml (1 tbsp) water to the honey and heat until boiling. Brush over the egg. Lay the icing over the egg. Smooth it to fit the shape – you will need to trim off excess icing, make a few pleats and smooth over the joins with a palette knife. Tuck the ends underneath the egg. With a sharp knife, cut a zig-zag down the middle of the egg, as though it has been cracked open, and ease it apart. Remove one or two of the zig-zag points to create a space to fit the dinosaur into. Place on the cake board or serving plate.

6 Use a little of the yellow icing to make a tongue for the dinosaur and fix it inside the mouth with water. With a cheese grater, grate the rest. Pile some into the open crack to represent the inside of the egg and let it spill over on to the board if you like. Fix the dinosaur and the tail into the egg. Rearrange the grated icing. Colour a little royal icing black. Pipe the eyes using white and black royal icing.

WRESTLING RING

T̲his fun cake will be a big hit with boys of all ages.
A cake to make by someone interested in moulding
as the figures require a little time.

350 g (12 oz) cake mixture, using
  350 g (12 oz) flour etc. (see page
  20 or 21)
jam, chocolate spread or ½
  quantity butter cream (see page
  25) for filling
30.5 cm (12 inch) square cake
  board (optional)
900 g (2 lb) ready-to-roll icing or
  sugar paste
blue, yellow and purple food
  colourings
100 g (4 oz) marzipan
30 ml (2 tbsp) clear honey
4 satay sticks
8 straws
2 wrestling figures (see page 185)

....

1 Grease and base line a 23 cm
  (9 inch) square cake tin.
Make the cake mixture and turn
into the prepared tin. Bake in the
oven at 180°C (350°F) mark 4 for
about 1 hour; cover the top of the
cake if it becomes too brown. Cool
on a wire rack.

2 Slice the cake in half and
  sandwich together with the
filling. Place on the cake board or a
serving plate. Colour 800 g (1¾ lb)
of the ready-to-roll icing sky blue
and 100 g (4 oz) bright yellow.
Colour the marzipan purple.

3 Add 15 ml (1 tbsp) water to
  the honey and heat until
boiling. Brush over the top and
sides of the cake. Lay the blue
icing over the cake and smooth
over the tops and side. Cut and
trim the corners to fit, then
smooth the joins with a palette
knife.

4 Using a ruler to guide you,
  mark the centre of the cake.
Cut a large star out of the centre of
the blue icing with a cutter or star
shaped cardboard template. Roll
out the yellow icing. Using the
same cutter or template, cut out a
yellow star and fit it into the space
in the blue icing. Smooth it to fit.

5 With the remaining yellow
  icing, cut out lots of stars
with a small cutter. Brush a very
small amount of honey around the
base of the cake and fix the small
stars to this.

6 Put a satay stick into each
  corner of sponge, pushing
them right down to the bottom.
Trim the tops so that they stand
about 7.5 cm (3 inches) above the
cake. Divide the marzipan into
four. Roll into sausages and fit over
the exposed stick like buffers. Trim
the straws so that they are just a
little longer than the gaps between
the marzipan buffers. Carefully
press them well into the marzipan
with two on each side. Set the
wrestling figures on top.

HINT
Remove the satay sticks from
the cake before cutting and
serving.

HOT LIPS

*F*illed with strawberries and cream, this adult theme
cake could be served as a dessert. Send any
message you like on the cake.

225 g (8 oz) cake mixture, using
  225 g (8 oz) flour etc. (see page
  20 or 21)
100 g (4 oz) strawberries, hulled
150 ml (¼ pint) double cream,
  whipped
30.5 × 20.5 cm (12 × 8 inch)
  cake board
550 g (1¼ lb) ready-to-roll icing or
  sugar paste
red and pink food colourings
30 ml (2 tbsp) honey
a little royal icing

....

HINT
The lettering can be transferred
to the cake by first tracing the
message on to greaseproof
paper, then pin-pricking the
outline on to the cake as an
icing guide (see page 130).

1 Grease and base line a deep
  baking tin, about 23 × 18 cm
(9 × 7 inches). Make the cake
mixture and turn into the prepared
tin. Bake in the oven at 190°C
(375°F) mark 5 for about 45
minutes. Cool on a wire rack.

2 To make a lip shaped
  template: cut a piece of
greaseproof paper the same size as
the baking tin. Fold in half
widthways. Draw the upper and
lower part of half a mouth and cut
out to the fold. Open out for the
whole lip shape.

3 Using a sharp knife and the
  template as a guide, cut the
cake into the shape of a pair of
lips. Slice the strawberries thinly
and fold into the whipped cream.
Slice the cake in half and sandwich
together with the strawberries and
cream. Set on the cake board or a
serving plate.

4 Colour 50 g (2 oz) of the
  ready-to-roll icing red and
the rest shocking pink. Roll out the
pink icing to cover the lips. Add
15 ml (1 tbsp) water to the honey
and heat until boiling. Brush the
cake all over with the hot honey.
Lay the icing over the cake,
trimming to fit neatly. With a
palette knife, mark the centre lip
line.

5 Fit a greaseproof piping bag
  with a fine writing nozzle and
fill with white royal icing. Write the
message along the centre line, such
as 'Be my Valentine' or 'Happy
Birthday Sweetie' with an
exclamation mark at the end.

6 Roll out the red icing and cut
  out a few small hearts. With
a dab of water to fix them,
arranging one heart at the end of
the written message. Arrange the
rest haphazardly around the side of
the cake.

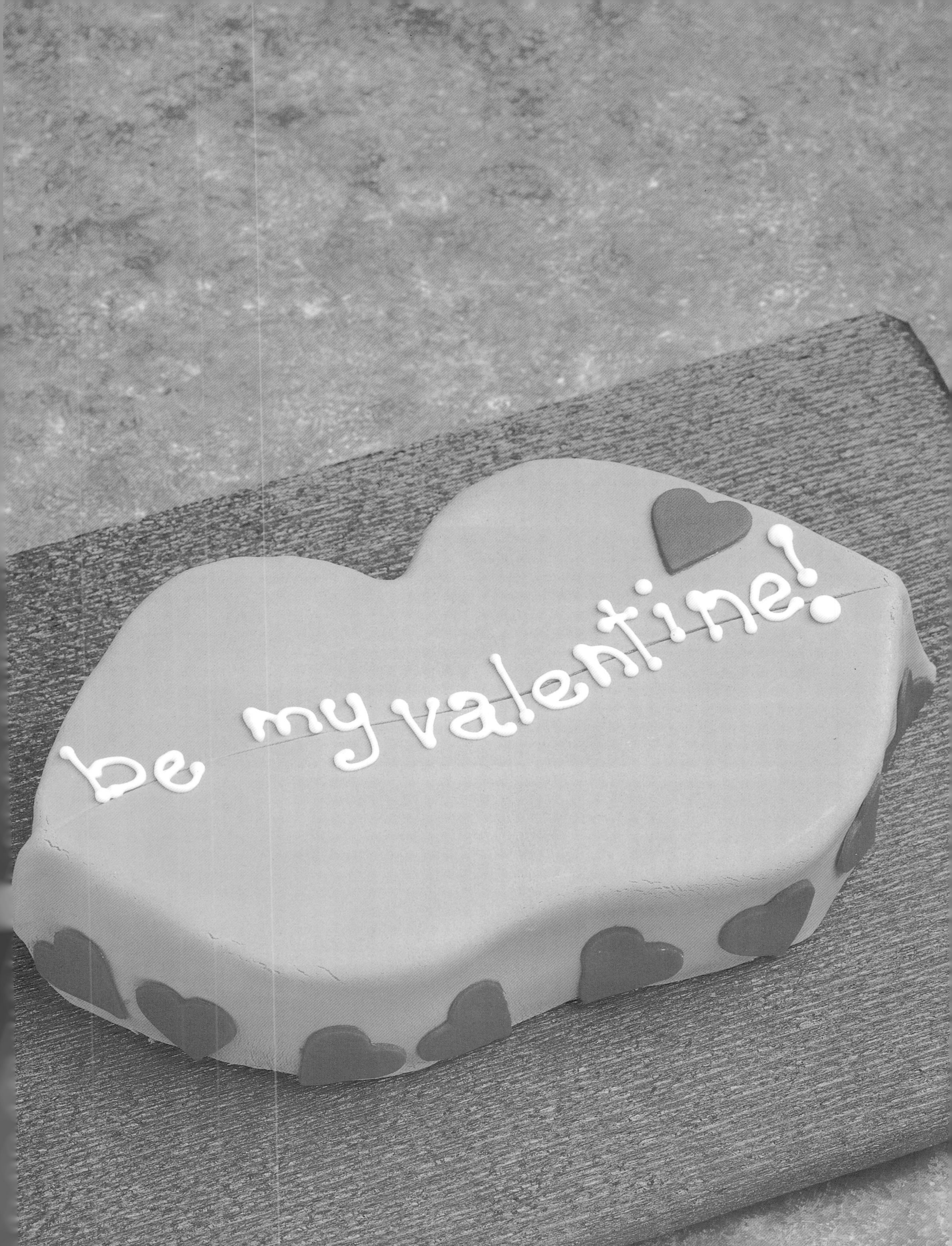
be my valentine!

TOADSTOOL

 cake to capture the imagination of young children. All kinds of sweetie insects can be included to add to the fun.

175 g (6 oz) cake mixture, using
 175 g (6 oz) flour etc. (see page
 20 or 21)
700 g (1½ lb) ready-to-roll icing or
 sugar paste
red, green, yellow and black food
 colourings
25.5 cm (10 inch) square cake
 board (optional)
½ quantity butter cream (see page
 25)
dolly mixtures and liquorice
 allsorts
a little royal icing

....

1 Grease and base line a 900 g (2 lb) food can and a 1.1 litre (2 pint) pudding basin. It doesn't matter how big the basin is as long as it holds at least 1.1 litres (2 pints). A wide shallow cake makes a better looking toadstool. Make the cake mixture, half fill the food can and put the remaining mixture into the pudding basin. Bake in the oven at 190°C (375°F) mark 5 for about 30 minutes for the food can and the pudding basin about 40 minutes. Cool on a wire rack.

2 Take 350 g (12 oz) of the ready-to-roll icing. Colour a walnut sized piece beige with gravy browning and the rest a not too bright red. Colour 100 g (4 oz) green and leave the rest white. Roll out the green icing and cut into a kidney shape as a 'grass' base for the cake. Fix to the cake board or a serving plate with a little water. Using the food can that the 'stalk' was baked in, cut a semi-circle from one side of the 'grass'.

3 Reserve 50 g (2 oz) of the white icing and roll out the rest as wide as the 'stalk' and long enough to fit all the way round. Trim to neaten the edges. Spread butter cream thinly round the cake. Holding the cake by the ends, set it at one end of the rolled out icing. Roll up and press the seam together. With a dab of butter cream, fix it upright into the semi-circle cut out of the green icing. Spread the uncovered top with butter cream.

4 Roll out the red icing to fit the pudding basin cake. Set the cake flat on the work surface and cover thinly with butter cream. Lay the icing over the cake smoothly. Trim the edges to the base of the cake. Dust the work surface lightly with cornflour and carefully turn the cake upside down.

5 Colour the remaining butter cream yellow and put into a piping bag fitted with a small fluted nozzle. Mark a circle where the stalk will fit on the centre of the cake. Pipe lines of butter cream on the underneath, starting at the mark you have made, to look like the 'gills' of a toadstool. Be sure to cover the sponge and icing join. Carefully turn the cake the right way up and set on top of the stalk.

6 Roll out the reserved white icing and the beige icing. Cut the white icing into dots. Using a little water to fix them, arrange over the top of the toadstool. Cut the beige icing into a door and windows.

7 Sweetie insects can be made any way you imagine. The ones in the picture are: caterpillar of assorted dolly mixtures and piped eyes. The snail is made from three liquorice allsorts stuck together with royal icing. He has piped eyes and sliced liquorice allsort for antennae. The bug is a sliced liquorice allsort with piped eyes. Use the red icing trimmings, rolled into small ovals, to make ladybird candle holders. Put the black royal icing in a bag fitted with a medium writing nozzle. Pipe dots and eyes on the ladybirds, a doorknob on the door and panes on the windows.

CAROUSEL CAKE

A spectacular cake for girls or a little boy, made using sponge, meringue and marshmallow. Any moulded or bought animals or figures can be used.

275 g (10 oz) lemon cake mixture,
  using 275 g (10 oz) flour etc. (see
  page 20 or 21)
lemon curd for filling
700 g (1½ lb) ready-to-roll icing or
  sugar paste
purple and yellow food colourings
30 ml (2 tbsp) honey
25.5 cm (10 inch) round cake
  board (optional)
little royal icing
5 satay sticks
5 marshmallow twists or straws
5 moulded animals (see pages
  184-185)
MERINGUE
2 egg whites
100 g (4 oz) caster sugar
pink food colouring

....

1 Grease and base line 20.5 cm (8 inch) cake tin. Make the cake mixture and turn into the prepared tin. Bake in the oven at 180°C (350°F) mark 4 for 1 hour. Turn out and cool on a wire rack.

2 To make the meringue canopy: lower the oven to 110°C (225°F) mark ¼. Line a baking sheet with non-stick baking parchment. Draw a 20.5 cm (8 inch) round on the paper. Whisk the egg whites until stiff. Gradually whisk in half the sugar, whisking after each addition until thoroughly incorporated.

3 Fold in the remaining sugar very lightly with a metal spoon. Colour the meringue pink. Spoon into a piping bag fitted with 1 cm (½ inch) plain nozzle. Pipe in rings to fill the circle. Separately pipe a whirl for the centre of the canopy and five tiny meringues. Bake for about 1½ hours until dry and crisp. Cool and store in an airtight container.

4 Slice the cake in half and fill with lemon curd. Colour one third of the ready-to-roll icing lilac and the rest lemon. Make a template: cut a 25.5 cm (10 inch) round from a sheet of greaseproof paper. Fold the paper into sixteenths. Draw a semi-circle at the bottom edge and cut out. Open up the paper and you will have a circle with a scalloped edge.

5 Add 15 ml (1 tbsp) water to the honey and heat until boiling. Roll out the purple icing into a long strip to fit around the side of the cake. Brush the side with the honey and, holding the cake upright, roll the sides on to

the icing. Set the cake on the cake board or a serving plate and smooth over the seam.

6 Roll out the yellow icing into a circle. Cut out using the template as a guide. Brush the top and edge of the cake with hot honey. Put the yellow icing over the top and smooth.

7 Colour the royal icing pink and put into a greaseproof bag fitted with a fine star nozzle. Pipe shells and dots around the purple sides of the cake.

the marshmallow twists or straws and attach to the cake at the marked points. Trim the tops.

9 Pipe a blob of royal icing on top of each pole and fix the canopy on top.

10 Attach the large whirl of meringue in the centre and the baby ones over the top of each pole.

8 Make five evenly spaced marks around the edge of the cake. Push the satay sticks through

11 Attach the animals by the side of the marshmallow sticks with royal icing.

WEDDING FAN CAKE (Page 149)

Fan-left hand side ×3

Middle
tier

Base
tier

Turn templates over for
right hand side fans

Top
tier

RIBBONED WEDDING CAKE
(PAGE 102)
Side templates

Base tier

Middle tier

Top tier

Side

RIBBONED WEDDING CAKE (Page 102)
Mark ribbon insertion lines following the outside edge of the template

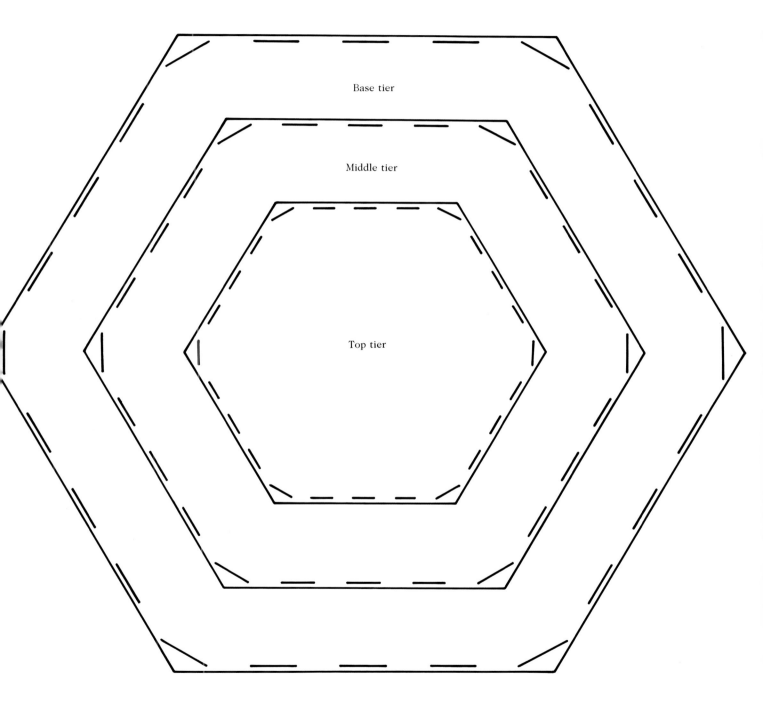

Base tier

Middle tier

Top tier

REBECCA'S CHRISTENING CAKE (Page 120)
Shoes

Toe piece

Back

Sole

DOILY CELEBRATION CAKE (Page 146)
Doily template

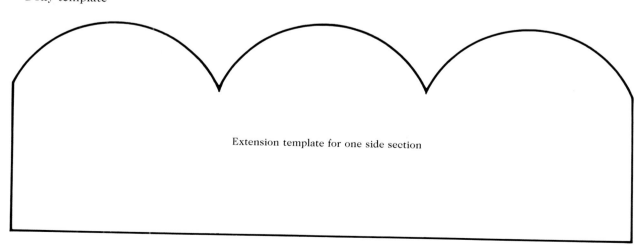

Extension template for one side section

EMBROIDERY CAKE (Page 140)
Embroidery pattern

DOILY CELEBRATION CAKE (Page 146)

Doily template

GOLDEN STAR CAKE (Page 118)
Star template

INDEX

A

acrylic boards, 80
acrylic rolling pins, 152
acrylic skewers, 81
albumen, 107, 108
almond paste *see*
    marzipan
American frosting, 27
anniversary heart cake,
    90-1
appliqué design cake,
    92-3
apricot glaze, 70
aspic cutters, 81

B

baking sheets, 8
basket weave, piping, 129
basket weave heart, 28-9
beads, piping, 128-9
birthday cakes:
    18th birthday cake,
        116-17
    happy birthday cake,
        74-5
    21st birthday cake,
        124-5
black and white gâteau,
    48-9
blossom, piping, 135
blossom plunger cutters,
    81, 88, 156
blueberries:
    kiwi and blueberry
        gâteau, 34-5
boards *see* cake boards
bone tools, 152
bows, ribbon, 176
boxes, 10
bridge, extension work,
    132, 133
brushes:
    glazing, 7, 8
    nozzle, 105
    paint, 81, 105
butter cream:
    covering cakes with, 24
    filling cakes with, 23

piping, 126-7
recipe, 25
buttercups and daisies,
    166-7

C

cake boards, 10, 16
    covering, 83
    royal icing, 111
calyx cutters, 152, 158
caramel, praline pyramid,
    40-1
carousel cake, 204-5
celebration cakes, 63-77
    anniversary heart cake,
        90-1
    chocolate celebration
        cake, 58-9
    doily celebration cake,
        146-8
    Easter cake, 76-7
    lemon geranium
        celebration cake,
        38-9
    Mother's Day cake,
        98-9
    rich fruit cake, 64-6
    special occasion cake,
        122-3
    see also birthday cakes;
        wedding cakes
cherries, Madeira cake,
    69
chocolate, 43-61
    black and white gâteau,
        48-9
    butter cream, 25
    chocolate box gâteau,
        50-1
    chocolate celebration
        cake, 58-9
    chocolate frosting, 27
    chocolate fruit ring,
        52-3
    chocolate fudge frosting,
        26
    chocolate ribbon cake,
        54-5

coating with, 45
crème au beurre, 25
cut-out pieces, 47
dipping, 45
filigree gâteau, 60-1
frills and curls, 46-7
frosted fruit ring, 32-3
glacé icing, 26
leaves, 45
melting, 44
piping, 46
ritzy mocha gâteau,
    36-7
rose leaf gâteau, 56-7
selecting, 44
Victoria sandwich cake,
    20
Christening cake,
    Rebecca's, 120-1
Christmas cakes:
    Christmas fruit garland,
        94-5
    Christmas greeting
        cake, 136-7
    Christmas wreath cake,
        112-113
    golden star cake, 118-19
cocktail sticks, 81
cocoa, 44
coconut:
    coffee coconut bombe,
        30-1
    Madeira cake, 69
coffee:
    butter cream, 25
    coffee coconut bombe,
        30-1
    coffee fudge frosting,
        26
    crème au beurre, 25
    glacé icing, 26
    ritzy mocha gâteau,
        36-7
    Victoria sandwich cake,
        20
colours, 78-9
    embossed designs, 84
    novelty cakes, 180
    sugar paste, 80
compasses, 105

cone tools, 152
consistency, royal icing,
    107
cornelli cake, 138-9
cornelli work, piping, 128
couverture chocolate, 44
covering cakes:
    icings and frostings, 24
    marzipanning, 71-2
    royal icing, 109-10
    sugar paste, 82
cream *see* butter cream;
    dairy cream
crème au beurre, 24, 25
crimpers, 81
crimping sugar paste, 84
crumbs, 182-3
curls, chocolate, 47
cut-outs:
    sugar flowers, 157-8
    sugar paste, 85, 87, 89
cutters, 8, 81, 152, 157
cutting cakes into layers,
    23

D

dairy cream:
    filling cakes, 23-4
    piping, 126-7
daisies, 135, 157, 166-7
daisy cake, 114-15
designing cakes, 17
dinosaur egg, 196-7
doily celebration cake,
    146-8
domed wedding cake,
    96-7
Doris pinks, 158, 168-9
dots, piping, 128-9
dowel, wooden, 81
dried fruit:
    light fruit cake, 67-8
    rich fruit cake, 64-6
dropped loop thread
    work, 128
duck, 184
dust, food colour,
    78-9

E

Easter cake, 76-7
egg albumen, 107, 108
eggs:
  dinosaur egg, 196-7
  sugar eggs, 76-7
18th birthday cake, 116-17
electric mixers, 7-8
embossing sugar paste, 81,
  84
embroidery, tube, 131-2
embroidery cake, 140-1
equipment, 7-10
  flower paste, 152-3
  piping, 126
  royal icing, 105
  sugar paste, 80-1
extension work:
  doily celebration cake,
    146-8
  piping, 132-3
  sugar paste, 86-7

F

fan-shaped run-outs,
  149-50
figures, moulding, 183-5
filigree, piping, 128
filigree, gâteau, 60-1
fillings, 23-4, 182
flat icing consistency, 107
floppy mats, 152
floral cascade, 168-9
floristry wire, 153
flower paste, 152-9
  plaques, 158-9
  recipe, 154
flowers:
  blossom plungers, 81, 88,
    156
  calyxes, 158
  cut-out sugar flowers,
    157-8
  cutters, 81, 152
  daisies, 135, 157, 166-7
  Doris pinks, 158, 168-9
  flower pads, 152
  flower spinner nails, 105
  flower spray cake, 172-3
  freesias, 156, 168-9
  fresh, 170-1

fuchsias, 155, 168-9
  Mexican hat flowers,
    154-5
  moulded sugar roses,
    89
  piping, 135
  silk, 171
  sugar-frosted, 170-1
  sugar paste, 88-9
  sweet peas, 157, 168-9
  wired sugar, 154
  wiring sprays, 159
food colourings, 78-9
food processors, 8
freesias, 156, 168-9
frills:
  chocolate, 46
  cutters, 81
  sugar paste, 83
frosted fruit ring, 32-3
frostings:
  American, 27
  chocolate, 27
  coffee fudge, 26
  covering cake with, 24
  seven-minute, 26
  vanilla, 27
  see also icings
fruit:
  chocolate fruit ring,
    52-3
  Christmas fruit garland,
    94-5
  crème au beurre, 25
  frosted fruit ring, 32-3
fruit cakes:
  light fruit cake, 67-8
  rich fruit cake, 64-6
fuchsias, 155, 168-9

G

garrett frill cutters, 81
gâteaux:
  black and white, 48-9
  chocolate box, 50-1
  filigree, 60-1
  kiwi and blueberry,
    34-5
  ritzy mocha, 36-7
  rose leaf, 56-7
Genoese sponge, 21

glacé icing, 26
glazes:
  apricot, 70
  gum arabic, 154
glazing brushes, 8
glitter flakes, 79
gold leaf, 79, 104
golden star cake, 118-19
good luck cake, 142-3
greaseproof paper piping
  bags, 105, 126, 129
gum arabic glaze, 154

H

hand mixers, 7
happy birthday cake,
  74-5
harvest cake, 160-2
haunted castle, 190-1
hazelnuts:
  praline pyramid,
    40-1
hot lips, 200-1
hygiene, 104

I

icings, 23-7
  covering cakes, 24
  crème au beurre, 25
  glacé, 26
  novelty cakes, 184
  piping, 126-35
  royal, 105-11
  run-outs, 133-4
  see also frostings

J

jam, filling cakes, 24

K

kitten castle, 186-7
kittens, 184-5
kiwi and blueberry gâteau,
  34-5
knives, 8, 80-1, 152-3

L

lace work, piping, 131
lattice garden cake, 144-5
layers:
  cutting, 23
  filling, 23-4
leaves:
  chocolate, 45
  cutters, 81, 152
  piping, 135
  sugar-frosted, 170-1
  sugar paste, 89
  wiring, 158
lemon:
  butter cream, 25
  crème au beurre, 25
  glacé icing, 26
  Madeira cake, 69
  Victoria sandwich cake,
    20
lemon geranium
  celebration cake, 38-9
lettering, 130
light fruit cake, 67-8
lines, piping, 128
lining tins, 11
liqueur:
  filigree gâteau, 60-1
  glacé icing, 26
liquid colours, 78
loops, ribbon, 176
lustre colours, 78-9

M

Madeira cake, 69-70
marbled sugar paste,
  174-5
marzipan:
  covering cakes, 71-3
  Easter cake, 76-7
  happy birthday cake,
    74-5
  moulding figures, 183-5
mats, floppy, 152
measuring jugs, 7
measuring spoons, 7
melting chocolate, 44
meringue:
  carousel cake, 204-5
  kitten castle, 186-7
  praline pyramid, 40-1

Mexican hat flowers, 154-5
milk chocolate, 44
mixers, 7-8
mocha:
glacé icing, 26
ritzy mocha gâteau, 36-7
modelling knives, 152-3
modelling tools, 81, 183
Mother's Day cake, 98-9
moulding:
figures, 183-5
sugar roses, 89
moulds, 8
mouse, sugar, 184
muncher, 194-5
muslin, 105

N
needles, scribing, 105, 152
novelty cakes, 180-205
carousel cake, 204-5
dinosaur egg, 196-7
haunted castle, 190-1
hot lips, 200-1
kitten castle, 186-7
muncher, 194-5
robot cake, 188-9
tiger cake, 192-3
toadstool, 202-3
wrestling ring, 198-9
nozzles brushes, 105
nozzles, piping, 10, 105, 126
nuts, Madeira cake, 69

O
one stage quick mix cake, 21
orange:
butter cream, 25
crème au beurre, 25
glacé icing, 26
Madeira cake, 69
Victoria sandwich cake, 20

P
paint brushes, 105
palette knives, 8, 80, 105
papers, 7, 8
paste colours, 78
patterned side scrapers, 105
peaked royal icing, 111
consistency, 107
pencils, 8, 105
pens, food colouring, 79
perspex, sheet, 105
petal paste, 152
pillars, 16, 17, 81
pinks, cut-out sugar flowers, 158, 168-9
pins, safety, 104
piping, 126-35
chocolate, 46
consistency, 107
equipment, 126
extension work, 132-3
flowers, 135
lace work, 131
leaves, 135
nozzles, 105, 126
run-outs, 133-4
techniques, 126-9
tube embroidery, 131-2
writing, 130
piping bags:
commercially made, 126
greaseproof paper, 105, 126, 129
nylon, 10
plain chocolate, 44
planning, 15-16
plaques:
flower paste, 158-9
piping writing on, 130
pollen dust, 79
portions, calculating, 14
praline pyramid, 40-1

R
rabbit, 184
racks, wire, 8
ready-to-roll icing, 182, 183
Rebecca's christening cake, 120-1
ribbon insertion, sugar

paste, 81, 86
ribbons, 104, 172, 176-7
bows, 176
loops, 176
ribbon slotters, 81
ribboned wedding cake, 102-3
ribbons and loops cake, 178-9
rich fruit cake, 64-6
ridge cone tools, 152
ritzy mocha gâteau, 36-7
robot cake, 188-9
rolling pins, 80, 152
rose leaf gâteau, 56-7
roses, moulded sugar, 89
rosewater glacé icing, 26
round cakes, royal icing, 110
royal icing, 105-11
consistencies, 107
equipment, 105
icing cake boards, 111
icing a round cake, 110
icing a square cake, 109
marzipanning cakes, 71-2
novelty cakes, 180
peaked royal icing, 111
piping, 127-8
quantity guide, 106
recipes, 108
rubbers, 105
rulers, 8, 105
run-outs:
icing consistency, 107
piping, 133-4
run-out film, 105
wedding fan cake, 149-50

S
safety, 104
sandwich cake, Victoria, 20
sandwich tins, lining, 11
scales, 7
scissors, 8, 153
scrapers, 105
scribing needles, 105, 152
scrolls, piping, 128
servings, calculating, 14
seven-minute frosting, 26

shells, piping, 128
side scrapers, 105
sieves, 8
silk flowers, 171
silver leaf, 79, 104
skewers, 81
smoothers, 80
spatulas, 8
special occasion cake, 122-3
sponge cakes:
Genoese sponge, 21
novelty cakes, 180
one stage quick mix cake, 21
Swiss roll, 22
Victoria sandwich, 20
whisked sponge cake, 22
spoons:
measuring, 7
wooden, 7
sprays:
flower spray cake, 172-3
plunger blossom flowers, 156
wiring, 159
square cakes, royal icing, 109
stamens, 153
stamps, embossing, 81
stars, piping, 128
stencils, lettering, 130
storing cakes, 13-14, 183
straight edges, 105
strawberries:
hot lips, 202-3
sugar-frosted heart, 174-5
sugar-frosting flowers and leaves, 170-1
sugar mouse, 184
sugar paste, 80-9
covering cake boards, 83
covering cakes with, 82
crimping, 84
cut-out designs, 85, 87, 89
embossing, 84
extension pieces, 86-7
flowers, 88-9
frills and flounces, 83
leaves, 89
marbled, 174-5

marzipanning cakes, 72-3
moulded roses, 89
novelty cakes, 180
recipe, 82
ribbon insertion, 86
sweet peas, 157, 168-9
swirls, piping, 128
Swiss roll, 22
lining tins, 11

T
tape, 153
templates, writing 130
testing cooked cakes, 13
thermometers, 10

tiered cakes, 15-16, 17
tiger cake, 192-3
tins, 7, 8
lining, 11
preparing, 10
toadstool, 202-3
trellis work:
lattice garden cake, 144-5
piping, 128
truffles, chocolate, 50-1
tube embroidery, 131-2
tulle, 176
turntables, 10, 105
tweezers, 81, 153
21st birthday cake, 124-5
two-tier oval wedding cake, 100-1

V
vanilla frosting, 27
Victoria sandwich cake, 20

W
wax paper, 105
wedding cakes:
domed wedding cake, 96-7
ribboned wedding cake, 102-3
two-tier oval wedding cake, 100-1
wedding fan cake, 149-50
weighing scales, 7
whisked sponge cake, 22

whisks, 7
white chocolate, 44, 47
wire, floristry, 153
wire-cutting scissors, 153
wiring:
flower sprays, 159
leaves, 158
plunger blossom flowers, 156
sugar flowers, 154
wooden dowel, 81
wooden spoons, 7
woodland cake, 163-4
wrestling figures, 185
wrestling ring, 198-9
writing, piping, 130

SUPPLIERS
AND USEFUL ADDRESSES

Squires Kitchen, Squire House, 3 Waverley Lane, Farnham,
Surrey GU9 8BB   Tel: 0252 734 309
Suppliers of cake-making and decorating equipment.
Mail order

V. V. Rouleaux, 201 New Kings Road, London SW10
Tel 071 371 5929
10 Symon Street, London SW3   Tel 071 730 4413
Suppliers of ribbons

Berisford Ribbons, PO Box 2, Congleton, Cheshire,
CW12 1EP

Cake Fayre, 11 Saddlers Walk, 44 East Street, Chichester,
West Sussex PO19 1HQ   Tel 0243 771857
Suppliers of cake-icing and decorating equipment